TRUTH-PROOF 2

Beyond The Thinking Mind

by

Paul Sinclair

Truth-Proof 2: Beyond The Thinking Mind
by Paul Sinclair

Paperback Edition
Published in Great Britain
by PBC Publishing 2017

E-Book also available

Drawings by Paul Sinclair

News clippings courtesy of
and copyright of Johnson Press Plc

Cover created by Jason Gleaves

ISBN: 978-1-9999165-0-3

TRUTH-PROOF 2:
Beyond The Thinking Mind

"There is nothing more exciting than being taken on a great adventure
by a guide who knows what he's doing,
and Paul Sinclair is just such a guide.
Expert research, a high level of credibility and a quiet,
deeply convincing sense of wonder.
A joy to read!"

Whitley Strieber

Bestselling author and writer of the definitive *Communion* books, renowned
lecturer on the subject of alien encounters
and director of the *Unknown Country* website.

"Truth Proof 2 is a fascinating and disturbing collection
of accounts of strange goings-on in East and North Yorkshire -
a part of the UK that seems to have more than its fair share of spookiness.
The Wilsthorpe Incident, in particular, sounds like
the sort of UFO encounter that you'd find in the X-Files,
complete with military involvement
and allegations of a sinister government cover-up"

Nick Pope

Bestselling author of 'Open Skies, Closed Minds'
and former Ministry Of Defence investigative spokesman
for unexplained phenomena.

"Once again, Yorkshire-based investigative writer Paul Sinclair
takes us on a tour of this beautiful, historic,
and at times completely unnerving region,
in search of the anomalous, the missing and the other-worldly.
Sinclair's resolve, tenacity, courage and curiosity
repeatedly manifest themselves in his investigations
and the reader is the beneficiary.
A most worthy follow-up to his first book, Truth-Proof."

Peter Robbins

Writer, researcher and international lecturer.

*"Thanks for my copy of the book.
I have enjoyed reading it and was impressed at the standard of investigation
and the many cases contained within it.
I understand that Paul Sinclair is currently writing a third book
and wish him well with his endeavours."*

Charles Halt

Retired US Air Force Colonel, author and public speaker.

*"Paul Sinclair has a flare for capturing your imagination
and his previous book was nothing less than excellent.
You will not be disappointed, as Truth-Proof 2
picks up where the first one left off,
plunging the reader straight back into the suspense and wonder.
A throughly entertaining read..."*

Steve Mera

*Author on the paranormal, lecturer and owner of
Phenomena Magazine.*

*"Paul Sinclair is a dedicated and thorough researcher
and this shines through his work
and the interviews he gives to people like me!
His work is refreshingly 'first-hand' and presented
in a clear and compelling way.
Truth-Proof 2 proves that strange happenings don't only occur
on isolated roads in Arizona or mountaintops in Colorado.
A lot of unexplained oddness happens right on our doorstep.
Best wishes."*

Howard Hughes

Broadcaster, journalist and presenter of the
hugely popular radio show The Unexplained.

*"Paul Sinclair's first book was a wonderfully weird explosion
of events of high strangeness in and around East and North Yorkshire.
Truth Proof 2 follows the same vein of incredible and weird events.
I know this new book will leave the reader in wonderment,
not just at the events themselves, but at the depth of work Paul
puts in to his investigations. Well done Paul."*

Chris Evers

Editor of *Outer Limits Magazine.*

CONTENTS

PART THREE:
THE WILSTHORPE INCIDENT IS BORN

ABOUT THE AUTHOR

ACKNOWLEDGEMENTS

I would like to thank the staff at King Street Library in Bridlington for all the help they have given me as I worked on Truth Proof 2. In particular; Sue, Sarah and Kathy, who unearthed an incredible amount of information for me.

My special thanks go to author and researcher Peter Robbins, who has been an inspiration whilst writing this book. I will never forget your words of support.

A special mention of thanks go to my friends Steve Ashbridge and Andi Ramsden who have spent countless hours with me at Bempton and the surrounding areas.

My grateful thanks go to my friend Al Carter for all his help and advice, and to my good friend Karl, because without his help, TP2 *and* TP1 would still be on my laptop in document form.

I may have done the research, walked miles and spent hours in archives, but this would mean very little if the accounts recorded in the book are of no interest. So I want to thank the people who have read my research during that process and took the time to give me their views; Chris Evers of Outer limits magazine and my wonderful wife Mary and daughters Jessica and Laura.

The internet is an amazing world that is open 24/7 and a place I never would have expected to find true friendship and genuine support. But even at five in the morning, my friend in the States; researcher, writer and radio host Debra Jane East, has been there for me, to offer help and advice. The same can be said of Derek Tiler, best selling author of 'Alien Contact: The Difficult Truth', who I consider to be one of the most knowledgeable people out there, especially when discussing some of my research. When Derek says he considers my work highly important, I take that as a compliment worth writing about.

So many people have given me their personal accounts of the strange and highly unusual. In many instances, I have had to change their names, but they know exactly who they are and without their accounts, this book would be nothing. Thank you for putting your trust in me and allowing me to share your very personal experiences.

My special thanks also go to Whitley Strieber, the writer who first asked me to talk about my own experiences on his radio show 'Unknown Country' back in 2006. I declined at the time, but you still offered me advice and encouragement and most importantly, a second chance to talk. After that, I completed the first book and now I sit here with the second. I will never forget this.

PREFACE

We are given a sanitised truth, a truth that fits the machine that we as human beings are all cogs within. No one power, be it religion or global power elite wants the populous to question anything. All truth and all proof must fit the mind-set of the machine.

The truth I search for is unsanitised and deemed unfit to be absorbed into the minds of the people caught inside the mind trap.

Human race, rat race - they are the same thing. Faces forced in the direction that society points them. Minds pressed and moulded into a single thinking block within the machine. A fish-ball of minds soaked in an ocean, where free thought and free speech must swim against the tide. Free thinking is never free inside the machine. The machine is at war with anything and everything that questions its code of conduct.

The price for free thinking is a world where the truth is bleached; diluted to the point where nothing is clear. The rules are made and broken by the rule makers.

INTRODUCTION

When I wrote the first Truth-Proof book, I never expected the volume of unexplained phenomena to continue to grow in front of my eyes. Truth-Proof 2 rolls on from the first book, like a ball of snow, gathering surreal stories from the minds of everyday people - people who have witnessed things beyond anything that is considered normal. I feel privileged to have spoken with so many of them. It was humbling to listen to these witnesses share such deep and personal encounters with the unknown. Some of them shared stories that had been locked in their minds for many years and others just wanted answers, which I just could not give.

In 2009 a weird kind of magic fell across East and North Yorkshire, bringing with it phenomena of every shape and form imaginable. But whatever is responsible is so distant, it cannot be seen or even understood.

While researching the incredible Wilsthorpe incident I questioned everything, including myself, for different reasons. Was a single intelligence responsible for all the phenomena? Or was there a kind of 'paranormal soup' of countless lifeforms, existing on the very fringes of human perception? The phenomena seems to act like a faceless chameleon, hiding on many different levels of our reality, but still able to interact with us at will.

Ultimately, I think we are faced with a mixture of many different and connected phenomena, which exist simultaneously. Although I cannot imagine how the silent black triangle, seen on Cliff Lane in Bempton, could be connected in any way to the stories of the ghost of Fimber Crossroads - but the connections are there.

The witnesses to these strange events may all be different, but the theme of their stories always runs along a similar path. The main difficulty, and it is one of the reasons people are so reluctant to talk, is that to accurately describe a genuinely bizarre experience is almost impossible. However, I have learned that nothing is truly impossible, but our minds must remain open. First, we need to accept that the lights seen under the sea and the lightforms out to sea are a genuine unknown, then perhaps we can create new words to explain and describe them. This has to happen before we can even begin to grasp the phenomena on any level.

'The fantasy of reality' is a phrase that I think describes the bubble which surrounds all of us, every day of our lives. We affectionately call it 'reality'. Truth-Proof 2 is a collection of strange and unexplained happenings that exist outside of that bubble.

I am not sure if these events of high strangeness affect our perception of what is real or whether, in those altered states of emotion, we can simply see further into the unknown. I think human emotion is a key that opens doors to some of the phenomena; be it trauma, fear or elation. I suspect it is a mixture of them all, at different levels, playing their part during an encounter. These emotions serve to detach us from the moment, allowing what we think as the unconscious, to seep in to what we call the real. There is nothing normal about the paranormal.

East and North Yorkshire are the main focus for my research. It does not surprise me in the slightest to discover, that many of the accounts contained in this book come from the same locations covered in the first one. Areas like this exist all over the world and I think researchers should focus on such places and the people/experiences within them, because location is key.

Interviewing a first-hand witness is like being given access to a Russian doll, because once opened they reveal many layers of experience - like stepping stones into the heart of the unexplained. Unearthing the details can take weeks, months, and sometimes years, but they *are* there. Many random incidents go unreported, due to the stigma of ridicule attached to the unexplained. These things simply defy explanation, but 'random' is not a word I would use for the accounts contained here. Throughout my years of research, I have learned that once discovered, one story invariably leads to another and patterns are revealed.

I don't get too uptight when scientific minds dismiss incredible witness accounts as impossible. Science is constantly evolving and its views change. Yesterday's dreams are tomorrow's innovations, and the fantasies of today are the realities of the future. Perhaps the Truth-Proof books are a study of nature at its most surreal. The unexplained events contained within their pages could all be part of some inharmonious coexistence. Is it possible that what we perceive as paranormal could actually be *normal* and simply an extension of what are natural occurrences in nature?

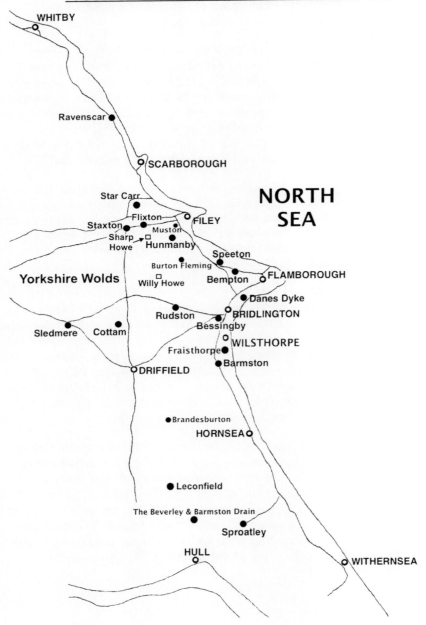

NORTH & EAST YORKSHIRE COASTLINE

WHITBY

Ravenscar ●

SCARBOROUGH

Star Carr ●

**NORTH
SEA**

Flixton
Staxton ● FILEY
Muston
Sharp Howe ● Hunmanby
Speeton

Burton Fleming
Yorkshire Wolds
Willy Howe
Bempton ● FLAMBOROUGH

● Danes Dyke

Rudston ●
Sledmere ● Cottam ● ● BRIDLINGTON
Bessingby
Fraisthorpe ● WILSTHORPE
● Barmston
DRIFFIELD

● Brandesburton
HORNSEA ○

● Leconfield

The Beverley & Barmston Drain
● Sproatley

HULL ○ ○ WITHERNSEA

Part One:
Stories From Strange-Land

Diary of a Lunar Watcher

I began researching and filming on the East and North Yorkshire Wolds early into 2005. Most of the time it is a cold and unrewarding place, so I am sure that anyone seeing Steve Ashbridge and me standing out there on cold and dark November nights must have thought we were lunatics.

Looking back now, it is clear that we never really capitalised on some of the things we both saw and experienced there. We were so blown away by the appearance of the intelligent lightforms that appeared in the sky, that we failed to pay enough attention to other less exciting anomalies that were presented to us.

In recent years our research has moved from the Wolds area to the clifftops of Bempton and Speeton and just like years before, other things are happening. After spending weeks, months and years hoping to catch sight of the spectacular but elusive lightforms, we *have* observed other anomalies. The difference now is that we are treating each one with the same level of importance.

These elements of the phenomena may not be as visually dramatic as the lightforms, but they are probably just as important. Yet these exotics are so random and detached that we are often caught off-guard.

The Exotics

I visit Bempton and the surrounding area with Steve Ashbridge at least once a week and Andi Ramsden usually accompanies me on Fridays. Other than that I go alone. It is however becoming an increasingly unwelcoming location. A combination of many things contribute to this feeling of unease, including the realisation that what I am writing about is real and happening.

Bempton after dark is not a place I would recommend visiting alone. *"But you go so often"* I hear you say. True, but even so, I'm not sure I will ever get that one bit of proof that will squeeze the air from the sceptic's lungs rendering them speechless. It is the only location I know of capable of giving me that proof. Don't get me wrong, I realise that unusual things are seen all over the world all the time. Ten years ago the East Yorkshire Wolds were active with unexplained phenomena and I am sure they will be again. But in this location the odds are greater than anywhere else I have been.

It must be difficult for people, who have no interest in all this, to get their heads around some of the things I research and report. But do the same people have the answers to any of the crazy things that have happened? Do the authorities? No, they choose not to think for themselves, preferring to follow official explanations, even though they rarely fit the circumstances. Did you ever wonder why there are no follow-up stories on the missing men of Bempton? What would the authorities say? '*People have gone missing and despite all our efforts and technical advancements in investigation, we still have no idea what happened to them. We will not say this to the public, but we hope everyone forgets.*'

I like to think that we shouldn't get blown away by every anomalous sparkling light or strange sound that we hear, and Truth-Proof is full of all things unusual. But people have to understand that both of my books are an accumulation of decades of activity, years of research and a lifetime of soul-searching. For me, the search for answers has become a huge part of my life. It is a full time job to gather information and observe, a job that offers little more than hope in return for my efforts.

Here is one such example of how unpredictable these events of high strangeness can be.

The Split-Second Observation

On the evening of February 13th 2017 Steve Ashbridge and I were on the cliff top at Bempton. We were looking out to sea from a viewing platform known as Big Railings, which sits on the very edge of the cliffs.

We had gone to Bempton to try and film the lightforms, which had been seen in recent times over the sea. Instead we came away with a split-second observation of something else entirely. This proved to me, once and for all, that there is nothing normal about the paranormal.

There was low-lying fog out on the horizon that night, but the sky above was clear and filled with stars. We had not seen the lightforms for a few weeks, but scanned the sky hoping they would make an appearance. Suddenly, out on the horizon I saw a faint red circle of light. This was it. This was our chance to catch the phenomena.

"Steve! Look, look. There's a red ball of light over there," I called out. *"Wow, its getting bigger."* I pulled the cover from my camcorder and began to film the shimmering red object. For the first thirty seconds it looked amazing. It was growing in size and appeared to be gaining altitude. As usual, I was filming and Steve had his high-powered binoculars trained on the light, which seemed now to be growing in luminosity through the fog.

"Paul I think it's the moon," said Steve. *"It's getting clearer now. Yes, it is definitely the moon."* I stopped recording. Steve's binoculars are very powerful, so I knew that if he said we were looking at the moon rising, that's what it was. For a few moments our sighting had looked promising and, in truth, if we had wanted to fake events at Bempton, the footage of the red moon rising out of the mist would have looked convincing. But we never have and never will play any of those games. The whole reason for our being there is to capture evidence of the genuinely unusual.

Thirty minutes later and the moon had lifted clear of the low-lying fog. I admit that it looked unusual, but this red moon was no match for the intelligent lightforms, whose sudden appearance is nothing less than spectacular for those fortunate enough to see them. This year we both purchased Nikon P900 cameras; an incredible piece of kit for close-up shots. If Steve and I had wanted to fake a sighting we could easily have

3

used images of that low, red moon in the mist and claimed we had captured a lightform.

The same night at around 10.15pm, I saw a light at the back of the nearby disused RAF base. It was brief. So fast in fact, that I made no mention of it to Steve. Less than a minute later Steve said, *"I think I just saw a flash of light on the base Paul."*
I told him I had also seen something moments before, but had dismissed it because it was so fast and I could not be sure. These strange anomalies happen so quickly, that at times we just accept them as part of the strangeness.

The evening passed with nothing more eventful than the occasional aircraft passing overhead. It was now quite late and we talked about making our way back to the car. Then I looked up towards the top of the field. The car park was over to our left and the old RAF base was on our right - both about five hundred metres away from us beyond the field ahead. But my eyes suddenly fixed and focused on the hedgerow at the top of the field, close to the perimeter of the old base.

"I just saw a flash of light Steve. It was very odd. It was in front of the hedge, just down from the base." At that point I hadn't told Steve that the light I saw was square or rectangular in shape, but that it just flicked on and off for the briefest of moments.
"I'm glad you said that Paul." Steve replied. *"Because I saw it as well. Was it at the top of the field - in the middle?"*
I described the position I had seen the light. My eyes had not moved from the spot and I pointed to the lower part of the hedgerow. Whatever it was must have been fast, because Steve insisted that it was in a different part of the field when he saw it. He said it was still along the hedgerow, but closer to the middle.

Steve and I have both been researching and observing for many years. We both share similar values and we trust each other's word. Steve's sighting of the light was confirmation of my own. Yet it happened so fast that I almost said nothing, but I was pleased I did when Steve began to describe what he saw.
"Paul this may sound daft, but the light was very pale, almost like those hedge lights we used to see out on the Wolds. But the strangest thing was, it was square-shaped."

Impression of the square-shaped lights witnessed by Steve Ashbridge and myself.

As soon as I heard Steve say 'square-shaped' I knew my mind was not just playing tricks on me. The light I saw had been more rectangular than square, but at least Steve's own observation confirmed it.

I realise this may sound crazy, but after standing out in cold for hours and only seeing the fleeting glimpse of something, we actually got excited. It was something foreign to our eyes but it had a shape. Everything has shape of course, but this had angled lines.

Only months before, I was there with Andi Ramsden one Friday evening. We were looking out towards the RAF base when, just above the base, we both saw a square of light open up in the sky. There were no words of suggestion from either of us. A square of light is exactly what we saw, but it is difficult to find the right words to clearly convey what we had observed. Anyone who has seen the sudden flash of a fluorescent strip-light, as it attempts to light up, may get the idea. It was a little like that, but not as bright.

In the past I have described the Wolds lightforms, as looking like tears in the sky - as though we were looking into another world. They seemed almost cartoonish. Could the locations contain a weakness in the fabric of our own perceived reality, that allows other things to punch through into our existence? The lightforms are real; the overwhelming number of eye-witness reports confirm this, but we are reluctant to consider anything that exists beyond our understanding – so we deny their reality.

We need new words to explain what our eyes have seen, but those words do not exist. Only when there is a shift towards accepting the reality of the lightforms, will new words grow around them and be used in the future. I also think that two people with limited funds will ever be able capture the full majesty of this phenomenon on film. It would take sophisticated cameras and round-the-clock monitoring to have any hope of success.

Steve had described the light he saw as 'square' and this was the only confirmation I needed. If he had just said it was a light, I would still have trusted his word, but he had said 'square-shaped'. I never told him the light I saw was that shape. Yet both of our observations were made in the same moment and our descriptions of its shape and position were so close, that it could not have been a mistake. I am sure that if I had been alone, I would have dismissed my sighting as nothing more than the darkness playing tricks on my mind. Yet suddenly, in the sky, this single white light had flicked on and off and we had both witnessed it. It was fast and it was small, no bigger than a spark.

For a while Steve and I just stood in the darkness, watching the top of the field. It was now after 11pm and nothing moved. We decided to walk along the edge of the field towards the old base and follow the route down to where we had seen the squares of light. As we walked, I wondered how many of the local rock-anglers had seen the exact same thing and because of its incredibly short duration, thought they had imagined it. I'm sure if I had been alone, I would have dismissed it just the same. But it took two of us to confirm that this briefest of surreal moments had actually registered in our conscious minds.

I had visited the area in the summer of 2016 with three other people; Andi Ramsden, Janet Wildman and her adult son, Karl. That evening both Janet and Andi claim to have seen a rectangular strip of light suddenly appear then disappear, in the entrance of one of the derelict RAF buildings. It blew their minds at the time and they still talk about it to this day.

We checked around the base, but there was no one around and the building where they had seen the light was empty. We left a short time afterwards because Janet's son Karl said he felt ill. As his mother and Andi were seeing the rectangular light (and for reasons he could not explain) a sudden wave of dizziness came over him. I noticed he seemed to be acting oddly and went over to speak with him - so I didn't see the light myself. He seemed confused and at one point, I took hold of his arm because I thought he was going to try and climb over the fence at the cliff edge.

Karl now says he never wants to go there again. His mother Janet believes something at Bempton had affected him and, after observing his sudden change in behaviour, I am inclined to agree. I also suspect this is not the first time people have felt confused or disorientated around this area. This is another element to sightings of the lightform phenomena and one that needs as much consideration as all the others. I wonder if, in the affected areas, we are witnessing some kind of overlap of dimensions, allowing other intelligences to interact and operate alongside of us?

At times, perhaps they are so close they touch our own existence, sometimes with fatal consequences. Is it something working on a much higher level than we could ever understand? We could call it 'new intelligence' - although I suspect it is ancient. Did the people using the bunker for satanic rituals at the old RAF base already know this? And did the people who built the prehistoric burial mounds and earthworks see and experience the same things?

After our own sighting, Steve Ashbridge and I made our way along the edge of the field. We already knew there would be nothing to see, but would have kicked ourselves later if we had not checked all possibilities. We had to be sure. We both had powerful torches but refrained from turning them on until we got to where we had seen the light-squares. I'm not sure why we act as though we can somehow catch the phenomena off-guard, because it's probably already aware of our every move. Everything that is happening is presenting itself on its own terms, and anything we think or do seems to make little or no difference.

We reached the hedgerow and as expected there was nothing. Only trees and darkness. All there was behind the trees were miles of open farmland, open skies and more questions.

Satanic RAF Bempton

One of the most difficult things I found, while obtaining information for my books, was to encourage witnesses to talk about the satanic activities that took place in the bunker at RAF Bempton. Over the years the activity at the base has become something of an urban legend; and like Chinese whispers many of the stories have grown out of rumour - but not all of them.

I am told that the bunker was used at various times for dark practices; from the 1970s to the late 90s. I do not know if the same people were involved throughout that period and it's not even possible to speculate what actually took place, but the information I have received over the years leaves me in no doubt that the Bempton bunker has been active.

Black magic is one of the rarest of human taboos and it is not hard to imagine why people are so reluctant to talk. They fear the unknown and the possibility that bad things might come to them if they do talk about it. Many seem to have heard about the strange goings-on below ground, but few are willing to share what they know. A few years ago I spoke to at least two members of a secret group. It was my one and only meeting and it did not end well. Their reactions towards me, when I asked questions about the alleged activities in the dark inner world of the bunker, changed from placid to hostile in an instant. My suspicions about their involvement were raised before we had even spoken, having previously been warned to be careful.

In 2017 I began visiting Bempton on very early mornings. I was hoping to photograph a sunrise behind the standing stones at the base for the cover of this book. During one of my early morning visits, I met and spoke with a man who claimed that as a teenager, he had found something unusual inside the bunker. In his own words he said;
"I think it would have been about 1994 or 95 and we decided to head up to the bunker. We were always exploring different places around the area and the bunker was a scary place. It was exciting. The stories of witchcraft and black magic were known by most people in the village - my Mum and Dad talked about it from time to time. They even warned me about going there and they were deadly serious.
It must have been the school holidays, because I remember it was a week day when we sneaked onto the base. We had to be careful because the farmer hated people on his land. His reaction was strange, I think he

was over-reacting really. It was not as though there was anything below ground that we could damage and above ground is just grassland. I suppose he can do whatever he wants, it is his own property.

Anyway, when we got inside it was obvious that people had been there during the night. There was a funny smell and we soon realised it was from burnt red candle-wax on the floors. It's hard to describe just how dark and enclosed it feels in that place. When we got into a larger area we found more candles, loads of them and it looked like they had been burning for hours.
It was creepy, knowing that people had been there a short time before us and by the looks of it, they were up to no good. But the candles were only part of what we found down there. We also found robes and face masks - but understand that these were not just bits of old sheet like you'd throw over your head with cut-out holes for the eyes. They were very well made. I took one of the hooded masks home with me and showed it to my parents. I told them where I had found it. They took one look at it and told me never to go there again. They went mad - I think my Dad cut it up and put it in the dustbin. They even told me never to talk about what I'd found."

The short account is not direct proof of witchcraft, satanic ritual or any other form of occult practice, but it does indicate that something weird took place inside the Bempton bunker as late as the mid-1990s. I believe people know that unexplained things happen around this area, but I wonder if those who focus their minds on dark thoughts are somehow able to evoke an interaction with something we don't understand. Satanic practice is a surreal and deep human pastime, but is it possible that the events of high strangeness in the area are heightened by such activities? If a secret group of people were able to evoke just one anomalous event, like those described in my first book, it would have been enough to turn an interest in the occult into an obsession that has spanned decades.

Nothing I write ever touches on the day to day running of the nearby Bempton Cliffs nature reserve and visitor centre. I'm sure the 80,000 visitors who came to the cliffs in 2016 have no idea about the darker side of this landscape. It might as well be another world. But peel back the layers of ordinary mundane life that cover East and North Yorkshire and we uncover a world of the unexplained as rich as anywhere else on the planet.

A Ghost By Any Other Name

On the evening of October 24th 2016 Steve Ashbridge and I paid a visit to Bempton cliffs. I had been visiting the area myself two or three times a week, in the hope of catching a glimpse of the lightforms that were being reported. I interviewed some of the sea anglers there, who fish off the four hundred foot high cliffs every year, and managed to collect some interesting accounts of sightings from them. I had been aware of the stories for many years and on a few occasions since, have been lucky enough to see the lightforms with my own eyes; but I have to say, what Steve and I witnessed on October 24th 2016 was incredible.

Steve and I arrived at Bempton nature reserve car park at 7.30pm and soon realised we were not alone on the clifftops. Six other cars were already there when we arrived and as we walked down towards the cliffs, we could see a faint line of lights spaced out evenly along the cliff edge, all the way from Bempton to Speeton. Rock angling season was in full swing and the fishermen's lights gave away their position on the clifftops. As we walked to our chosen observation point a faint orange light suddenly appeared low in the sky. I don't think it was as far away as the horizon, which, due to our elevated position at the time, I was able to estimate to be about twenty miles away.

This object was closer and seemed to be in front of the lights of a boat out in the distance. I have to confess that it was a very dark night so the light could in fact have been further away. We both watched it for a few moments and then it was gone. It was an unusual sight and a positive start to our night of observation. We set up our cameras and prepared to wait in the darkness, hoping that the lightforms would appear. I knew our chances were good - I had already received several texts and calls during the week from anglers who had seen them – and we were not disappointed. At approximately 8.05pm we saw an intense orange ball of light suddenly switch on in the sky, just a few miles out at sea.

"Wow Steve, look, look." I called out. *"There's another light out there. It's just appeared."* By the time Steve had turned around, the light in the sky had switched off. I did not have to say anything more. Steve knew that if I told him I had seen it, then it *had* appeared. Then about 8.20pm it reappeared, in what seemed to be the same position. This time Steve saw it seconds before it switched off once more. It happened so fast that I could not get the camcorder started and in position in time to catch it.

Steve had his own camera but he was so taken aback by the incredible sight that he never even tried to record it; he just wanted to observe the phenomena. At 8.30pm we decided to move a little further down the coast, towards Flamborough. We were in close proximity to the rock anglers who all wore head lamps. Quite unintentionally they would flash in our direction from time to time. It was a little off-putting, so we began to gather up our things to move on.

Just then, a huge orange globe lit up in the sky. It was over to our right and closer to us this time. It's hard to describe the vivid colour and intensity of the light. Saying it appeared soft may sound crazy, but to my eyes it looked like a soft orange/red ball and it was so vivid - that the word 'vivid' does not do it justice. Moments later it switched off. I tried to catch it on camera but it was so fast, I had no chance. Steve simply observed it, trying to gather as much information as possible, before it vanished. Usually, we are a good combination, since my first instinct is to film objects as they appear, where Steve's is always to observe.
"I could see a structure to that Paul. I think it was square. It definitely had some kind of structure to it."

A short time later the light reappeared. It was in the same position and lit up in the sky exactly as before, but we were packed and ready to set off towards Flamborough, so I did not have my camcorder to hand. I had no alternative other than to observe it. To my eyes it did have more than just a circular shape. I would have said oval, but an oval that was upright and a bit like an egg. But I think there was more; I think the intense orange light was just a glimpse of something much bigger and darker hiding behind it. I realise I only have my word and Steve's to show for the sighting and like all UFO-related reports before it, this really is a truth that leaves no proof.

A short time later we settled on a position further down the cliffs towards Flamborough and we stayed there until approximately 11pm. The objects made a few brief appearances in that time, but nothing that could compare to the earlier show we had been treated to; their vivid arrival and exit being over in less than a few seconds. The rock anglers who have seen them over the years have lots of theories of what they think the lights are. Some actually think the lightforms are something alien-related, though most look for an Earthly explanation.

A few years ago I was given explanations by two men who were fishing up at Speeton; one said the afterburners of jet aircraft were responsible, the other thought they were flares. Both agreed that the objects they saw were silent and had the ability to appear from nowhere, then vanish just as quickly, only to reappear seconds later in a different location. People are reluctant to consider that a true unknown might responsible. Everyone from a fool to a genius wants to pigeon-hole the unexplained into a box that requires no hard thinking.

So what did Steve and I see that made these lights different? Well, the colour for a start. It's hard to explain, but there was such a richness to it and it was as though there was more 'inside' it. But were they flares? I would have to lean towards saying no to that question - because these things were quite large and simply appeared then vanished, as fast as they arrived. We observed nothing that would suggest they *were* flares. There was no smoke, no sound of anything being discharged. Nothing. So it would be a pretty useless flare if it just appeared and disappeared in seconds. And we could not hear aircraft. The boat on the horizon gave us a good reference point to indicate the divide between sky and sea and except for a few patches cloud, the sky that night was very bright.

Some witnesses say the lightforms appear below the clouds, but it is worth noting that some never illuminate the cloud around them. For me, all of this rules out the possibility that flares were responsible for what Steve and I saw. There was no smoke, no aircraft, no loud noise to suggest a discharge of any kind. There was no illumination of the cloud area around them and when I say the light was intense, I cannot stress that enough. Does that sound like flare activity?

I am not sure if these things were projecting a light of some kind onto the surface of the sea, but from a short clip of footage I captured in the last moments of our sighting, the sea is clearly glowing an orange-colour below the object. *(Clip available on my YouTube channel)*
I don't know what this means, if anything, but it strengthens the case that flares can be ruled out. Because if they were close enough to see a reflection on the surface of the sea, I am sure we would have heard aircraft. Could they have been meteors or some strange kind of atmospheric effect? The word meteor conjures up images of something fast moving in the sky, but these things just appeared, sometimes in the same location a short time later.

Maybe they remained in the same place all the time but were invisible and they did not streak away, they just switched off.

The next day I spoke about the lights with a man who works for the Royal National Lifeboat Institution. I wanted to ask if they knew of any military exercises that might have been responsible for the lights. I was basically trying to arm myself with as much information as possible and be one step ahead of the debunkers. I described what we had seen on the previous night and I was informed that nothing unusual had been reported and there had been nothing happening out at sea involving aircraft. We spoke at length about what we thought the lights may have been and I explained how a single light could appear and then suddenly become five.

The man was intrigued and said, *"Paul, if that is how they appeared it would rule out flares fired from a vessel because they usually go up in pairs. I used to work on submarines so have considerable experience. I am familiar with most types of flare activity and nocturnal lights that civilians might find unusual when seen from the land. I have to say that, going by what you have described, I am not sure what they could have been."*

The Bempton lights had now got me hooked. They were just like the lightforms seen over land at the Wolds years before. I thought they had to be connected in some way, since their behaviour was very similar. Although the sea lights were much richer in colour and, in the words of Steve Ashbridge, they were 'eerie to look at'.

The next night I packed a few things together and told my wife I was going back to Bempton for a few hours. I was determined to get these objects on film. At six-thirty I was standing alone on the remote clifftops, with my camera set on its tripod and my eyes fixed to the sky. It was getting dark and it's always colder out there than it is inland, at any time of the year, but I had to remain positive. I wanted documented proof of the Bempton lightforms. At approximately 7.05pm a single light appeared in view, north of Flamborough Head and I would estimate about ten miles offshore. I was unable to get the camcorder started before it vanished. So now I stood there ready, with my fingers on the switch of the camcorder, waiting to throw it into action if the light reappeared. Is that dedication or the comfort of madness?

So many researchers sit at computer screens gathering information or they rely on the word of a witness. I just feel the need to prove to the world that we are actually seeing these objects. Of course, online research is valid, but I sometimes feel it is only right that I try to see with my own eyes the things that others are seeing and experiencing. Proving what they are is a page in a book that I have not yet turned. At 7.15pm a single gold light appeared. This one caught me off guard, because it was parallel to where I was standing and straight out to sea. It vanished before I could even gather my thoughts. Then, just before 7.30pm, two lights switched on in the sky, roughly in the same position as the first one I had seen. I did manage to capture a fleeting glimpse of them on camera before the last one switched off.

A single light appeared at 7.40pm, then it suddenly jumped in the sky to become a row of five, evenly spaced spheres. They all seemed to be blinking independently of each other and then, all at once, they just vanished as fast as they arrived. My phone rang at 7.45 and it was Steve calling to talk about the lights we had seen. He was surprised when I told him I was out on the clifftops. He had no plans to come and join me, but as we spoke, a single light appeared in front of me. When I told him, his mind was instantly changed and he said he'd be there in thirty minutes.

In that time the lights had appeared and disappeared in rows of five in various places in the sky. I was able to capture their last moments on film a few times. I wondered again if they were still out there, but were just invisible to my eyes. I cannot understand how this phenomena seems to be constantly ahead of our thinking. I have to conclude that it somehow knows the workings of our minds.

Steve arrived just before 8.35pm and we stayed on the clifftops until about 11pm. I think he must have dragged the clouds along with him from Hornsea on his way, as the sky slowly closed in. Soon, all we could see was the beam from Flamborough lighthouse, flashing every four seconds, as it reached out into the lonely night. We saw nothing more of the lights and I felt guilty now, after telling him about them on the phone hours before.

The next day I received a phone call from one of the sea anglers who had also been on the clifftops the previous night. His exact words were, *"did you see the light show?"* I told him I had and asked what he thought they could have been. He said, *"Flares or meteors. I don't know what else they could have been. I have never seen anything like them."*

This seems to be the general opinion of many of the anglers who fish off the cliffs at Bempton and nearby Speeton. That is, until they have a close and personal encounter - which some of them have experienced. The day these lightforms become an officially recognised phenomenon, they will never be called flares, meteors or an unusual atmospheric effect again.

The Ghost Of Big Railings

Big Railings is the name given by local fisherman to a large wooden viewing platform on top of Bempton Cliffs, overlooking Breil Nook. Perched almost 200ft above sea level, the platform was built by the RSPB nature reserve and is used by bird watchers during the day and sea anglers during winter evenings. I spoke to one of the anglers who told me that many of the men who fish from the platform had seen something they call 'the ghost of Big Railings'.

I found this of particular interest due to my own sighting of a white ball of light on the clifftops. First documented in Truth-Proof (2016), I was working through the night, fitting a floor-safe inside the RSPB visitor centre, when I observed the ball of light in the direction of Breil Nook. Was this a coincidence? I asked the fisherman to describe the 'ghost'. *"I have seen it a few times over the years. Sometimes we see it as we walk down the path towards the cliff and we think someone is already there fishing. It spooks us when we actually get there and no one is around. Loads of us have seen it, but none of us can say what it is."*

He was standing by the visitor centre gate looking down towards the cliffs at the time of this sighting - which made it even more interesting, because I was standing by the same gate when I had my sighting of the ball of light. Maybe what I saw is what the anglers call the ghost of Big Railings. But are the fishermen really seeing a ghost out on the cliffs?

"You call it the ghost of Big Railings?" I asked. *"But I haven't heard you say that it's the shape of a dead person - you know what I mean? When I imagine a ghost I think of something in the shape of a man or woman, but you seem to be talking about something else."*

I made a point of asking in a quite blunt way because my interpretation of a ghost seemed slightly different to what the angler was describing. I have heard similar descriptions before; like the ghost of the White Lady at Danes Dyke. The name conjures up images of a female apparition, but up to this moment the reports from Danes Dyke only describe spheres of white light - not unlike what I was hearing now from the angler. He looked at me and a slightly puzzled frown formed on his face. For a moment I could not tell if he was annoyed or felt tricked, so I asked again. *"So you never actually saw the shape of a person or anything suggesting it was a human form?"*

I had to push the question, because nothing about what the anglers were seeing suggested to me that this was a standard ghost, if such a thing exists. I know what I saw close to Big Railings on the night I fitted the safe - and it was nothing but a ball of white light. To me, the word *ghost* is just another term used to fit something unexplained into a box that we can accept and understand. So I asked the angler again.

"We have all seen the same light," he said. *"Loads of the guys have seen it. It's about the size of a headlamp and very bright. But like I said before, when we arrive at the place we've seen it there is never anyone there. We've also seen it on the edge of the cliff, just off the path. It gets us every time; we walk up thinking someone is already fishing. But just like at Big Railings, there is never anyone around when we get there. We just call it the ghost of Big Railings; I suppose your right though, it is just a ball of light."*

Many years ago I began to consider if such a thing as 'living lightforms' could somehow exist in this area; this might then explain the similarities between the Danes Dyke reports and those from the Wolds and Breil Nook. Perhaps this a step too far into the abyss of the unproven - although after further investigation, I learned that this phantom light has been seen by generations of men and women around the same coastal location. For the moment I would settle for acceptance that this unknown phenomenon is real. I know of similar accounts of 'ghost lights' seen twenty miles inland, as the crow flies, close to the village of Fimber on the East Yorkshire Wolds. Locals call it the ghost of Fimber Crossroads, but it is not until we begin to look more closely at what has actually been seen, that we realise, in most instances, that people are actually seeing luminous balls of light - hardly the ghostly form of a dead person. My point is, that no one seems to have looked beyond the word *ghost*; usually the shadowy form of a deceased human being.

Regardless of that fact, I have no doubt that something unusual is happening around the clifftops of Bempton. It is a phenomena that also extends out to sea and at times, is responsible for the reports of distress flares that never were. The impact these lightforms have on witnesses can range from shock and amazement, to outright fear and sometimes I wonder if such an interaction has ever ended in fatal consequences. All of these things have to be considered, but no matter how hostile and uninviting the area may be, I have to continue with my research.

The Ghost Of Fimber Crossroads

As I read about ghosts and railway crossings, I wonder if the crossings themselves might contain some sort of concentration of human energy and emotion. These are just my own thoughts, as I study a few accounts of ghostly activity from my own county of East Yorkshire.

The stories originate around the old Fimber railway station that once existed between the villages of Fridaythorpe and Sledmere. Both locations are noted today for sightings of big cats and UFOs, so it seems only fitting that reports of ghosts should also come into this mix of the unexplained.

Since its closure in November 1958, the station itself is now nothing more than a memory. It was opened in 1853 as Fimber station, renamed Sledmere station in 1858, then finally Sledmere and Fimber station in May 1859. For almost a hundred years it gave passengers the perfect opportunity for observation in a remote location, where strange things had been seen and continue to be seen, through to the present day.

Local folklore tells of a haunted crossroads where Fimber station used to be, but reports of strange ghost lights and mysterious animal apparitions were recorded long before the existence of the railway. It is in fact a location where two deep valleys cross and, although it was once a focal point for human activity, all physical traces of the railway station have long gone. The area is now known locally as Fimber Crossroads.

Travellers and local people have reported seeing ghosts and hobgoblins in this area for hundreds of years. The roads and wooded areas surrounding Fimber were not considered a good place to find yourself on a dark night - and having spent many hours there myself over the years, I have to agree. The ghosts of Fimber Crossroads are said to come in many forms and cause feelings of fear in the people who claim to have seen them. Yet over the many years I have spent observing in this location, I have only ever seen unusual spheres of light.

There are tales told by grown men who have been terrified by the sight of a ghostly hound with red eyes, that appears like a phantom out of the darkness. There are other amazing accounts, including that of a headless woman, whose ghostly form is said to drift by and just vanish into the night. While others claim to have seen a ghostly woman on horseback gallop past them. Personally, I wonder if witnesses to these historical sightings have simply added elements to their experience, to make them more identifiable - and maybe some deep human instinct is triggered, filling the mind with dread when such things are seen.

When Chris Evers, the editor of Outer Limits online magazine, asked if I would write something about ghosts connected to railway crossings, I already knew of the ghosts of Fimber Crossroads - but finding a local ghost story with a beginning and an end is difficult. For the moment, all I can do is report what people claim to have seen in the area throughout the years.

Whilst researching UFOs seen over the Yorkshire Wolds back in 2009, I spoke with a couple who live in Fimber village. They were very keen to tell me about some 'ghost cats' they had seen around Fimber crossroads. *'Ghost cats?'* I thought to myself - but I asked the question and they told me what they saw. The couple claimed to have seen two black cats, which looked so real, except they seemed out of place. They said they appeared as real and sharp to human eyes as any other domestic cat. That was, until they vanished before their eyes.

The couple admitted to being scared by the experience and, as they spoke to me, I could tell they were clearly embarrassed to be even talking about it. They said that if they had not seen them with their own eyes they would never have believed it. They said that if anyone else had told them the same thing before this, they would have laughed - but now they think the area is haunted by strange cats.

There *are* reports of black panthers, which have been seen in the adjoining woodland around Fimber. So I have no doubts that large phantom cats *have* been seen in the area, but I do not think they are wild 'flesh and blood' predators. After all my years of research I have concluded that there must be something about the location which allows these bizarre things to happen.

In my first book, I reported on a different kind of sighting of my own from 2002. It was at Sledmere, just a few miles away from Fimber, that I saw a huge tubular-shaped UFO that simply vanished. I also wrote about the time Peter Easterby and his family saw a very similar object, which they said vanished in front of their eyes. All of this happened in the same concentrated area. Even the reports of phantom dogs have never gone away. There are infrequent sightings of the beast at Flixton and Danes Dyke, which is less than 15 miles away from Fimber, as the crow flies. These huge animals just appear and disappear in such a way that they cannot be real flesh and blood beasts.

All of these things seem connected to other parts of East and North Yorkshire. But I do not know why so many accounts of ghosts come from the area around Fimber Crossroads. I am not sure whether they are even ghosts. Perhaps we just give them that label because it fits in with human belief and what we perceive. Could the ghosts, the lightforms and the phantom animals all be showing us a glimpse into another world that is as alive and vibrant as our own?

Travellers passing through Fimber have also reported seeing glowing lights over in Besendale valley, just a few miles away. This is another location where I have spent many hours watching the skies at night. I realise now, after observing the very same things myself, that the ghost lights seen over many years are the same lightforms that we are still seeing today. The only thing that has changed over the years is our interpretation of them.

The Cliff Lane Triangle

In the summer of 1995 four young lads from Bempton were walking along Cliff Lane, close to the track known as Blakehowe Lane.

Peter is one of the four who gave me his account in early 2017. Now in his thirties, he told me he had never spoken to anyone about it since that time. His experience is another example of a phenomenon which appears out of thin air, which leaves witnesses with nothing but a visual memory which cannot be proved. Neither can it be processed because there is nothing to compare it with.

Peter told me that, as far as he can remember, it was a warm evening and the sky was clear and blue. He said it was early enough in the evening, so the four of them decided to take a walk up to Bempton Cliffs, their final destination most probably would have been the underground bunker. The bunker is sealed today, but it used to be like a magnet to the youth of the village, who considered it to be an exciting, if not forbidden, place to explore.

They were close to the junction of Blakehowe Lane when one of his friends pointed into the sky and called out, *'Look at that.'* Peter told me he is unsure exactly what his friend said but it was enough for them all to look in the direction he was pointing - and they were astonished by what they saw.

Right in front of them hovered a black triangle, it was low in the sky and directly over Cliff Lane. They all could see it clearly and Peter estimated its size to be approximately 25ft by 15ft. He said it was less than 200ft above the ground, but was not directly above them when they saw it. They seemed to be looking at it from the back, as the pointed end was furthest away from them. Peter described seeing a huge bank of lights which slowly flashed in every colour.

I made a point of asking Peter about the colour of the lights, because he had described them as 'every colour imaginable' and that was something I had never heard before. He told me they looked like LEDs and thinks they were in a horizontal strip. The lights did not appear to flash in any sequence and the triangle made no sound. Apart from the lights, he told me that it all looked to be seamless and black. He also said it appeared to be very flat and probably measured no more than 8ft thick.

The four lads were more excited than frightened by what they were seeing, and they ran up the lane towards the object to try and get directly beneath it. Peter told me he was not sure if it began to move away as they approached, but he said that it did appear to keep the same distance from them the whole time.

He said they followed the triangle as it moved above them along the lane. It maintained a slow speed and for a short time they were able to keep up with it. Then he told me that its speed gradually increased and pursuit soon became impossible. Peter said he was sure the object had no windows and even as it gained speed, it remained silent. The four friends continued to follow the object as they ran along Cliff Lane and down towards the cliffs. From there they watched it fly over the clifftops and out to sea until it was so distant, that they could only see its lights.

I saw the look on Peter's face when I asked him to describe the black triangle they all saw. It was reminiscent of the same expression I see on the faces of many witnesses I interview. I could tell that he found it difficult, because his eyes were remembering something so unique that his mind could not understand. Observing the expressions of witnesses is just as important to me as hearing them recall their experiences – and this was a close-up sighting that gave the four of them an amazing view of something truly unknown.

The fact this black triangle had just appeared from nowhere makes me wonder whether it was able to materialise into view. Or perhaps it had some kind of cloaking device making it invisible at first. I think the way it appeared may be connected to the actual location. This often seems to play a major role in the manifestation of objects that are sometimes so off-the-scale, their appearance is nothing short of magic.

We think we are the supreme intelligence on this little blue ball of light but we should consider the possibility of worlds beyond our own. I think the intelligence behind the Cliff Lane triangle may belong to something our minds cannot even imagine, but I don't think the question of whether they come from some distant world is of any importance. Before we answer that question, we have to develop ways to understand them as they appear in this world - because they are already here.

Next page: impression of the Cliff Lane triangular craft.

The Bempton Blue Light

In March 2015 I spoke with a Bempton man named David Ellis. He had a story to share about some strange lights he had witnessed from the clifftops during the summer of 2004.

It was early evening and David was out walking with his two Labrador Retrievers, close to Bempton RSPB nature reserve. He cannot remember the exact date but thinks it was mid-summer, either June or July, because it was a warm evening and the grass was green and lush. He had left his home in Bempton village at about 6.30pm to walk up Cliff Lane - a journey he did many many times over the years throughout summer and winter.

David told me he had seen spheres of light suddenly appear and disappear on more than one occasion over the years, but they were nothing in comparison to what he saw on the clifftop this time around.

The evening began as uneventfully as all the others before it, as he proceeded to walk down towards the RSPB nature reserve. David remembers a car passed by as he walked, so he shouted his dogs to the side of the road and did the statutory nod to the driver as their eyes met. His dogs know the route well and a short time later all three of them entered a field to the right of the nature reserve. Access to the field is now restricted to the public but it looks no different today than when David had his unusual encounter. I cannot identify any mystery to the fact that this field is now off limits, but for some reason the RSPB has simply restricted public access.

As he continued walking David recalled seeing an owl flying low over the old RAF base, hunting for voles and mice. He remembers watching its flight path as it skimmed the contours of the land. His dogs were oblivious as they ran back and forth, seemingly unaware of anything out of the ordinary. This was just another summer evening. Then David turned to his right and was now looking out over the cliffs towards Flamborough. That was when he saw it. A most unusual sight on the edge of the cliff path. Suddenly, the day had switched from ordinary to extraordinary.

At first he just stood there, staring in disbelief and trying to work out what he was actually looking at. He had never seen anything like it before, so had nothing to compare it with. Thoughts of hunting owls had now gone from his mind entirely and were replaced by confusion. He glanced over towards his dogs, who seemed unaware of the huge mass of sparkling light that was now on view on the edge of the cliffs. Whatever it was remained still and silent.

David leaned forward as he spoke to me and looked around, as though not wanting anyone else to hear what he had to say.

"Paul, the atmosphere seemed to change from the first second that I looked at it. It felt like I had stepped into another world. It was like a vacuum had sucked out all the sound and left me in a sound-proof room. Like the moment when you suddenly realise nothing else matters and you are 'in the moment' - that's how it made me feel. I had never seen or experienced anything like it before or since. I remember tipping my head from side to side, just like a dog does when it's confused..."

More than ten years later and David still found it difficult to describe what he saw and experienced. He said it was just a huge luminous mass that was sitting on the edge of the cliffs. It was on the main clifftop path inland, but over the edge actually hanging out to sea.

"At first I thought it was some kind of marsh-gas because I can remember seeing some years ago in Norfolk. But you have to realise at that point I was desperately trying to understand what I was looking at. Marsh-gas was the closest thing I could think of, even though it was nothing like it."

David dismissed that idea as fast as it formed in his mind. This anomaly was nothing like what he had seen in Norfolk and the composition of the land and the clifftop location could not support theories of marsh-gas anyway. As he spoke, my mind was taken back to Lesley Buttle's 1977 account, first reported in Truth-Proof, of the large oval-shaped UFO seen close to Bessingby Industrial Estate. Lesley saw the UFO with two friends, who all described seeing an unusual misty cloud hanging above some nearby garden allotments.

In the Bessingby case the mist seemed to evaporate revealing a large oval object that hung in the sky in front of the terrified ladies. The difference here was that David could not see any solid structure within the luminous blue-green light in front of him, only the sparkling lights that danced within it.

I asked him if he felt the urge to get any closer to the light.

"No I did not. I don't know what I felt exactly. Uneasy and a bit scared I think. It just wasn't right. I should have stayed and watched what happened, but for some reason I turned away and walked back towards the bird centre. I have asked myself why I didn't at least just stand and observe it, after all, it was like nothing I had ever seen before. But it gave me a feeling of fear. I just don't know, its hard to explain the feeling."

I have to admit that I am unsure which paranormal category David's stationary light fits into. Most of the lightforms seen from the cliffs of Flamborough and Bempton have been up in the air and are red, amber or white in colour. The sharp sparkling lights he saw within the mass suggest to me that something was hidden within it, but this is speculation and something we will never know about for sure.

What kind of energy could create such a change to the surroundings as David had described? Did this really happen or was the sparkling mass having a direct effect on David? I wonder if the outcome of such an encounter would have been different if he had stumbled upon the light and it was blocking his path as he walked along the clifftops. I know this strange phenomenon has been seen at least once, so there is a good chance it has been seen earlier still.

I know the lightforms are real and I have no reason to believe David's account is anything less, but I wonder, would an 'up close and personal' encounter like this be a positive or a negative? Has such an encounter already happened, as I suspect it has? As a gauge, if we use the witness accounts I have collected over the years, it would appear that the deeper, more vibrant lights have a more sinister and unnerving effect on the people who see them. But David's account is totally different. Here, the light mass was ground-based and different in colour, but it still had a negative effect on the witness.

Without feet-on-the-ground, eyes-to-the-sky observation over long periods of time, the various lightforms of Bempton and surrounding areas will forever remain a mystery. I have said many times that no one is better placed to observed them than the local rock anglers and fishermen. Unfortunately they seem to have no interest, other than finding them a curious sight on a cold winter's night.

Blake Howe: Window To Another World

The following account was given to me on April 14th 2017. It is one of those rare stories that we only seem to hear about from friends of friends. Yet I had the opportunity to hear a first-hand account from a man I have known for over twenty years.

In all that time we never talked about UFOs or anything relating to the unexplained. We used to work together years ago and we still run into each other occasionally. If I was asked to describe Dan I would say he is a genuine 'what you see is what you get' kind of a man. He got in touch quite out of the blue, after I had posted a copy of Truth-Proof to an address in Buckton on the outskirts of Bridlington. I hadn't realised that I was sending the book to the address of my friend of over twenty years.

Two weeks later Dan called me to say he had read the book and thought I might be interested in hearing something he had to say. Over the phone he gave me an outline of what he wanted to share, and I have to say, it was something I never expected to hear. We both agreed it might be better if he related the story from the actual location where his experience occurred. So on the 14th at around 6.30am we met up and drove the short distance from his home to Cliff Lane in Bempton. This time of day suited us both, since I would often see Dan out dog walking if I decided to visit Bempton in the early mornings to take photographs. It's funny how Cliff Lane seems to be the starting point for many of Truth-Proof's unusual happenings.

As we walked, Dan began to tell me about his amazing encounter. He said it was a blistering hot day in July 2012, when he and his wife Jane decided to go for a walk - something they often did during the summer months - and they went suitably dressed for the occasion in shorts and T-shirts. They walked up Cliff Lane until they reached the entrance of Blake Howe Lane, a narrow dirt-track that runs between fields of wheat and barley and an area of open land called the Moor. The path is rarely used by anyone who is not local to the area, even though the entrance is only about half a mile from the RSPB nature reserve.

Dan told me they had been walking for about thirty minutes when Jane suddenly called out, *"Look at him! Where has he come from?"*

"I had no idea what she was talking about at first," Dan told me. "Until I looked in the direction Jane was pointing. I have to admit I was as surprised as she was when I saw him. I would even go as far as to say we were both shocked by his sudden appearance. It was about here Paul; where we are standing now, when we first saw him."

I glanced around at our surroundings. Today the fields on both sides were glowing yellow with rapeseed plants, but on the day Dan and Jane saw the stranger he told me the fields were growing crops of barley. From where Dan and I were now standing we could see in all directions without any obstructions. The narrow path we were walking rose ahead of us on a steady incline. At the highest point we could still see the North Sea and I estimate our distance from the cliffs at that point was about a mile.

"We didn't have a clue where he came from Paul," Dan continued. "I mean he was just there. We had been walking for about half an hour and he just appeared in front of us. We should have seen him at any point in our walk. We would not have been able to miss him, but he literally just appeared from nowhere."

Looking at the surroundings I had to agree. There is no cover for anyone to hide, not even a hint of a tree. There are just crops on each side of the path and the North Sea cliffs out in front. I find it impossible to imagine how this person could not have been seen, if he were ahead of Dan and Jane on the path we now walked. "He looked so strange Paul. He was tall. Very tall. We never saw his face, he had his back to us, but he was all wrong."

I asked Dan what he meant by 'all wrong'.
"It was how he was dressed Paul - or more to the point, what he was dressed in. I mean, it was probably one of the hottest days of the year and this bloke in front of us had on a black Crombie overcoat that went down below his knees. He was wearing a Fedora hat too – the kind with the brim and he was unusually tall and I think he was thin. In that coat it was hard to tell, but it's even harder to explain just how unusual he looked. We were mesmerised."

I remember Jane kept asking where he could have come from, because he just appeared out of the blue. We were curious, but at the same time we were a bit unnerved by his sudden appearance. We were the only people on the path, I am sure of that, but he appeared like magic. For about ten minutes we never took our eyes off him, as he walked up the track. I reckon he was only about forty metres ahead of us the whole time. It actually freaked Jane out a bit. Well both of us I suppose, because he was definitely one of the strangest sights I have ever seen.

Here we were in shorts and T-shirts and this stranger just appeared from nowhere, dressed in clothes that belonged in an old gangster movie. It seemed impossible to us. We didn't have a clue where he could have come from. He wasn't there one moment, then the next he was. I don't know how to explain it."

Dan stopped and pointed to a slight rise in the path and I took a few photographs of the track and the surrounding landscape. Looking at the surroundings and playing over what I had just been told, I could understand how they must have felt when they saw the stranger dressed in black. Then I actually uttered my thoughts out loud, "Where could he have come from? There is nowhere to hide..."

"Exactly my point Paul," said Dan. "Now you can understand why we were so shocked to see him. He walked up that rise in the path, we knew it dropped down on the other side, but it's a steady slope just down to the cliffs. We knew he couldn't get away. As the stranger approached the highest part of the path we stepped up our pace. We wanted to make sense of what was happening. It didn't take us long to reach the top of the path, so imagine our faces when we looked down the path and saw no one was there. He had vanished. It was impossible, but that's what happened."

I visited the same spot that Dan and Jane had been in back in 2012. It has unobstructed views of Flamborough to the right and RAF Bempton to the left. I believed him, but I didn't know what to say and I could offer no explanation. As we carried on straight ahead towards the cliffs, I wish I had been able to offer him some words of wisdom, but I had no experience of such an out-of-this-world encounter as this. I thought about the strange man that my wife Mary and I had met in 2014, but he wasn't dressed anything like the man Dan had described.

Next page: impression of the appearance of the mysterious stranger.

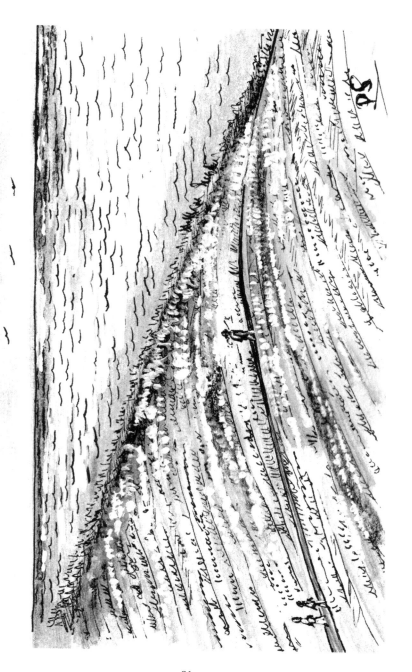

31

I find it intriguing that so much unexplained activity comes out of this small clifftop area in Bempton. And the fact that Dan and Jane had sat on their story for years suggests to me that others may also have similar unusual stories to tell. Dan pointed down the track with his outstretched arm and said, *"Paul it was just impossible for him to do what he did - to just appear and then disappear, but that's what he did. It sounds mad but there was nowhere for him to go. You can see for yourself how, after about half a mile, the path ends on the clifftops between Bempton and Flamborough. But when Jane and I got to the brow of the hill, he had gone. Vanished. How you do explain that?"*

Dan was right I could not explain it. No one could and that's the reason most people never step forward to tell these incredible stories. I think something unique exists here that throws everything we understand as normal, up into the air. Everything I have researched over the years suggests that this location allows many different things to manifest.

Maybe there exists some kind of all-knowing 'chameleon intelligence' that hits our senses with an overdose of the unexplained? Does the fact that these events strike in isolated areas mean this intelligence actually thinks and understands? Is it a calculated predator? I thought about all of the missing men who seemed to have just vanished. For now connecting the two is an impossibility. I have to steer clear of doing that, even though the question of whatever happened to them remains.

Dan explained further by saying *"Jane started to look along the sides of the fields, thinking the stranger might have collapsed, but in truth, we knew he hadn't. We would have seen him easily and if he had gone into the crop we would have seen where he had walked. We spent ages looking for him and talked about nothing else for days."*

When I stood in the exact spot where this sighting had happened, I have to say I could understand Dan and Jane's reaction. There was no chance anyone could have slipped out of sight; there was literally nowhere to go. The walk to the cliff edge would have taken another ten to fifteen minutes and in that time anyone out walking would have been easily seen by Dan and his wife.

Some people share their experiences with me and I often choose to sit on the story, until other information surfaces that adds weight to what I have been told. Other times I only have to hear a witness account once and I instinctively know it's the real deal. Dan and Jane's story left me in no doubt it was authentic. Dan has always been a man of few words. He is deep and honest, to the point of sounding blunt. This is something I like because I know where I stand. I now believe he and Jane had a genuine encounter with an MIB [Man In Black].

My first thought after hearing Dan's story was to ask *why* this stranger was there, I believe there had to be a reason. Was it simply to show himself to Dan and Jane? Or did he just walk into the fabric of our world and back into his own, like a fish leaping from water. Perhaps this is all these locations really are; areas of interdimensional weakness that simply exist, creating a special soup of unexplained events that we have no understanding or control of.

On our walk that morning Dan told me that, during the many years he had lived in Buckton, he had walked Blake Howe Lane lots of times. He even admitted that in the past, after occasionally seeing lights suddenly appear in the sky, he had felt so unnerved that he had turned around and gone home. We stood for a few moments on the brow of the path looking down towards the cliffs. What he had described made no sense and within in the parameters of what we knew was possible it should not have happened - but it had.

Dan turned to me, and looking me right in the eye, said, *"Paul, this place here, where we are standing now and down there, is strange. Not just because of that man. On more than one occasion I have felt as though I was being watched. Like eyes were on me. I don't how else to explain it. When I read in your book about the lights in the sky, I can tell you I have seen them – and seen them more than once.*

One early morning, a few years back, I walked up to the top of Cliff Lane and looked over towards the old RAF base. It was just getting light and I saw something blue on the ground. It was lights glowing blue. They were weird, like misty-blue lights, but definitely on the ground. They were big but I could not tell what they were. It felt strange, so I turned back. They made me feel really uneasy. I have also seen the orange ones and red ones you talk about in Truth-Proof. But that blue one was the strangest."

Before returning to our respective homes we drove to the top of Cliff Lane and Dan pointed out where he had seen the glowing blue light mass. It was in an open field just below the old RAF base, about half a mile away from where David Ellis had reported seeing the sparkling light mass on the cliff path. I cannot help but draw comparisons between the two sightings. Both men had attempted to describe what they saw – and I say *attempted,* because they simply could not explain what they saw. This tells me just how unusual the lights must have looked.

It strikes me that the majority of these encounters happen when witnesses are alone and isolated, and although we all react differently to situations, who could say what might happen if someone got too close to such a phenomena.

Dan said, *"I remember walking down Cliff Lane one morning and passing an old woman. I remember thinking it was a bit strange because she was alone and it was very early. As I passed her I said hello, then I turned around a short time later and she had gone. There are also two places on Cliff Lane where the radio on my phone cuts out, same place every time."*

Later I spent some time studying a few old maps of the area, taking special note of some of the unusual place names. To understand them better I considered the local dialect - as spoken by the born and bred residents of Flamborough and Bempton. For instance they don't say *yes* they say *yiss,* and they call a *turkey* a *tocky.* It has taken me years of talking with these close-knit people to understand half of what true Flamborians say. A *football* is a *fertball*, a *post hole* is a *possstol.* And so it goes on.

I find the name for Blake Howe Lane most interesting, as locally it is pronounced Black Howe – but why would it be named *black*? Is it because things of an unnaturally dark nature once occurred there? On one map I found the area where Dan and Jane had their MIB sighting. This is in very close proximity to an ancient burial mound, also called Blake-Howe, located in a field known as the Leys - which in itself is an interesting old name.

Without doubt I think something about this area makes it suitable for producing strange phenomena, only a lack of suitable explanations or the right words prevents our understanding of them. But this place, and others in the world just like it, are where we should be focusing our research. As always, I think location is key.

Time Experiments: November 2016

This chapter sounds more grand than it actually is, but I feel we have to take steps to provide data, wherever possible, to prove and expose this phenomena to a wider audience.

So far it evades us, no matter what we do, leaving nothing but a confused mind in its wake. Over time we begin to question what we have seen and experienced, eventually allowing ourselves to slip into the belief that it could have been something rational or mundane. Some of us, however, remain on track. We write down what we have experienced as soon as it happens and we try to document every detail, no matter how bizarre. If we do not, we can be sure all the little bits of detail will dissipate from our mind over the course of time.

I have said before and will say again; I am not so sure if we simply forget. It is as though some inbuilt mechanism kicks in, which make us overlook the most incredible things we experience. I have listened to so many people recall phenomenal events - events that should be a life changer. I have seen the awe in their eyes and felt the emotion rise and fall as the words leave their lips. I have watched them struggle to conjure the right sentence as they play the event over in their mind's eye - and then in the next breath, almost denounce it ever happened. That's the inbuilt mechanism. That's when we question our own minds, almost to the point of overriding the true experience.

In July, during the summer of 2014, my wife Mary and I decided to visit Bempton. Mary has always disliked the place. I do not know why, but it was an instant dislike. Maybe it has something to do with my research. Maybe the things I have exposed and written about have given her a negative view towards the place. For Mary to be there was quite a thing; she had been suffering with panic attacks for a number of years and was quite reluctant to go many places, but on this occasion we were having a good day.

We arrived around 4pm and although there were a few cars parked at the nature reserve, the clifftops were relatively free of people. As we made our way from the car park to the cliffs I remember Mary asking how long we would be, because she did not want to stay long. I assured her we would only have a short walk and the fresh air would do us both good. Once at the cliff edge we walked along the path in the direction of the RAF base. I never tire of seeing the skeletal remains of RAF Bempton, because I know it still holds many secrets, both above ground and below it.

At this point I noticed a few bumblebees in the grass on either side of the path. I had not really bothered looking down until now, but with my eyes turned to the grass that grew along the path I saw lots of bees - hundreds in fact, all around us and they were either dead or dying. I wish now that I had collected a few and arranged to have them analysed to establish what killed them. They were literally everywhere along the clifftop and not just one type of bee, but lots of different kinds.

We walked until we were almost level with the old base, then Mary said she had had enough and wanted to go back. I never forced the issue with her and asked if we could just take a few pictures before we left.

We were on the path standing by the last section of timber fence, which protects walkers from the cliff edge, before it changes to a metre-high tensioned wire fence, supported on solid posts. The old base has a surrounding fence of its own, about the same height, but of barbed wire. A few old eight-foot high concrete posts can still be seen, left over from the days when the base was operational. The distance between the cliff-edge fence on our left and the base fence on our right was about 50ft.

I asked Mary to stand with her back to the base so I could get a few shots of her with the old RAF buildings in the background. Then we swapped places and Mary took a few of me from the same position. *"Now a few of you Mary with the sea in the background,"* I said, and she stepped closer to the cliff-edge fence so I could take a few random photos. As Mary positioned herself by the fence she took hold of the top strand of taught wire. With a jolt she recoiled and let out a loud yell, shaking her hand in front of her. *"Ow! That fence just gave me an electric shock. You told me it was not electrified."*

Although she was clearly uninjured, I was surprised this could have even happened. I know for fact that the cliff-edge fence, and even the fence around the base, are not electrified and never have been. I asked her if she dare to touch it again and nervously she did. This time she only felt a small tingle of electricity through her fingertips. It was nothing like the first shock she received. This did not make sense to me, so I walked over to the fence myself and just grabbed a hold of the top strand of wire. I felt nothing. Mary did not have to convince me. I knew by her reaction that she'd had a shock. The look on her face told me she felt the pain of it, yet I felt nothing at all.

"Mary it's not electrified. Look. I can't feel anything when I touch it." I even lent forwards to touch the wire with the tip of my tongue, as if to prove my point further and still I felt nothing. Mary had clearly received a painful shock, but there was no explanation for it that I could think of. Then I thought about the bumblebees we had seen and wondered why so many had lost their lives on the clifftop that day. I cannot imagine they had been poisoned by insecticide from nearby fields, since the land around the nature reserve is designated for the conservation of wildlife - and there is nothing but open ocean to the other side of the fence. So what killed them?

Recalling the events of the day in my mind, I scribbled down a few notes of interest when I got home. At that point I did not consider any of this strange enough to be included in my first book. I just continued to collect stories from the local area without giving much thought to the shock Mary received or the dead bees. Then in July 2016 all of that changed.

We had not revisited the area together since July 2014, but now things had improved considerably for Mary. Her panic attacks had all but gone and life seemed to be getting back to normal. We were at Bempton nature reserve by around 4.45pm. It was a glorious day and in no time at all we were on the clifftops soaking up some late afternoon sun. I specifically wanted to know whether the bees around the cliffs were thriving or not. After visiting a few times on my own in July 2015 I was happy to find that they seemed to be doing well. In some way, I guess I did not consider Mary's electric shock two years earlier as important as the dead bees, but I know for sure that if I had asked her to accompany me in 2015 she would have declined.

We took a similar route up towards the old RAF base, stopping at various places to take photos and observe the many seabirds that were nesting on the sheer rock face of Bempton's mighty cliffs. The gannets in particular are an amazing sight to see, as they glide effortlessly on air currents rising from the North Sea.

We eventually found ourselves opposite the RAF base, with its arrangement of strange-looking concrete pillars; standing like twenty-one giant figures from Easter Island looking out over the North Sea. I paused in thought and wondered why no conservation order had ever been placed on these huge stones, after all they were unique. They were originally constructed as part of a high speed passive radar array.

I wanted a few pictures of myself with the pillars behind me and Mary obliged with the camera. Then we swapped places and I took a few photos of her. We never gave a thought to what happened in 2014; Mary's panic attacks now seemed under control and her electric shock was the last thing on our minds.

I wanted a few more shots, this time with the sea in the background. Mary moved towards the cliff-side fence and reached out with her left arm. She intended to take hold of the top strand of fence wire, but only got as far as touching it with her fingertips before letting out an almighty yell. *"Aargh! I just got another electric shock. I am never touching that fence again. Its electrified. It has to be."*

Of course it wasn't and never has been. Mary was more annoyed than hurt, but once again the fence suddenly became an interesting feature. The odds of Mary getting another electric shock from the same ordinary fence must have been very slim.

"I want to go now, I do not feel right, Paul can we go? I hate this place. I only came for you. I can tell you now that I won't be coming back here again."

I looked at my wife. She was angry and did seem unnerved by the experience. Part of me wanted to laugh, because I could not believe it had happened a second time. I also realised this had to mean something and I really felt there was something deeper happening here. Receiving an electric shock from a build-up of static electricity once is more than possible, but the same person in same place, years apart? I'm not so sure. But the last thing I wanted was for this to prevent Mary ever going out again. It had taken us so long to get her over the panic attacks, so I did not pressure her to stay any longer and this was not the time for sarcastic comments.

"You do believe me Paul don't you? I felt another shock when I touched the wire." I assured her I did and I genuinely believed her. After thirty-four years of marriage we have gained enough insight to know whether

each of us are telling the truth or not. *"Ok Mary,"* I said. *"We'll head back to the car. What time is it?"*
She looked at her watch. *"Its 5.20, now can we go? I really don't like this place, it has a bad feel to it."*

As we walked back to the car park, we passed a few people along the way who were watching the sea birds and looking out to sea. I noticed that some had their hands on the wire fence and I wanted to ask if they felt anything when they touched it, but I didn't bother. If static shocks were a danger to the public, I am sure the RSPB would have erected signs along the route, advising people to not touch the fence. Mary always said that Bempton made her feel uneasy. Now all she wanted to do was get in the car and go home, so that's what we did. Once we reached the car, the relief on her face was obvious.

We said very little on the journey home, but I realised we would not be visiting Bempton again together anytime soon. As we drove through Bridlington I glanced up at the clock on the spire of Trinity Church. It said 6.30, so I commented that we would just get back in time to catch the local news on TV. Mary nodded then glanced down at her watch. *"My watch has stopped Paul. It still says 5.20."*

I could not believe my eyes when I looked at her wristwatch. It *had* stopped at 5.20, but could the electric shock from the fence really have stopped the hands from turning?

Everything seemed to point to it doing exactly that, but what could have caused it? This was the start of my time experiments. I knew I wanted to try something, but at that point I had no idea what. I kept Mary's watch without altering it. I looked at it occasionally, half expecting it to spring back to life and half expecting to suddenly understand why it had stopped in the first place. After several failed attempts at coaxing Mary into revisiting Bempton clifftops, I realised there was no way she was going to touch that fence again, so I had to find another way to experiment.

In September 2016 I decided I had to try to replicate the situation again somehow. The best way would be to use Mary as a human guinea pig, but that was not going to happen, so I devised a plan to use wristwatches instead. Mary's watch had a traditional analogue display with quartz movement - and since I believe something affected the quartz, I purchased four similar watches for my experiment. My plan was to bury them in the ground close to where Mary had her experience - and then wait.

I took the four watches with me to Bempton, made sure they all showed the exact same time, then I placed two inside one plastic bag and two inside another. I put each bag inside its own sealed plastic container, taking great care that no one was around when I buried them. After burying the first container I walked approximately 100 paces along the cliff path to bury the other. This was Sunday, September 11th 2016 - day one of the experiment - and all four watches displayed the time of 4.35pm when I put them into the ground.

Three days later, at approximately the same time of day, I returned to Bempton to retrieve the four watches. The first pair displayed the same time of 4.40pm. By the time I had walked the distance to find the second pair, five or six minutes had passed and the second set of watches showed 4.45pm. So far, so good.

I continued with my experiment throughout September and October, repeating the same sequence of events, checking the watches, with little or nothing to report. On Wednesday, November 23rd I returned once more to check the watches. It was a cold day and had been raining on and off for most of the afternoon. The sky was overcast and it was just getting dark when I lifted the clump of grass that hid the first container of two watches. I could see that both were still running, but they were both over an *hour* behind. It was one of those surreal moments. I felt like a scientist who had made a momentous discovery. I was elated. Now I had an edge on the phenomena, but even if I did, I knew I had to remain silent for the time being.

Something had caused two of the wristwatches to lose an hour and six minutes each. Even with the bad weather, the container they were inside of was bone dry, yet both watches had been affected at roughly the same time, give or take a few seconds. I placed them back in the ground as they were, without correcting them and made notes as I went along. Further up the path and the other two watches were entirely unaffected. They continued ticking as normal showing the right time and I placed them back in the ground as they were. Besides the other two watches showing exactly the same *incorrect* time, there was nothing else unusual to report. I have no idea what all this meant, but something had clearly affected them.

I still continue with the experiment today and I know for sure, that at some point in the future, there will be an unexplained event in the area. It may be an unusual sighting; perhaps a lightform, although I fear it may be a missing aircraft or even a missing person. These things are too regular in this area for them to be random. But when this happens I hope the watches will reveal something unusual in time - and time is the keyword here. They may give an indication that a type of an unusual energy is at work in the area, but I have to be patient.

After the lost hour of time shown by the watches in November 2016 I took part in a radio interview about my work. I mentioned my time experiments but stopped short of sharing the details. We need more data than simply a pair of watches losing an hour. Also, if there *is* an outside intelligence involved in all this, talking about a result so soon might even affect the experiment.

Time Experiment Update: December 2016

Although nothing significant has happened since that one result from last November, I still check the watches on a weekly basis. On Saturday December 3rd 2016 I was up before first light. I wanted to arrive at Bempton nature reserve before any bird watchers or dog walkers, so that I could check out my buried watches.

Around 7.45am on that cold and dark December morning I arrived at the bird sanctuary armed with my GoPro camera and a small trowel. I made my way along the cliff-edge path towards the same area I had visited so many times in the previous weeks. The only thing I saw on my way there was a dead rat, which I kicked to one side and wondered why it had not been taken by whatever had killed it.

The week before, November 26th, I had been up to Bempton and buried two extra boxes of paired watches and, as before, I buried them along the cliff path approximately 100 paces apart from the others. I have to confess that I had done this in a bit of a rush, as I was actually with Mary and our two young grandchildren; who needed our careful attention at the time. Now I was back again and eager to check all eight watches. As I approached the area along the clifftops I suddenly realised that I was unsure where I was meant to be looking. In my haste on the previous week I had not noted the exact position of the two new sealed containers. After more than an hour of trying to locate them and feeling frustrated, I gave up and headed home. The only thing I noticed on my way back to the car was the rat. It had gone. When I arrived home Mary asked if the watches had shown the right time. *"In a word - no."* I said.

I was embarrassed and explained that I couldn't find them. She laughed, then told me I had lost them. Fortunately Mary could remember where I had buried them and after a bit of pleading she agreed to come back with me later that day. 3.00pm arrived and we were back at Bempton together. I never doubted Mary and knew we would find the watches. True to her word she led me to the correct spot, but unfortunately there was nothing to report. Both pairs of watches displayed the identical time. This really was becoming a very uneventful day.

We carefully placed them back in their boxes, then into the ground. This time I carefully noted their location before we headed back to the car. It was a cold, but bright day, with broken cloud and blue sky over the sea.

Inland the clouds seemed thicker, but the sky was still crisp and sharp. At a distance we could see a few final visitors dotted along the cliff path. Before we reached the car park I turned to say something to Mary. At that moment I saw a flash of bright silver light close to her right shoulder. It was so fast I could have missed it in a blink.

It was one of those surreal moments when you question your own truth. I told her instantly about what I saw, then moments later took my trusty Olympus voice recorder from my pocket and pressed the record button. I began to ask questions out loud, directing them to the great volume of nothingness that is the sky. I know how crazy this must sound, but just moments before I had seen a brilliant flash of silver light that looked as if it belonged more in a cartoon, than in reality. So, to be inspired to try a little 'electronic voice phenomenon' recording seemed a natural and perhaps even a logical thing to do. Trying to sound as normal as I could, I asked out loud, *"What just flashed at Mary's side? Can you give us a sign of your presence? Please show us something. Please do it again."*

Nothing happened. We heard nothing and we saw nothing, so we continued on our way. As we approached the Big Railings viewing platform, I asked if Mary would stand with me to take in the amazing views from Bempton's mighty white cliffs. It was getting cold, very cold, which was why I asked if she minded. My enthusiasm for these locations is not always shared by others and thinking about Mary's past experiences out here is no exception. But she nodded in agreement, so I set my box of equipment on the ground and we both looked out to sea.

The few people who were still around were near to the visitor centre behind us; its doors would soon be closing for another day. I turned to Mary to ask why I should have seen the light that came so close to her. Then, as I tried to visualise what I had just seen, the words *"you have to stop bringing down the light"* echoed through my mind. The phrase 'stop bringing down the light' is recorded in my first book, after an encounter with a stranger who we both thought was other-worldly.

Just then something caught my eye - just to the right of the visitor centre. A brilliant, shining, silver object, vivid and clear in front of the clouds. *"A UFO. Mary a UFO,"* I wanted her to see it too. I dived down and scrambled to get my camcorder from its box; quite why I didn't have it in my hands already is beyond me. As I rose with the camcorder in hand, the object was already turning on its axis.

Pointing, I urged Mary to look in the right direction, but as fast as she turned, the object itself seemed to be moving in what appeared to be a fixed position. A bit like a weather vane side on, which slowly turns until all you see is the point. At first it looked like a double-ended bullet, but then it seemed to morph into a silver circle that slowly diminished in size, until it could no longer be seen. Between trying to point it out to Mary and aiming my camcorder, it was gone. Had I immediately flipped open my box of equipment, instead of processing what I was seeing, I might have been able to capture a small amount of footage. This was a failed attempt. The phenomena had beaten me once again.

We both hung around, looking in the direction I had seen this 'silver bullet', but it was over. The moment of magic presented itself as if to prove a point and then vanished. The image was etched in my mind and I had to be content with that. All I could do now was retell the tale and hope I would be believed. Mary and I have been together so long, I no longer have to convince her that I have seen or experienced something. In fact, we have both experienced so many things over the years that we trust each other. Mary turned to me and said, *"Paul you asked the question. You asked to be shown. I think you have just been shown."*

I thought about it and wondered if that was really what happened. Had an unknown intelligence heard my words and reached out to make contact? Suddenly the time experiment had progressed from boxes of watches buried in the earth to silver shapes in the sky. I kicked myself all the way home for not capturing even the minutest part of what I saw. After all, I even had my GoPro camera strapped to my chest, but it was not switched on. I also had my old Sony VX2100 camcorder with me and it was more than capable of capturing the object.

Only days before, my daughter had given me a brand new fishing box to carry my increasing array of cameras and equipment, which I always take with me on location. Any day before this and I would have been ready with a camera around my neck. The problem had been me. Once again, the phenomena had caught me off guard, leaving me with that elusive truth that leaves no proof.

Next page: impression of the silver UFO seen by Mary and myself.

The object turned in a fixed position
to become nothing more
than a dot of light

46

The Andrew Eeles Report

On November 23rd 2016, my friend Bob Brown paid me a visit at home. Bob is the host of his own online radio show called *Over The Rainbow.* He has interviewed me a few times in the past about my research, particularly regarding the lightforms reported locally. Bob brought a friend with him named Andrew Eeles, who was interested in buying a copy of my book. I had never met Andrew before but found him a very interesting man.

Andrew told me he was interested in visiting the clifftops at Bempton. I said I would be going back up there this Thursday, which was in two days time, and he was welcome to come along if he wanted. Since Andrew is a geophysicist, I thought it would be a good opportunity to take someone with me who had a scientific background. When Thursday came Andrew was unable to join me, but the next day he visited Bempton with his cousin, to view the area where the lightforms had been reported. A few days later Andrew sent me this detailed report of their experience (his cousin chose to be excluded from it altogether).

Report: *UFO Encounter*
Date: *Friday 25th November.* Time: *18:00 hrs approx.*
Location: *RSBP Wildlife Centre Bempton.*
Lat/Long: *54.14609N, -0.16889E*

Meteorological Conditions: *Some stratus, patchy.* Temp: *8°C approx.* Wind: *Southerly 5-8 mph.* Visibility: *Sky clearing 80% clear of cloud.* Seeing conditions: *Good, except on the horizon, where there was some patchy mist out to sea.* Sea state: *Calm. Visibility, mostly clear, +10 miles.*

Description:
I (Andrew Eeles) arrived at Bempton Wildlife Centre at approx 18:00. It was quite dark at this time as the sun set at 3.45pm approx. I had been observing the night sky for around ten minutes when I made my way over to the bird viewing gallery, approximately 100m from the Centre.

Looking out to the horizon I observed a number of orange/red lights in a row (between 3-6 lights). It was difficult to make out any silhouette as they emanated from a misty part of the horizon to the east. Given the elevation of 130m this should give a distance to the horizon of up to

40kms approx. The lights appeared to blink independently of each other (this may have been caused by the viewing conditions).

At one point a bright white tubular object appeared to launch from their right-hand side at 45 degrees, in a straight line through the clouds. I lost contact with the white object in less than 1 second. It moved very quickly. The flashing lights then appeared to lift to their left-hand side and rise to 45 degrees to approx 500ft. They held this position for approximately ten seconds, before again resuming their previous horizontal position. All visual contact was then lost after approximately ten minutes. There was no noise during this contact.

I think Andrew's report speaks for itself. His sighting doesn't sound like he saw anything like flares, meteorites or unusual atmospherics. This does not demean the reports given to me by the fishermen – their accounts are as important as any other – but it is often the case that the word of an academic is the only one accepted as valid proof.

His report adds to a growing number of excellent first-hand accounts. If it encourages those who are sceptical about my own claims to think again, then this can only be a good thing. I only wish more people from a scientific background would spend time in locations of high strangeness, such as Bempton. Andrew Eeles was fortunate to have the experience he did on his first visit there. He may find that he never sees them again, but his eyes and mind are now more open to the truth of what I am reporting. Believing, without knowing how or why, is one step nearer to understanding.

Encounter At Big Railings

I doubt this location will ever stop surprising me, because just when you think you have seen everything, something different happens.

Throughout 2016, after spending many hours observing the sky and surrounding areas of land and sea off Bempton and Flamborough, I was still able to discover a few things I never knew before. The lightforms were the main reason I spent so much time investigating at Bempton in 2016. They appear too quickly to be flares and they 'switch off' in seconds after seeing them. They are too far out at sea to be Chinese lanterns - which is one of the possible explanations given by people who see the lightforms. But quite how a Chinese lantern could appear as a huge ball of light, then suddenly become five in the blink of an eye, is beyond me.

On November 11th my friend Andi Ramsden and I made a night-time visit to Bempton. It was a cold evening at around 6.15pm when Andi collected me in his car. We talked en route about the lightforms, which had been seen locally in the days and weeks before, and I remember noting that on November 14th we would be treated to the sight of a super-moon. It was said that the moon would look bigger on that date than it had since records began. So it was no surprise to find that visibility was quite good, as there was just some light cloud in the sky with the moon shining brightly through them.

When we arrived at the RSPB nature reserve we saw one other car in the car park; a maroon-coloured saloon. Walking down the cliff path we saw no tell-tale signs that anyone was out fishing off the clifftops. The fishermen only go out there if the tides and weather conditions are favourable, but because we had seen the other car, we knew someone was around. We decided to head for Breil Newk or Big Railings, as the local fishermen call it, because it offers amazing views up and down the coast. We saw a few lonely boats out on the horizon, but all in all, the night was quite uneventful, apart from the occasional sound of fireworks coming from miles inland.

At about 7.30pm I decided to take some photos in the darkness with my small Olympus camera. I pointed the camera towards the old RAF base and took a few snaps. The flash brightened up the darkness, but I captured nothing unusual in any of the pictures - not unless you consider dust orbs something unusual, which I do not.

However, we have noticed on very rare occasions that a strange, sparkling mist is caught in some of the photographs, which cannot be seen by the naked eye. Similar pictures have been taken in other areas of high strangeness all over the world. If my investigations were ever funded I would like to have a camera set up over a long period of time, to take pictures at two-second intervals. I actually think the results could be startling.

After I had taken five or six photographs, we saw a single white light on the clifftops. It was about 500 metres from our position in the direction of Speeton. We only saw it for five to ten seconds, but our immediate thought was that it was a lone fisherman. Besides the dramatic moonlit sky, the light on the clifftop was the only thing of interest we had seen.

From Big Railings looking towards Speeton we could see the skeletal outline of the old RAF base, silhouetted against the dark grey sky. Ahead of us were Speeton Cliffs, rising at their highest point to 120 metres. The towns of Filey and Scarborough cannot be seen from this point, as they are somewhere in the distance beyond the cliff's mighty wall of white.

Just then, in the sky above the old base, we saw a white square-shaped light suddenly switch on and off. It lasted only for a moment, but we both saw it. It was just like a light in the sky being switched on and off - but this was square. We waited for it to happen again, but it never did. Andi made a tongue-in-cheek comment that the light might have been responding to my camera flash, so I took a few more shots just in case his theory was right. The strange square light never returned and now the light on the clifftop had gone too.

A few hours passed, but nothing more interesting happened except Andi's phone sounding to remind him that his battery was almost dead. It was just before 10pm and getting colder, so we made our way back to the car along the remote clifftop path. As we walked I took a few more photographs; the camera flash punching holes in the darkness.

Once again a single light appeared on the clifftop, in a similar position to where we had seen it hours before. We watched it as we walked and noticed that it was quite low to the ground, but it seemed to be moving to the right and then to the left. We just assumed it was the fisherman, it had to be. After a few minutes we were on higher ground and could see his light more clearly, but why was he moving around so much?

It was strange enough that we never saw it in the first place, as we walked down to Big Railings from the car park when we first arrived - but here it was. It is important to realise that these fishermen have to climb the cliff-side fence in the dark to reach the edge of the cliffs for fishing. And with sheer drops below of between three and four hundred feet, once they have set up their fishing gear, they don't move around much in the darkness. The men fish there during the hours of darkness because the RSPB nature reserve does not permit fishing during the day time - but they always wear powerful head torches, which are switched on constantly.

There really is no room for error on the top of these cliffs. If you find yourself on the wrong side of the fence up there in the darkness, it could be fatal. This is what makes the light that Andi and I saw so unusual. As we rounded the corner into the car park we gave the clifftops a final glance, but they were in darkness. The car we had seen on our arrival had now gone, which deepened the mystery for a time. I did however learn, later on, that it belonged to a member of cleaning staff who worked at the visitor centre on a few evenings a week after closing time.

With no safe explanation for what Andi and I had seen on the clifftop – besides the unusual square light above the base that had appeared and disappeared in a flash - I now wonder if we had witnessed what the local fishermen call the Ghost of Big Railings? I can imagine many people, even those local to the area, would just roll their eyes when they hear a story like this. These are the same people who never look at the sky and never question anything.

Dead Man Running

In Truth-Proof I wrote about the mysterious disappearances of men around the East and North Yorkshire coastline. So I was not surprised to learn of additional unexplained deaths and disappearances locally, while researching for this book. Regardless of what anyone might think, they have disappeared or been found dead in unusual circumstances, but do I have any ideas or clues about why these things are happening?

The clues lie in the pattern of events that unfold when these tragedies happen. Throughout my research I have discovered that other unexplained events happen around the same time a person vanishes. Yet there appears to be nothing to connect one event to the other, *except* that they occur around the same time. The professional services who search for the missing individuals find nothing, and apart from some media coverage at the time, they seem to let the disappearances just fade into the background. Whatever is responsible - and that covers everything from the normal to the paranormal - has so far outwitted us all, but it is the apex; the Alpha Omega.

One case of an unusual death goes back twenty-five years to December 1992 and, as usual, the archive in Bridlington library proved invaluable to me. There I found a related news article from the Bridlington Free Press, published in January 1993. It is because of such cases, that I always knew I would write a second book, but this article really is an unusual piece of writing. It states that the police want to solve the mystery of Raymond Johnston's final hours, how he was found dead with massive head and internal injuries – but that they were *not* looking to blame anyone. It tells how Mr Johnston's naked body was found in a pool of blood at around 5.35pm on December 15th 1992, after he had been seen running along Bempton Lane for almost a mile, with injuries so severe that it sounds impossible.

The police state they believe he was in a collision with a light commercial vehicle, which may have been fitted with bull bars. This almost sounds as if they are describing a vehicle hitting a wall; but he was not driving, he was a pedestrian.

They also state that they were sure Mr Johnston had removed his own clothing because his body thermostat would have collapsed and he would have overheated. They also say that the body would have continued to run on auto-pilot - but 'the body' seems a strange way to describe a person who was still alive at that point. If they are using that term because he was technically brain-dead how would have been able to remove his clothing?

I had to read the article a few times to actually take it in. The fact the article states Mr Johnston's 'body' was able to remove his clothing after the accident amazed me. His injuries were horrific. Among them he had a broken shoulder blade. Extreme force is usually required to break a shoulder blade; such as impact from a vehicle, high-speed sports accident or extreme fall. After speaking with medical professionals about this, I do not think it would have been possible for Mr Johnston to remove his own clothing, even with one such debilitating injury. So it would have been impossible for him to move his arm, regardless of the body's thermostat. Combined with his other injuries, that makes the suggested scenario impossible for me to accept.

The article states that he was seen running naked down Bempton Lane, after being in a collision with an unidentified vehicle. Reading the article carefully we see that it never actually mentions there were any witnesses to a collision with a vehicle. It goes on to say that, before collapsing at the entrance of Windmill Farm he was able to run for almost a mile, during which time we are also expected to believe he was able to *remove* his clothing.

Talking to a reporter in January 1993, Detective Chief Inspector Hewson said that the person responsible for causing the accident may be *"unaware or too frightened"* to come forward. Surely it would be more correct to call this 'a hit and run'? How could anyone fail to realise they had hit someone with their vehicle? Even hitting a rabbit whilst driving can make quite a bump, but this was not a rabbit. Raymond Johnston was a fully grown man. DCI Hewson also said, *"We are not trying to blame anybody - we are trying to clear this up."* Now I know at this stage I may be reading between the lines, but the Mr Johnston was dead. He was found to have massive head injuries, a broken shoulder blade, seven cracked ribs and severe internal injuries and all the police wanted was for the person responsible to come forward so they could clear the matter up and not blame anyone. This suggests to me that, at the time, they did *not know* how Mr Johnston came to have his injuries.

Tel: (0262) 606606; News 677338   Thursday, January 7, 1993   No 7843

Help police solve mystery of this man's final hours

POLICE unravelling the mysterious death of a man found in a Bridlington lane are appealing for help from Free Press readers.

Raymond Johnston was seen running naked down Bempton Lane after being in collision with an unidentified vehicle. Shortly afterwards he was discovered unconscious in the entrance to Windmill Farm. Despite exhaustive inquiries police have not traced the driver.

By Emma Barnes

Until that person comes forward, the body cannot be released for burial.

Now, in an attempt to shed new light on the mystery, police have revealed important information - including Mr Johnston's photograph - in the hope readers will be able to piece together his final hours.

"We think it is purely an accident of which the person responsible is unaware or too frightened to come and tell us," said Det Chief Insp Trevor Hewson, leading the inquiry.

The 33-year-old unemployed loner from Leeds was found in a pool of blood at 5.35pm on December 15. He had sustained massive head injuries, a broken shoulder blade, seven cracked ribs and severe internal injuries. Despite the injuries he was able to run almost a mile before collapsing. Police believe he was in collision with a light commercial or off-road vehicle, possibly fitted with 'bull bars' at the junction of Bempton Lane and Bempton Back Lane.

"He is not a man of the road but he was prepared to sleep rough."

DCI Hewson said they were sure Mr Johnston had shed his clothes himself:

"The body would go on running on automatic pilot. Because the body thermostat had collapsed he started to overheat to keep cool and discarded clothing. We are not trying to blame anybody, we are trying to clear this up."

● DCI Trevor Hewson displays Mr Johnston's distinctive purple rucksack, with a balloon logo and 'Freedom' on the back.

'We are not trying to blame anybody – we are trying to clear this up'

54

In March 2016 a police officer came to my home to speak to me about an unrelated incident. I was sitting at my kitchen table, as I often do when working, and was surrounded by newspaper clippings and missing people reports. The officer glanced down at the scattered papers and gave them a curious look. I pointed to the clippings and asked, *"Have you any idea how many people have vanished or died in strange circumstances around Bempton?"*

He gave me a puzzled look, then I held up a 1993 news clipping with the headline, *"Help Police Solve Mystery Of This Man's Final Hours."* *"I remember this,"* he said. *"I attended the scene. It was on Bempton Lane. Am I right?"* Surprised, I said yes and watched his reaction as he read through the article. *"Yes it was a strange one,"* the officer continued. *"We just couldn't understand how he came to have so many injuries. It was like he had fallen from the air; like he had been dropped from a plane or something. That's what we thought at first."*

Now this *was* interesting. But why he would say such a thing? The newspaper article said the police thought Raymond Johnston had been involved in an accident with a light commercial vehicle. Of course this was very vague and only one possible scenario, but now I had testimony from someone who was there - and the suggestion of the body being dropped was an intriguing one. So perhaps I was right before. Perhaps the police had no real clue how Mr Johnston had come to have such horrific injuries.

I searched newspapers after that date but found no other information relating to Raymond Johnston's death - and there was nothing to show that anyone had ever coming forward claiming responsibility for his death either. Surely someone should have come forward in all that time? After all, in the words of the police, they only wanted *"to clear this up."* They did not want to *"blame anybody."* Yet the way this reads it was as though they were referring to a stray dog that had been hit, not a man.

Knowing the area as I do, very few ideas sprang to mind. In fact, I am sorry to say that none of my ideas have ever come close to explaining the mystery. In 1993 there were no properties between where Raymond Johnston was found and where he was supposedly hit by a mystery vehicle. He did not live in the immediate area, so why would he have been on that desolate back road out of Bridlington in the first place? What could have placed him there on a cold December night, where he

would have been exposed to the elements - and for what reason?
In March 2016, a few days after my conversation with the police officer,
I decided to try and find out a little more about this tragedy and on a
spur of the moment decision, I jumped into my car and headed off
towards Bempton Lane. I knew there were two disused windmills on
either side of Short Lane in the direction of Bempton. They were roughly
a mile apart and both situated amongst farm buildings. I needed to find
out which of these belonged to Windmill Farm. I paused at the entrance
of Short Lane trying to imagine the circumstances of that freezing
winter's night back in 1992. The road has no street lighting and apart
from four private homes at the top of Short Lane, there is nothing
between it and the first farm.

I continued in the direction of the first windmill, carefully timing my
journey. The distance was closer to one and a half miles, so that part of
the reported story was inaccurate, but something just did not add up
with this story. It was as though I could feel it. I stopped at the entrance
to a farm. The old windmill had now been restored and had a glass
viewing bay on top. After taking a few photographs I walked up the long
driveway and proceeded to knock on the door of the farmhouse.
Moments later a couple in their late fifties came to the door.

"Sorry to bother you," I said. *"I wonder if you could help me with a little
information. I am researching for a book and came across this unusual
article in the Bridlington Free Press from 1993."*
The lady glanced down at the news clipping I had with me, then lifted
her hand gesturing for me to stop talking.
*"We didn't live here in 1993 so I don't think we can help you. We do
know about this though, you would have to speak with Mr Bailey who
lived here when it happened. He lives in Bempton now, he will be able
to help you, I'm sure of it."*

I had found Windmill Farm, but needed to speak with the previous
owner. Thankfully, the lady gave me directions and a description of Mr
Bailey's current home. I was soon on my way to Bempton, where I hoped
to find out more about the circumstances surrounding Mr Johnston'
death. Before leaving I snapped a few more images of the windmill and
the entrance of the driveway where the police had said his body was
found. Less than fifteen minutes later I was outside the home of Mr
Bailey. I knocked on the front door and waited. I could hear movement

inside and moments later the door opened. My first impressions of Mr Bailey were of a big man in his sixties who showed all the signs of a hard-working life. I explained that I was writing a book and researching unexplained events in the area, then showed him the newspaper clipping. He smiled, turned his head to the inside of the house and shouted, *"There's a man at the door asking about that bloke I found in front of our window years ago."* A voice inside called back *"Are you going to tell him?"*

Mr Bailey pointed to an entrance about fifty feet away with two double gates. *"If you go through those gates and walk up the garden, along the front of the house, we can have a talk in the kitchen. I'll see if I can help you."* I followed Mr Bailey's directions and after a few minutes I found myself sitting at the kitchen table of the former owner of Windmill Farm. He told me to call him by his first name, David, and we chatting as though we had know each other for years.

I explained about my work on Truth Proof and some of the things covered in the book, and he began to understand why I found the death of Raymond Johnston so interesting. I handed him the Free Press news clipping to read. *"Um I see. I don't remember reading this, but I suppose I must have done. Well the paper says he was found at the entrance of the farm - it's a long time ago now, but I can tell you that is simply not true. I think it was around five o'clock in the evening when it happened. I was in the bathroom and my wife and daughter were downstairs - in the kitchen I think. Well our daughter was for sure. I suddenly heard a very loud crack - just one loud sharp bang."*

I asked if he could describe the sound for me. *"I want to say it sounded like someone shutting a car boot really fast and hard, but I think it was a bit sharper than that and louder. My daughter heard it and shouted to me from the kitchen, 'did you just hear that noise?' That's how I know she was in the kitchen. She'd heard it and she was in another part of the house. It was a freezing cold night so all the windows and doors were shut tight, so it must have been loud for us to hear it.*
About five minutes later I saw the reflection of headlights on the drive, then heard my son's voice shouting from outside, 'Dad, Dad you have to come out here quick.' He had just arrived home and I thought he was messing about, but I opened the bathroom window and looked out. That's when I saw the man lying there."

I asked Mr Bailey if he was able to see the entrance to the farm from his position at the bathroom window? *"No I couldn't. That's why I said that part was not true. This man was in the middle of our drive, under the window. I was looking down at him and he was still alive. I know that because I heard him make a groaning sound. I could not believe it to be honest. I grabbed a blanket and ran downstairs. Then I ran out and put it over him, but he was in a right state. He had a big hole in the side of his head and he was naked. I just don't know how he ended up there the way he did. I wondered if he had tried to climb the windmill and fell, but that would not explain all of the injuries. And he was between the windmill and the house, I just didn't understand it."*

Johnston's body lay on the driveway near the main house and forty feet away from the windmill. This was in the time before the mill was restored and it still had no roof. Even so, the mill was locked at night, so how would he have gained access - and who would even attempt to climb a windmill while naked, in such horrendous weather conditions? Such a scenario seems impossible.

Map and photo of Windmill Farm.

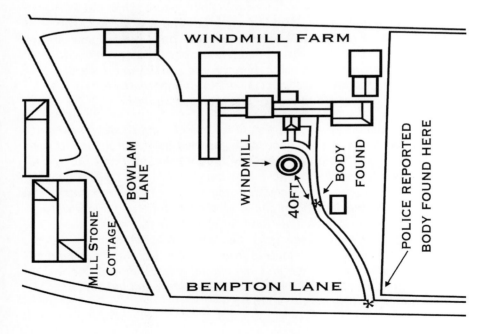

I asked Mr Bailey if he remembered seeing any clothing near to where Johnston was found. He said there were none to be seen, although he did remember noticing that Mr Johnston did not even have any socks on. However, he did tell me that his son had seen a pile of clothing at the end of Short Lane over a mile away. I think it makes sense to assume they belonged to Johnston. If this is all true, I wonder why the police said the body removed his clothing as he ran down Bempton Lane. Exactly *how* does a dead man remove his own clothing? And why had they reported he was found at the *entrance* to Windmill Farm, when that was simply *not* the case.

Many of the accounts I write about are often years after the event, but they are not so old that witnesses cannot be traced. Most of what was reported in the Free Press article from 1993 is pure speculation. What was responsible for Raymond Johnston's horrific injuries is not known, so again, a theory that fits human understanding is suggested. A vehicle, possibly fitted with bull-bars, is claimed to have led to his death - yet no witness to that accident has ever been identified. These are just suggested scenarios, created to fit an event that defies explanation.

I believe there is much more mystery surrounding the tragic death of Raymond Johnston, perhaps more than anyone could ever imagine. We should expect to hear more about this case in the future.

Missing Men, Missing Clues

When researching the many cases of missing people for my first book, I came across a few obscure pieces of information that had been staring me in the face from day one. At first it did not register because it was so unimaginable. This was one of those 'hidden in plain sight' type scenarios, but newspaper archives did reveal that something was happening. However, I was so engrossed in the missing men cases, that for a long time I had missed possible clues. When the penny finally dropped, I discovered there were some unusual occurrences that seemed to happen at the same time as these men went missing. Although they were unusual, perhaps 'ridiculously odd' might be a better way to describe them.

The gap between my research and actual proof is immeasurable and high strangeness never leaves any clues. Now I was stepping up the level of craziness by uncovering even more bizarre information from reports published at the same time some of these men had disappeared. When I began to look more closely I saw these things had cropped up so many times, I knew I would eventually have to follow them up. It was during my research into the case of James Gorman that I first noticed strange stories of missing cats and power cuts. Ultimately, although none of these events may be connected, I feel it is only right they are documented in Truth-Proof.

James Gorman - Jimmy to his friends and family - disappeared on February 8th 2010. His bruised and partially-clothed body was found four days later in the grounds of St.Oswald's church in the town of Filey. Twenty days after the discovery of Jimmy's body, a second man was reported missing just a few miles down the coast, at Bempton. On March 2nd 2010 nineteen year old Russell Bohling's abandoned car was found in the RSPB car park at Bempton. No clues of what happened to Russell have ever been found. He seemed to have just vanished from the face of the Earth.

It was only after rechecking my notes from 2010 that I noticed a most curious thing. There were reports of large numbers of missing cats and reports of electricity blackouts. Of course there may be no direct connection between these things and the tragic loss of these two men, but I soon discovered it was not the first time someone had gone missing locally when similar things had been reported. My first hint of these events came after looking through a news article in the Bridlington Free Press from Thursday April 1st 2010. The opening headline read, *Missing Cat Worries* and the report described how large numbers of cats had simply vanished in the weeks and months leading up the article being published. I noticed the date and hoped the Free Press had not been playing an April Fools' joke on their readers.

So domestic cats had been disappearing in large numbers around February and March 2010, but between all the years I researched - from the 1930s to present day - large numbers in animal disappearances were rare. Yet these cat disappearances coincided with the recent disappearances of people so I could not ignore them, but what might it mean? Dare I even suggest they were connected in some way? They were certainly connected through their location, since they were happening in the same area; the newspaper article was proof of this. However, no other clues were available to tie one into the other, despite spending many hours of searching. It was another one of those challenges for me to 'prove the unprovable'.

At first glance this all seemed ridiculous. It took a while before I even shared my suspicions with anyone else, let alone write them down. Up until now, I doubt that anyone had placed these events side by side before. Yet the evidence was there, but evidence of what exactly? Even in my own mind, I wondered whether I was searching too far into the darkness in my quest for answers.

I have not yet formed an opinion about *why* I think there could be a connection between missing cats and missing men, but it is happening; and with alarming regularity. By highlighting this now I hope that researchers in other areas will look for similar connections, no matter how unusual the association might appear. We must never stop looking for clues that suggest or even predict these unusual happenings in the future. If all this seems too far-fetched, we should remember the empty conclusions drawn by reporters, the police and other professionals, who do not adequately explain these disappearances. Although it might run against the tide of public opinion, there is nothing normal about the paranormal. I do not pair these things together lightly. These are tragic events with tragic consequences and I have no evidence to prove a connection, except to say they all occurred within the same timeframe.

Thousands of properties lose power

A POWER cut left homes and businesses without electricity in a large area of Bridlington on Sunday morning.

Electricity network operator Yorkshire Electricity Distribution (YEDL) confirmed 2,667 homes and businesses went without power from around 9.25am until the power was restored at 12.18pm.

Areas stretching from one side of Martongate down as far as York Road were affected.

A spokesman for YEDL said: "The problem was a high area voltage fault with wiring which is underground.

"When we were notified of the problem we switched around our resources and managed to bring power back to the area as quickly as we could.

"The underground wires will need to be excavated and repaired but there should be no further disruption to electricity services, and we expect the work to be completed by the end of next week.

"We apologise to anyone in the area affected by the power shortage."

Shops in the area managed to cope during the cut, with the Somerfield store in York Road ferrying stock to fridges and freezers at its sister store in Martongate.

The Co-operative store in Wheatley Drive had to close as tills were unusable but stock in the store survived until the power came back on.

Missing cats worries

By Mike Brown

mike.brown@yrnltd.co.uk

CAT owners in Bridlington have been warned to keep an eye on their pets after a recent spate of missing cats in the town.

Felines from homes around Queensgate and the Amy Johnson Avenue areas of town have been reported missing throughout March, leading the RSPCA to appeal for pet owners to be vigilant.

Kay Harrison of Bridlington RSPCA said that a 'disturbing number' of cats had gone missing in recent weeks.

"We had a similar problem a couple of years ago with cats going missing and being poisoned by anti-freeze," she said.

"I've been speaking to several people who have told me their cats have gone missing, or that they know of friends' cats which have simply disappeared.

"One lady rang me to tell me that her heavily pregnant cat went missing last week and it is very unusual for pregnant cats to stray far from home.

"It is very upsetting for all these owners left worrying about what might have happened to their pets."

Mrs Harrison warned owners in these areas in particular to take steps to ensure the safety of their cats, such as micro-chipping them at the local vets, which costs just £5.

"If a cat is wearing a safety collar with the disc showing it is chipped it might just put someone off stealing them and if they end up as a reported stray we would be able to re-unite them with their owners once they had been scanned and the chip found," said Mrs Harrison.

One cat owner on St Wilfred Grove, who asked not to be named, had his ginger tom cat Rocky go missing.

The two-year-old is one of

Two-year-old Rocky, who went missing from St Wilfred's Grove at the beginning of March.

five cats that went missing from Queensgate, or its surrounding roads, between March 1 and March 10.

The owner said: "I think it is very strange how all of the cats from one area are going missing at the same time, Rocky went missing on March 4.

"We got Rocky from the RSPCA when he was a kitten and he has been trained as a house cat, he never stays out overnight so the first time he didn't come back we knew there was something wrong.

"If anyone has taken in a cat, or knows what might have happened to Rocky, call us on 07882 569599."

Cats disappearing in the town is not something new.

In May last year, the RSPCA issued a similar plea to pet owners after cats were attacked and killed on the Havenfield Estate, as well as a number of other ginger cats going missing.

Besides finding reports of missing cats, power cuts and missing men during my research, I recall noting that UFOs had also been seen and reported around the same time these events occurred. So now we have an unlikely but powerful combination of events, without one shred of physical proof linking one to the other. No matter how weak and absurd all this might appear to the brain-washed public, who consume anything that the mainstream media push into their retinas, the only evidence I have is that it *is* happening. All I can do is present what I find, even if it goes against the grain of what many want to believe.

Researchers before and after me will know only too well the difficulties of looking into the unexplained. The population as a whole are steered into a fixed mindset. These are the same people who laugh in your face or snigger behind your back, while worshipping a cross and having their children christened in church. I don't even think many even question what they are worshipping; they just follow rules and guidelines ingrained from birth, creating generation after generation of sheep. To me this suggests blind faith and ignorance of what is really going on and I think this attitude stands in the way of ever understanding truly unexplained phenomena.

Missing cats and power cuts are such absurd partners alongside my research into the missing men, that I may never understand where they fit. I am not even sure what could create such an unusual set of circumstances. It is possible that some mechanism - on the very edge of our perception - is at work, but on such a high level, that as observers, we may not even be considered worthy of its acknowledgment. I suspect that we are seen as simply the visual residue it encounters, as it passes through our lives without any concept of the confusion it leaves in its wake. Maybe it is all of the above and more, like a blameless carnivore with a cold and calculated intelligence capable of reading any situation.

The questions are endless and the more I search the more confusing it becomes. These cats cannot all be falling into a black hole along with the missing people. But to look through the eyes of a sceptic and dismiss it all as pure coincidence would be wrong. Scientific thinking has so far failed to produce any logical answers or solutions. Rather than suggest something we don't understand could be responsible, scientists remain silent. To suggest anything more would expose their inadequacies and mean they have to admit something is happening that defies understanding. If other clues are there, we must continue to search - even if it means looking outside of the physical world.

Power cuts, missing cats and missing men could all be coincidence, but I don't think so. I think the gaps between the coincidences just cannot be filled by anything that would make sense. The reason no one has ever discovered why these unfortunate events have happened, suggests to me that nothing of human understanding or scientific reasoning exists to explain them. The pressure appears to be on the researcher to make the evidence fit, but the facts we often uncover make little sense within the boundaries of what is considered normal.

All I have to share are a series of events that seem to keep repeating themselves in a vicious circle of tragedy. If I continue unearthing these strange events, will I find a predictable pattern is forming? Could that pattern then be applied as evidence in some way, without even understanding how?

In April 2010 the Bridlington Free Press reported that a disturbing number of cats had recently gone missing from the Queensgate area of Bridlington. The report even told of heavily pregnant cats vanishing. I think this in itself is unusual, since pregnant cats tend to stay close to home when they ready to give birth. Yet between March 1st and 5th, a total of five cats were reported to have vanished from a concentrated area of Queensgate. Many more vanished in the weeks before these five were reported missing and all from the same area.

Body In The Graveyard

The missing cats are a curious puzzle that seem to shadow the reports of missing people. The strange circumstances surrounding the case of a man found in a graveyard in Filey are no less puzzling.

The body of 58 year old James Patrick Gorman from Queensgate in Bridlington was discovered at 11.50am by two walkers as they passed through the grounds of St.Oswald's Church in Filey on February 12th 2010. According to the Bridlington Free Press, Jimmy had discharged himself from Scarborough Hospital and it was thought he had tried to make it home on foot. His friends and family have no idea why or how he ended up nine miles away in Filey.

The newspaper also points out that Jimmy had no reason to be in Filey, since his home was in Queensgate, Bridlington, which is eighteen miles from the hospital. So just how and why did he come to be there?

Body in churchyard

THE body of a man in his 50s has been found in a Filey churchyard.

It is believed it could be that of a Bridlington man who had been reported missing since February 8.

The body was discovered on Tuesday in St Oswald's Church yard in Filey.

Police said they were not treating the death as suspicious, but cannot make a formal identification.

An inquest was due to be opened today in Scarborough.

Man found dead was trying to walk home

A MAN found dead in a Filey churchyard could have been making his way on foot to his Bridlington home.

James Patrick Gorman, 58, of Queensgate, had discharged himself from Scarborough hospital but failed to return home.

Police issued a missing person alert and his body was found by a couple of walkers around lunchtime on Thursday February 11 at St Oswald's church in Filey .

His brother, Danny Gorman, 50, who lives in the West Hill area of Bridlington, said he believed his brother, who had an alcohol problem, had been making his way back to Bridlington on foot.

"He did not have any money, or a mobile phone. I don't know why he should have been in Filey, there is no family connection with the town," said Mr Gorman.

His brother, who was divorced, originally came from Bradford and had lived in Bridlington for some years. He has a son living in York, a sister in Ilkley and a niece who lives in Bridlington.

He had been a skilled engineer and for a short time had worked at the former Sara Lee factory on Carnaby Industrial Estate.

An inquest into his death was opened and adjourned in Scarborough last Thursday.

Bridlington Free Press article - Sept 22nd 2010

A man whose body was found slumped over a grave in a Filey cemetery, died of natural causes, a coroner has ruled. James Gorman, 58, of Queensgate, Bridlington, was admitted to Scarborough Hospital after complaining of seizures on February 7th, but the following day he went missing from the hospital after discharging himself. Four days later, a member of the public found his body in the cemetery of St.Oswald's Church in Filey.
Dr Peter Cooper, consultant pathologist at the Royal Victoria Infirmary in Newcastle, who carried out a post-mortem on February 13th, said despite evidence of 36 separate injuries to Mr Gorman's body, including "substantial bruises", he concluded the death was not suspicious.

Dr Cooper said many of the injuries were consistent with Mr Gorman's well-documented drinking problem, while his liver showed signs of "fatty change" - the stage before cirrhosis sets in. Mud and dirt on his clothes suggested he had been "crawling and stumbling around" in the graveyard shortly before his death. He said because Mr Gorman had temporarily stopped drinking, he had died from alcoholic ketoacidosis, which affects those with a recent history of binge drinking and little or no nutritional intake. Dr Cooper explained, "The end result can be the same as diabetics. They may complain of abdominal pain and lapse into a coma."

Answering questions from members of Mr Gorman's family about when he died, Dr Cooper said: "He had been missing for four days, and logic would suggest he probably died near the beginning of that. It could have been two or three days." He added that while the early stages of hypothermia could have begun, he did not believe it was the cause of death. A statement from the deceased's brother, Daniel Gorman, said the pair had shared a love of horse racing and James had recently found a new girlfriend. He said: "When I received the news I was in shock. I'd always been concerned about the amount of alcohol he drank. I knew it would kill him but not this soon."

Coroner Michael Oakley said: "It is significant that while at the hospital he had received treatment for alcohol withdrawal." Some four days after he had discharged himself his body was found in a graveyard. He had clearly been dead for some time." Although he may have been in the early stages of hypothermia, Dr Cooper has found he died as a result of ketoacidosis which follows withdrawal from alcohol."

This article sounds pretty convincing and if I had not discovered one or two other things about Jimmy Gorman, I may never have decided to look into his death. But certain things, while reading between the lines, told me something was not right. I thought long and hard about whether or not to make contact with the Gorman family. Regardless of the actual circumstances surrounding Jimmy's death, it seemed clear to me that something did not add up.

I have found no more evidence than what was available around the time of Jimmy's death, but with the kind permission of his family I have attempted to lay out that evidence here, in a fair and honest way. To the best of my knowledge I have not lied or tried to make the events surrounding this tragedy any more unusual than they already are.

Meeting Daniel Gorman

On January 19th 2017 Jimmy Gorman's brother Danny agreed to meet me. He wanted to share his thoughts about the unusual circumstances surrounding the death of his brother. I don't think it was a decision he took lightly either, because it was only after speaking with his sister and brother-in-law that he agreed to meet me at all. I had spent a long time deliberating whether I should contact Danny. I was unsure how he would feel about a stranger asking questions about, what must have been, one of the most painful times in his family's life, but I pride myself on talking to people with respect and that is exactly what I did. My books may cover the unexplained but I try not to step over the line. Danny knows his family will always have my full support and respect.

I have not found solid proof to explain why these people have vanished or been found dead in strange circumstances and I made that clear in our first meeting. All I know is that people *are* disappearing and I am the only one highlighting these mysteries years after the event. If my work eventually leads to an answer then it can only be good - even if the answer we find is not the one we expect. That, in part, is the reason I never say that one event is responsible for the other. I do suspect that some unknown element is at work that we do not understand, but without proof of how that mechanism works, I have to stop short of saying that A is responsible for B.

I met Danny Gorman at 2pm in Bridlington town centre and we spoke for over two hours about the circumstances surrounding his brother's death. I went armed with a few questions but I had no idea how our meeting would go. I found Danny to be a very warm and genuine man who had more questions about his brother's death than I could have imagined. The Gorman family had never stopped asking why and how Jimmy had ended up in grounds of St.Oswald's church at Filey. It was a question they had asked over and over since the day he was discovered. The details of Jimmy's disappearance and death are highly unusual. It is a mystery that definitely belongs within the pages of Truth-Proof.

Jimmy Absconds From Hospital

Jimmy Gorman was thought to have left Scarborough Hospital and made his way on foot back to Bridlington - a journey of 18 miles. Despite the newspapers reporting that he discharged himself, he did in fact just leave the hospital sometime before 12 noon on February 8th 2010 without so much as a word.

Jimmy's partially-clothed body was found four days later in the ancient graveyard of St.Oswald's Church in Filey. He was not slumped over a grave as reported in the paper; Jimmy's body lay face-up with his arms raised above him. One of the walkers who discovered his body explained that Jimmy's arms felt very stiff when touched and that they did not move. An interesting point that Danny made was that any walkers passing by the church should have been able to see his brother's body from the path that runs alongside the graveyard.

I put Danny's theory to the test in February 2017 by walking the route myself and agree that it would have been possible to see Jimmy's body from parts of the path. So how could he have gone unnoticed for four days?

I could see Danny's frustration when he told me that the coroner couldn't give them an approximate time for Jimmy's death. It appeared to the Gorman family that it could have been anytime within the four days he had been missing. Now I am no expert in such things, but I do wonder if an estimate could have been made, at least to within a day of his death. Although Jimmy left the hospital on February 8th and was found on February 12th, nothing is known about what happened to him between those dates. He was reported to the police as a missing person, but it is unknown exactly when hospital staff raised their concerns.

Jimmy had no money or means of contacting anyone and from the moment he left the hospital to being found, he appears to have just vanished off the face of the Earth. Neither were there any reported sightings of Jimmy on the eighteen mile walk between Scarborough and his home in Bridlington. So just what happened in that four day period?

I had read in the press that Jimmy had substantial bruising to his body; the report said thirty-six bruises to be exact. Yet when Jimmy was admitted into hospital the medical staff who examined him had said nothing about marks or bruising. I asked Danny if he was given an explanation for his brother having so many injuries on his body. He said the family were told that they probably occurred as his brother stumbled around the graveyard during the night.

It is known that Jimmy had bruises to the front of his thighs, which could perhaps be attributed to falling forwards. He also had 8inch by 5inch bruises on his calves. Personally, I am at a loss to understand how a person could receive such bruises by falling either backwards or forwards. I also wonder whether the approximate time of death could have been established from the condition of the bruising. Some of the bruises were red, which implies that some of them had occurred shortly before death. Now we all bruise at slightly different rates, but red bruising is fresh bruising. The family tell me that Jimmy's body had many red and blue bruises, which must mean they were not all received at the same time. Surely the older blue bruises on his body would have been seen when he was first admitted to hospital, yet no one ever mentioned it.

The pathologist report states that the thirty-six bruises were not considered suspicious, since Jimmy was believed to have sustained them as he moved around the graveyard in the dark. Was this before or after he had attempted to remove his own clothing? Reports state that Jimmy had died soon after leaving hospital, but I wonder why it was not possible to ascertain how long his body had been in the graveyard. I always thought it was possible to learn these things, but I am not an expert and there may have been circumstances I am not aware of. The pathologists word and conclusions have to be respected.

The Bridlington Free Press reported that when Jimmy was found he was wearing just one shoe. This intrigued me because missing or removed footwear seems to be a feature in many of these unexplained deaths and disappearances. I wanted to ask Danny this question about his brother's footwear, but I needed to assure him that he could stop talking about his brother's death at any time. The last thing I wanted to do was cause any additional stress, but Danny said he was happy to continue so I began to ask a few more questions:

"Danny, can you tell me if the police or anyone involved in the investigation, think that your brother had walked for any length of time without wearing his right shoe? Because I am sure the sole of his foot would have shown evidence of this."

"They never said Paul. All they did talk about was the mud on his clothing and the heavy bruising, which they say came from scrambling around in the churchyard in the darkness. He was wearing his socks though and I don't think they were ripped or torn. Lots of things didn't add up at the time and they still don't. He was not even wearing the same shoes that he wore to the hospital. I think that's something the police seem to have overlooked. To me, that has to mean that he must have got home or he went somewhere else before he ended up in the church grounds."

"What do you mean 'not wearing the same shoes' Danny?"

Now the strangeness had just stepped up a level. If I had heard Danny correctly, he was telling me that his brother Jimmy had been found wearing totally different footwear to that which he had on his feet when he was first admitted to the hospital. To me, if I had been a police detective, this should have sent alarm bells ringing. I wondered why this had never been followed up in more detail at the time.

"I know for a fact Paul, that when our Jimmy went into the hospital he was wearing white trainers. Even one of the nurses remembered he was wearing white trainers when he was admitted. When me and my sister had gone back to the hospital to ask questions they were sure he had white trainers on - and jeans. We told the police this and we told the coroner, but they did not seem to listen. To us it proves that Jimmy either made it home or something else happened to him, because he was found wearing a black brogue on his left foot.

I don't think he could have been there all that time either, someone would have seen him. We went with the police to the place where the walkers found him and anyone could have seen him from the path. There were other things too. Not just the shoe - which was strange on its own - but the fact the shoe was different is only part of it.

Paul it just does not add up. His shirt was on wrong and it was a different shirt to the one he was wearing at the hospital. All his clothing was wrong. He didn't have his sweater on, but it was freezing cold. He went into hospital wearing a black sweater, where was it?

We asked questions and said what we thought, but it didn't seem to matter. They found Jimmy's body between two graves, not on top of a gravestone like they said in the papers. Paul, his tracksuit bottoms were around his knees when they found him, but he was wearing jeans when he went into hospital. Then the authorities said that his partial state of undress could have been, in some way, due to the onset of hyperthermia. They said he would have started to feel too hot, so he was trying to remove his clothes. They said that the early stages of hyperthermia might have begun, but it either had or it hadn't.

Then they said they didn't think it was hyperthermia that killed him. The coroner said his death was more likely because of his sudden withdrawal from alcohol. The witness who found him says both of his arms were raised above his head and that they touched his hand to see if he was still alive. They said he was rigid and that sounds like rigor mortis to me, but the coroner says he only found evidence of slight rigor mortis in his lower legs."

An inquest and autopsy was carried out at Scarborough Hospital on the 13th, the day after Jimmy's body was found. In his report the pathologist states that Jimmy was admitted into hospital on the 8th and went missing at 1.25pm on the 9th. This is wrong, because Jimmy was admitted to hospital on the 7th and went missing on the 8th. If the experts could not even get the actual dates right, I wonder if this could have had some bearing on their final conclusions. With the evidence they had in front of them I would have thought they could easily have predicted certain details. I still cannot understand how Jimmy's time of death could not have been narrowed down - unless the evidence they were presented with did not add up. Knowing the correct dates might have helped.

Jimmy had been found four days after his disappearance from hospital and it was suggested that his death occurred a short time after that. So was this on the same day or the next - and if so, where was he? If his body had been in the graveyard for four days, surely someone would have seen him? Even though the public footpath is lower than the graveyard itself, the grass and the gravestones can be seen easily. Danny Gorman visited the church grounds himself and is sure that anyone passing by could have seen his brother's body. There are so many unanswered questions. For example, no one can explain why the clothing he was found in was different to those he was originally wearing. Had he been elsewhere after leaving the hospital and found a change of clothes?

When Jimmy was found on February 12th he was wearing tracksuit bottoms, a dark T-shirt and his green parker coat. The staff nurse who saw him on February 7th said in a statement that, to the best of his knowledge, Jimmy was wearing a black sweater, white T-shirt, jeans and white trainers when he was admitted. When Jimmy left hospital that morning it was a bitterly cold day, so there is a strong possibility he would have been wearing his sweater, but there was no mention of it ever being found. Had Jimmy taken off his coat, removed his sweater, then put his coat back on?

He was also found wearing a single black brogue shoe on his left foot. During the investigation the right shoe was found ten metres away, on the other side of the church path. Reports also state that Jimmy's clothes was caked in mud when he was found, but the ground was frozen hard, so where had he come into contact with soft mud?

None of this was ever discussed with the Gorman family during the investigation, even though they asked several times why their brother was found wearing different clothes to those he had on when he first arrived at the hospital. The pathologist told the family that their brother may have been suffering from the onset of hyperthermia. This can make someone feel very cold, then very hot, as a result, they can begin removing clothing - which is why he thought Jimmy's tracksuit bottoms were down around his legs. But why did Jimmy begin to remove them and then stop? Would it have been possible for him to move around the graveyard with them down around his lower legs?

I realise that the job of the pathologist is to find the cause of death and I have the greatest respect for their expertise, but none of this fully explains the different clothing and how Jimmy came to be found where he was. When I asked Danny why he thought his brother ended up nine miles away in Filey, he told me the police had suggested Jimmy had walked along the clifftops following the coastal route known as the Cleveland Way. The estimated walking time from Scarborough, along the Cleveland Way, to Filey is about three hours and fifteen minutes. Add to that another hour to walk from Scarborough Hospital to the clifftops makes a journey of four hours and fifteen minutes. Had Jimmy done this wearing shoes that might not have been his own? Walking the clifftops in terrible winter weather would have made this journey even worse.

Even if Jimmy had left Scarborough Hospital before noon on Monday February 8th , walking non-stop without interruption, he could have made it to Filey at around 5.30pm. This still leaves a gap of over four days until he was found on Friday February 12th. Danny says his brother was a good walker, so it is possible he could have walked non-stop to Filey, but this does not explain why he walked there in the first place. His family say he had no connections to Filey. There was simply no reason for him to go there.

There are so many unanswered questions about what happened to Jimmy Gorman. There are gaps in time that makes no sense, gaps that appear to have been filled with half answers and there are impossible scenarios - and I have no answers. Even the time that Jimmy was reported to have left the hospital was wrong, which must impact on the final conclusions of the investigation.

It would be wrong to say that mistakes were made or even that there was a cover-up in the investigation of Jimmy Gorman's death. I would never make such a statement. But it is clear that many things about his tragic death do not add up. For a time, I could not stop thinking about the location that Jimmy was found. So on February 8th 2017 I made another visit to St.Oswald's Church. As I walked towards the church my first thoughts were of Jimmy. It was a freezing cold day and I wondered if he really could have taken the coastal path seven years earlier. The idea of him walking nine miles along the Cleveland Way in similar weather conditions just did not make any sense.

There are three entrances to the grounds of St Oswald's church. One has a pair of wrought iron gates at the end of a path which crosses a ravine bridge. The gates, which do not lock, lead up a sloping path to the top of the graveyard where another entrance can be found. This one has no gates and is about 30ft wide and is used for vehicle access and funerals. There is a third entrance found along the ravine path, which I suspect Jimmy would have used if he had walked the Cleveland Way.

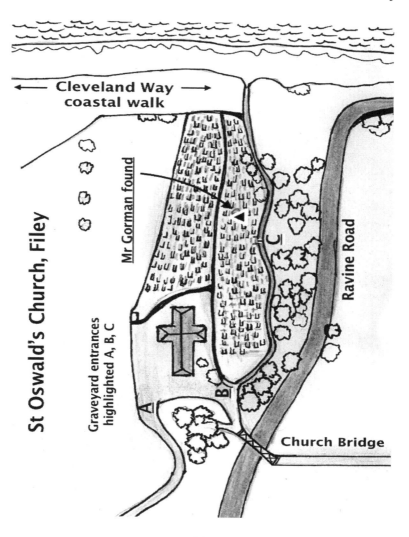

While I was there I wanted to check whether either of the gates were locked during the evenings. I thought this might help to explain why it had been suggested Jimmy had been stumbling around in the darkness.

The drawing shows the three entry points into the church grounds; including the third gate which is further along the graveyard and close to where Jimmy's body was discovered. There is a path towards this gate which runs parallel to nearby Ravine Road. At this point all we can do is speculate, but I do not believe Jimmy could have become trapped in the graveyard and even if he *had* entered by this path. Also, why was his right shoe ten metres away on the other side of the graveyard?

This path is unlit at night with a sheer drop of eighty to a hundred feet down onto Ravine Road below. There is no safety fence either and in February 2010 it was freezing cold with snow and ice, so it would have been deadly to walk at night. Could Jimmy have negotiated that path in a confused state and still found the graveyard? The entrance to the graveyard is easy enough to miss in the daytime, so I am unsure how Jimmy could have found it. Over the weeks that followed I visited the area a few times, both day and night. If Jimmy's body had been in the graveyard for days I needed to feel sure that it could have easily gone unnoticed, so I had to get an idea of just who might have been around at that time of year. During the daytime I noticed the ravine path was used by dog walkers, joggers and people just out for a walk.

Prior to this visit in February I had contacted Danny to ask if he had any objections to me speaking with staff at St.Oswald's Church. I wanted to know if they had any information that could help. Danny thought it was a good idea so on Monday January 23rd I gave them a call. A lady named Jill answered and told me she could remember the incident, but knew very little about it. She said the area had been taped off and out of bounds for a while but the grounds were always quite busy with dog walkers passing through and people visiting graves. She then asked me if I was the same person who had called recently to ask about Mr Gorman's death. I assured her that I had never phoned the church before and she remarked how strange it was, because I was the second person to ask about it in the last few weeks.

I checked with Danny's family to be sure they had not contacted the church, but they said they had never even thought about it until I suggested it. So who could have been asking?

Jill promised to ask around to see what she could find out for me, then said I should phone back the following week. That same evening I contacted Jimmy Gorman's sister and brother-in-law, Jacky and Steve Wade. I wanted to tell them about my call to St.Oswald's Church and I mentioned Jill by name. As agreed, the following week I called the church again. I asked to speak with Jill, but was told she was not there. After giving a brief summary of our previous conversation I was told that they would contact her for me. Less than ten minutes later my phone rang. *"Hello is that Mr Sinclair?"*

I said yes and went on to remind the lady of our conversation from the previous week. To my surprise she did not remember the conversation at all. Now I have to admit that I began to feel a little embarrassed. I apologised and assured her I had spoken to someone at the church on the Monday of last week. She told me she knew nothing about it but would ask around for me. I even told her that whoever I had spoken with before had asked me if I was the same person who had been enquiring about Jimmy's death a few weeks earlier. Our call ended with a polite thank you and good bye, but I don't mind saying felt a bit confused. I was sure this was the lady I had spoken with a week earlier.

Minutes later my phone rang again.
"Hello is that Paul? It's Jill here again from St.Oswald's Church. I think I understand the confusion now about who you spoke to."
I thanked her for calling me back and she continued.
"The lady you first called today has just told me you asked her today about the death in the graveyard. That's where the confusion has come from, no one else has asked. You asked one of my colleagues today and that's the mix up."

Now I was completely lost. I had called the week before and spoken with someone named Jill. I thought this was the same lady. I had to say something, even though this had no bearing on my inquiry into Jimmy's death. *"No I'm sorry but that's not true. I don't mean to sound rude, but I definitely, definitely spoke with a lady last Monday who told me I was the second person recently who had called to ask about Mr Gorman's death. I phoned to ask if someone could look through the records for me to see whether anything of significance had happened at the church between the 8th and 12th of February 2010. The lady I spoke with said she would ask for me. She also told me the grounds were always quite busy with dog walkers passing through and people visiting graves."*

Before our conversation ended I asked if she could recall anyone finding any items of footwear or clothing in the church grounds; it was a long shot but was worth asking. She told me that she knew nothing and could not help any further and our conversation ended. Speaking later with Steve and Jacky Wade, they confirmed I had told them about my original call to the church. They remembered it was a Monday evening and that I had spoken with someone named Jill. They even remembered the part where she said someone else had been asking about Jimmy's death. At least I was not going mad.

Foreground of image below is where Mr Gorman was discovered.
Entrance C to the graveyard can just be seen along the fence, top-right.

Jimmy Gorman's mysterious change of clothing has puzzled me as much as anything else in this bizarre story. Steve and Jacky Wade say the hospital insisted he wore white trainers, jeans and a black sweater when he was admitted on February 7th. The fact he was found in an entirely different set of clothes should have alerted detectives to speak with hospital staff. Maybe they did. Maybe they thought it was not relevant.

This has to rule out Jimmy walking the Cleveland Way and his life ending in the graveyard. He had to have made it home to change his clothes. But could Jimmy have made it eighteen miles back to his home in Queensgate? He had no money with him and could not drive. If he did, why was he then found ten miles north in the graveyard of St.Oswald's church? Maybe he was intercepted during the journey and later placed in the graveyard, but if so, by who or by what? If this is true then how could such a thing have happened?

If Jimmy died soon after leaving the hospital, as suggested, then where had he been to be later found wearing a change of clothing? There is also the question of all the bruising on his body. If the blue bruises signify older injuries and the red bruises indicate he had sustained recent injuries, what could this mean? Although Jimmy's injuries may not have been responsible for his death, they are hard to explain. Reports state there were 36 bruises found on his body, but that is not correct. The list of injuries records observations of 36 different areas of his body and some of these areas contained multiple injuries.

Nothing seems to add up when looking back at the details of this tragic story. Maybe in time more evidence will come to light. There is much about this disappearance that I feel will forever remain unexplained, but this does not mean they should not be addressed or spoken about.

Truth Proof would not be the book it is if it did not raise questions the scientific community dare not even consider answering. Is it just a coincidence that so many domestic cats vanished from around the area of Queensgate, Jimmy's home, around the time of his disappearance? There is nothing to link them at all, apart from location and approximate timeframe. Unless there is proof of a connection this will remain an oddity – one that continues to occur when tragedy strikes. If the missing cats and the large-scale power cuts seem hard to believe, at least newspaper reports exist to prove something happened.

I would end this chapter here if it was not for something Danny Gorman told me in our very first conversation. There was even more to this story than even I was prepared for. The phrase 'beyond belief' jumped into my mind when I heard the account that follows. It is one of the most amazing visions into the future I have ever heard.

Conversation with Danny Gorman

During our first meeting to discuss the death of his brother, Danny Gorman told me that his brother-in-law Steve Wade had been having strange dreams before Jimmy disappeared. Danny explained that these dreams occurred and had been discussed between family members, weeks before the event itself.

Danny told me that Steve had experienced two surreal dreams, both about Jimmy and both about death. He said Steve dreamed with such clarity and they contained such important details that I personally think they were more than just pure chance or coincidence. His dreams were about searching for Jimmy, but this was before he even went missing. The main dream involved a ravine - which was almost a premonition in itself; a clue to things that had not yet happened. St.Oswald's church, where Jimmy's body was later found, is on Ravine Road. Is this pure coincidence? I don't think so. I am sure there has to be a connection and perhaps the answers lie behind the thinking mind.

After so many years of being immersed in the unknown, I get a feel for the stories that tip the balance - the stories that leave no proof and leave the authorities scratching their heads. I believe something else played a part in the tragic death of Jimmy Gorman. This dream occurred before the family had any knowledge that Jimmy was missing and before he was found dead. It is not too much of a leap of imagination to suggest that some form of telepathic interaction could have been taking place.

We should examine things that science and the mainstream avoid, the unexplained that happens and defies all explanation, the events that simply will not fit into any box they can think of or create. It is the desire to understand that leads me to believe that many answers might be found if we could gain access to unconscious thought. All I can do is speculate, I cannot prove this, any more than I can prove God exists.

Steven Wade's Premonition

I spoke with Jacky and Steve Wade on the evening of January 23rd 2017. They did not live in Bridlington at the time of Jimmy's death, they lived in Ilkley, West Yorkshire, after moving from Bridlington on Good Friday 2009. Jacky told me that she and her brothers, Danny and Jimmy, all kept in touch by phone. Jacky explained that years before she had helped her brother Jimmy through some difficult times and said they were always there for him when he needed them.

They told me about being present at Jimmy's inquest and how they felt shell-shocked and unable to think straight. Jacky remembered a police woman holding a photograph of Jimmy, which had been taken at the scene. She told the family they would not want to see it, because it would be too upsetting to look at, but Jacky spoke up. She did want to see the picture. It was her brother and she wanted to see it.

Jacky told me the police woman handed her the photograph, which Jacky showed to her husband Steve. But before he could look at it in any detail, the police woman snatched the image back and seemed annoyed. She said that because Steve never asked to see it, she should not have shown it him. They found her attitude quite troubling - almost as though they were being patronised. They admit to being so shocked and upset at the time, that they did not think to ask enough questions.

Then Jacky's husband Steve wanted to tell me about his strange dream experiences. They occurred in January 2010, perhaps two or three weeks before Jimmy had gone missing. Steve said he could not get them out of his mind. He talked about them constantly with his wife Jacky and other members of the family. They had such a lasting effect on him that he knew they were no ordinary dreams.

"I had the strangest dream Paul. One that did not make any sense at the time, but I knew right away that it was important and had deep meaning. I remember it as clear as day though and I told Jacky about it soon as I woke up. I told Danny and even our daughter Mandy about it. At the time I did not understand its meaning, it was just really weird and unsettling. For me to make such a fuss, it had to have been a strange dream. I mean, it still amazes me to this day. How could I have known location names and seen actual places while I was in the dream state,

without ever visiting them before. That's what happened Paul. I saw where Jimmy died.

In the dream I was in a hospital with Jacky. I knew it was about death - don't ask me how, I just did. At the time I thought it was about Jacky's death. I think that was because of how Jimmy was dressed in the dream. It's all I could think as I tried to understand what I was seeing. That's another odd thing. I remember trying to understand what was happening as I was actually having the dream. It's so hard to explain, it was like I was looking into my own dream while another part of my mind was asking questions. It wasn't like an ordinary dream, if that doesn't sound too daft. I even woke during the dream and went to the bathroom. As soon as I went back to bed I was able to re-enter the dream.

I remember telling Jacky the next morning I'd dreamt that someone close had died. I recognised Jimmy in the dream and Jacky, but I knew she was not dead in the dream - except I knew the dream was about death. It's hard to explain. I remember it being vivid and so real. I was looking into the distance through a window. I could see some corridors and two doctors. I know they were doctors, because they had the white coats on like doctors wear and there was someone with them. It was a man with short grey hair and he was standing behind them with two nurses. In the dream I remember thinking to myself it was our Jimmy. But then immediately I thought it can't be because whoever it is was wearing a pink dressing gown.

It was confusing. For a moment I thought it might have been Jacky, because she owns a similar dressing gown, but I knew it was definitely Jimmy and wondered why I was questioning myself. I also remember saying to myself that it isn't Jacky, because she has long blonde hair – this is Jimmy, I know it is. But he seemed somehow different, distant and vague. It was like I could see him, but he had gone.

The next thing I remember is, there was a nurse standing with me and Jacky. She was telling us to go home because there was nothing more we could do. I knew in the dream that it was one of those talks they give you before or after someone one dies. The nurse said the time has come - meaning it was their time to die. I knew the meaning of her words. Even in the dream I just knew this Paul. At the time I didn't understand any of it, except that it was very important.

In the dream the nurse said that it was time to go, that there is nothing more you can do and you should go home. All the time I was thinking 'but who did she mean?' The only people I recognised were Jacky and our Jimmy. Jacky was standing beside me and she seemed sad and Jimmy seemed distant and lost. When I woke up I thought it meant Jacky had died.

I was confused about why I saw Jimmy wearing the pink dressing gown. I thought it had something to do with Jacky because she does have a pink dressing gown. I understood the nurse's message to mean that someone had to die and it was their time, but I kept thinking that Jacky wasn't that old, so surely it can't be her. Jimmy was there, but he was distant and seemed lost - and he was in pink, which really confused me. Anyone who knew him when he was alive would tell you he would never dress like that.

Paul, I know this must sound weird but I was actually trying to understand this complicated dream as it was happening. It was all I could think of for days and weeks afterwards. It was like I was one person but had two minds. I don't know how else to explain it. Here I was in a dream and I was watching myself in a strange place, in an even stranger situation.

The dream seemed to jump back and forwards as well Paul, because after they told us to go home the next thing I remember was getting on a bus. I think I was going to the place where I was meant to live in the dream. But this is what I mean by having two minds. I could see myself getting off the bus and I remember thinking that I must live here. It was just like watching myself on film.

I remember getting off the bus and sitting under a tree. Then I was thinking about things and getting upset. Then I stood up and started walking towards this house and I thought this must be where I am supposed to live. It was a big stone house and I remember by the side of it there was like a path going up into, what looked like, a field and I was walking along the path..."

I interrupted Steve at this point, because I thought I recognised the place he was describing. It seemed as though he was talking about the land surrounding St.Oswald's Church. I asked if he had ever been there before having this dream, but Steve assured me he had never been to the area before; and his wife Jacky echoed his words.

These are the parts of his story that fascinate me. This man was telling me the truth, I have no doubt about that, but how could he describe a place when he had never been there? Had he experienced some sort of mind time travel? Not only had he seen events unfold that his thinking mind could not understand, he was seeing them in advance of the event.

There are so many things that scientific thinking seems reluctant to address. Perhaps accessing the unconscious mind is a way into these unknown areas of existence. The way Steve described looking at himself in the dream was almost like he was looking into another world. I was fascinated to hear more.

"Paul, I had another dream about the same place, all within weeks before Jimmy died. In this second dream I was in the back of a car with our Jimmy. I remember that it was very dark and there were two men sitting in front, but I don't know who they were. I asked them to stop the car because I needed to pee. When I got out the car, it drove away and I could see our Jimmy still inside and he was looking back at me through the rear window.

After that I remember walking back along the path towards the field, away from the stone house I thought was my home. Further along the path began to drop down into a steep ravine. Then suddenly, I was down at the bottom of this ravine and I don't know how I got there, I just was. I remember looking around and seeing what looked like lobster and crab pots. Then I could hear voices, so I scrambled up the bank to see who it was.

When I looked back I saw a sleeping bag - at least I think that's what it was. It was high up on top of this big stone wall. I remember thinking it was a reservoir wall. I tried to make sense of what I was seeing, but all I could think was that I was looking at a reservoir."

All sorts of images flashed through my mind as I listened to Steve. I remember hearing that Jimmy's parker coat had been pulled up high over his head. Could this have resembled a sleeping bag as in Steve's dream? Could the stone house on the hill he was telling me about, really have been St.Oswald's Church at Filey? And what were the chances of him dreaming of a ravine when the road that runs parallel to the church is named Ravine Road? It was not long after Steve had painted these images in my mind that confirmation came.

"Paul, it all became clear after Jimmy's death. I looked online at Google Earth for the place he had been found and I knew it was the same place I'd visited in my dream. Looking at the map I realised instantly that what I dreamt was a reservoir, was actually the sea and the top of the reservoir wall was the narrow strip of sandy beach. I don't know how else to explain it. The weeks I spent trying to make sense of the dream and it all fell into place instantly. As soon as I saw the map I realised I had somehow been dreaming of Ravine Road looking towards the beach."

I thought about how Steve was describing this and could not help but draw a comparison to remote viewing or an out-of-body experience.

"In the dream Paul, I was on the path by the side of the church that runs parallel to Ravine Road and the field I saw was the graveyard. I did not have to make any of it fit. This was the place where our Jimmy's body was found. It was exactly what I was shown. I was shocked - we all were - but it's true. I saw all this before he died. It's not something I would or could make up. I talked about the dream as soon I woke up, weeks before anything happened.

I could not get it out of my mind for weeks Paul. It was all I could think about. The ravine, the stone house, the field and path. It all went round and round in my mind, over and over. I talked about it all the time. I told other people as well; not just Jacky, Danny and Mandy. I had no idea what it meant until the day we found out about our Jimmy.

The pink dressing gown Jimmy wore in the dream always puzzled Jacky and me. It was the only bit that never seemed to add up, but then about four weeks ago, we spoke to Danny and his partner Tanya. We were talking about Jimmy and all the things you had asked us about. We talked about my strange dream and Danny was telling me about how far he'd got with a letter he wrote to the hospital. Then out of the blue, Tanya talked about how she went to see Jimmy at the chapel of rest before the funeral. Then she said; 'Our Jimmy would have gone mad if he knew the undertakers had dressed him in a pink robe for his funeral.'

I think Steve's account is an amazing example of the mind's ability travel. His experience offers an insight into a parallel world that can only be accessed when the thinking mind is inactive or disabled. But what kind of intelligence projects images from the future into the unconscious mind? And what could be the reason for it? What if the intelligence *wanted* Steve to see events before they happened? Could it have simply been a mistake or is the unconscious mind an active participant in the outer nowhere. Maybe it was *because* these future events were so traumatic that they bled through into his subconscious, as some form of incontinent thinking?

Something happened to Steve Wade as he was sleeping that allowed the unknown to work within his unconscious thoughts. Perhaps his pure unconscious mind had somehow connected to future events. Can the answers to some of life's great mysteries be found behind the thinking mind? At the time they happened Steve's dreams made no sense and I suppose in this world of black and white they still don't.

Is it possible that future events have already happened and can be placed into the human mind? What if all of human life is pre-recorded and every move we make is planned and known about in advance. It would explain everything; why no one who sees a UFO or ghost ever brings back proof or why in fact, nothing is ever captured in advance. It is a frightening thought, but as I sit at home now writing this, at 5.30am in March 2017, knowing that the night before I had 'asked' for a moment of understanding - an epiphany if you like - I am wondering if I have just had one.

I have written about this before - the idea that where emotions run high, due to traumatic events, people can experience paranormal activity around this time of stress. Other examples being the near-death-experience, where the thinking mind has become detached. Some who are unconscious, after an accident or under anaesthetic during surgery, report leaving their bodies and observing themselves. I think this is clearly an example of the mind having two parts. Other examples come from the stories some people tell after using hallucinogenic drugs; DMT being a prime example. They describe meeting other beings while the thinking mind is detached from reality.

When the thinking mind is detached perhaps the unconscious mind is able to enter other spheres of existence and realities that parallel our own and engage in a world that we are only allowed to glimpse. The memories we bring back are usually fragmented and so disjointed that all a person feels is confused. I can think of no other way to justify Steve Wade's premonition than to say I believe he entered such a place and brought back more than fragmented memories. But we must not read about his premonition and simply roll our eyes, as though it is not worthy of our consideration. Valuable clues into the circumstances surrounding Jimmy's death may still be hidden. If the sleeping bag Steve saw on the reservoir wall in his dream really was a sleeping bag, what could that mean? Could it be a clue to solving the mystery of what happened?

How could Steve have found himself on the ravine path by the side of the church in his dream? He never saw the place in real time until after Jimmy's death - but if he had described it to a local resident of Filey, they would have known exactly the place he was talking about.

* * *

After the discovery of Jimmy's body in the church grounds the family went to Filey to look for clues about why he might have been there. Both Danny and Steve told me they visited a few places and asked lots of people if they had seen or heard anything suspicious. They took a photo of Jimmy to show the people they asked. They were convinced someone must have seen him around Filey between the 8th and 12th of February.

Much to Danny's surprise some people they asked said Jimmy was known in the area as a local drug dealer. Both Danny and Steve said they were amazed to hear this, because Jimmy couldn't even drive. He didn't smoke and he didn't have a penny to his name. His only vice was alcohol and nothing before or since ever hinted at Jimmy being involved in the sale of drugs. So was someone spreading untruths at the time – and if so, why? The toxicology report after his death proved no illegal substances were found in his body.

Another point of interest - one that I don't think anyone picked up on at the time - was about the alcohol levels in Jimmy's body when he was found. At the inquest the pathologist said Jimmy did not have any traces of alcohol in his system, although the cause of death was ketoacidosis, which is often the result of a sudden withdrawal from alcohol. I cannot dispute the observations of a trained professional, but if Jimmy died soon after leaving hospital, where did he die? He was found days later and in different clothing, so he had to have been somewhere else before he was found. Was his body placed in the graveyard after death. If it was, then how? If Jimmy did not walk the Cleveland Way, as his family believe, then where did he go and how did he receive all of his injuries? It is as though, between February 8th and February 12th, Jimmy Gorman had just vanished off the face of the Earth.

Jimmy was still wearing his hospital wristband when he was found. If he was somewhere else, his wristband would have been of no consequence. Would he really have worn it for days? Could he have been dead before being placed in the graveyard? This 'somewhere else' raises a massive question when considering Steve Wade's premonition.

Could there have been paranormal elements that link to Jimmy's four-day disappearance? I don't know whether there is a connection with the other strange occurrences at the time. Perhaps it is pure coincidence that the vanishing cats all disappeared close to the location of Jimmy's home in Queensgate. Maybe the power cuts were also a coincidence, even though they often seem to happen around the time similar tragedies strike. If there is a link, we have a clash of the surreal meeting the real, none of which ever leave a clue to the questions why or how.

It was said that rigor mortis was detected in Jimmy's legs, but not found anywhere else when he was examined. So I wonder why the witness who found him said his arms were raised and were very stiff, when the post mortem recorded only one of Jimmy's arms was raised. The witness did say *arms*, not *arm*. It was also suggested that the 36 bruises on his body were caused by Jimmy stumbling in the graveyard. When in fact there were 42 bruises on his body and a collection of cuts and abrasions.

All of this may be exactly the way things happened, but there are still many unanswered questions. Why was he in the graveyard? Why was he wearing different clothing? Could a man who was dependent on alcohol survive four days without a drink? And if he had been in the church grounds that long, why had no one found his body?

I'm not sure all the answers will ever be found to solve this mystery. It seems clear to me that the people looking into Jimmy's death at the time did not get very far. Steve Wade actually told the police and the coroner about his strange dreams, but they were of no interest during what was a scientific investigation. I suppose it is understandable, even though they might have offered more clues than were ever found. The truth is Steve saw a sequence of events before they happened. If a first-hand witness had come forward to tell the police the things that Steve saw in his premonition, they would have been a key part of the investigation.

What Steve saw took place beyond the thinking mind, a place we cannot access or understand. This does not make the facts any less real, but these things will never be accepted if they cannot be understood. When unexplained events occur within the parameters of scientific thinking, they are disregarded - but many of the minds who dismiss these truths still pray to a God we have no proof of. These are the same minds who laugh in the face of a man who has a dream that foretells a future event.

I believe much of the great unknown operates behind the conscious mind. Our thoughts are like an instant firewall that blocks the unknown every time it seeps through from the unconscious. I can understand why people walk away from the paranormal. It can drive you to the point where your own thoughts make no sense. Like chasing cobwebs in the mist, it can be too much to bear. But we continue, even though in our hearts we realise we might go to our graves no wiser. Perhaps the answers we crave *will* become clear after death. Knowing there is a connection to all of this pushes me on. Perhaps it is my job to find the pieces of the puzzle, until someone higher up the brain chain solves it.

If the unconscious mind can see events, weeks in advance of them happening, talking about them has to be easier than trying to understand them. This is the barrier that cannot be broken down by any means conceived by academic or scientific minds. Unconscious recall of events only seems to occur when the events are so dramatic, they are pulled through to the here and now and stamped onto the thinking mind for a reason. Is this evidence of a pre-recorded life? Or proof that evidence exists? I thought about this and all the people in my area who have vanished or been found dead in unusual circumstances.

Most are alone when they disappear and the places they disappear from are remote. They are detached from the trappings of this materialist and fast-paced world, where we rarely concentrate on anything. Perhaps this helps the blank canvas of our own pure thought to open up to the outer nowhere, allowing an interaction with a truth that leaves no proof.

Missing Men Revisited

The lack of understanding from all levels of academia means nothing; no one wants to step into my world or even dares to ask the same questions as I do. The creation of 'Prozac explanations' mean even less when the only published explanations remotely close to the truth, are simple placebos designed to pacify.

My observations about disappearing cats and power cuts had now grown from mild curiosity, to the point where I decided to re-examine some of the reports of missing men. Could there be a connection? Part of me did not want to find confirmation of my suspicions. The disappearances were unsolved and this would only throw more confusion into the mix of high strangeness.

I thought the best place to look should be the first missing person case covered in TP1. The mystery surrounding the disappearance of John Deakin in 2004 has never been solved. If I could discover a pattern that connects these mysteries, at least that would be a starting point. While I have no intention of repeating any of my research from TP1, I wish to outline further unusual events that I have discovered, from before and after John Deakin vanished.

Over the following pages I present cases of missing men in the order they occurred. They are interspersed with reports of missing cats and power cuts from around the same timeframe.

Man Jumps from Bempton Cliffs

The first unexplained tragedy of 2004 was that of a 22-year-old man who died after jumping from the cliffs at Bempton, on Tuesday August 24th. His body was found below the 200ft cliffs just half a mile from the RSPB bird sanctuary and nature reserve.

The report states that he jumped, but makes no mention of witnesses to the incident and makes no mention of his death being suicide. The article, from the Bridlington Free Press, was the first and only reference ever made about this tragedy. Nothing more was ever reported on this incident and not even the name of the deceased was published.

The article does state that he was a Bridlington man and, although there were no suspicious circumstances, police were appealing for anyone who might have seen him that day. I have been unable to discover who this man was; it is possible his death was nothing more than an unexplained tragedy. Much of the mystery surrounding this case is the obvious lack of background information.

After the death of Raymond Johnston in December 1992 the police suggested he had been hit by a vehicle, possibly fitted with bull bars. The truth is, they had no idea. This was a guess based on his injuries. The same lack of knowledge is seen in this 2004 report of the 22-year-old man falling to his death at Bempton. Without additional facts, there is just guesswork.

The Cats and the Power Cuts

On October 7th 2004 the Bridlington Free Press reported that Flamborough and parts of Bridlington had been hit by an electricity blackout two days earlier. On page seven, the same newspaper had an article entitled *Mystery of Missing Cats*. The article stated that throughout the previous August and September, over twenty cats had mysteriously vanished. One owner who had lost a cat locally had even moved to a new home and lost a second cat. This was not a random advertisement in the lost and found section asking if anyone had seen Felix - it was an article describing how lots of cats in and around Bridlington were vanishing for no apparent reason.

I thought long and hard about these missing cats. Just what could have been happening? It was a cause of great concern to animal welfare organisations, who were at a complete loss for an explanation. Anyone who has ever owned a cat will know they can be elusive creatures. Armed with sharp claws, keen eyes and the ability to move fast in any direction, they are not generally known to be so easy to catch. Whatever was doing this was outsmarting these felines on a grand scale.

Every cat has its own unique personality and most, although affectionate to strangers in their own home, would never allow anyone to get close enough to capture them. I checked with local veterinary practices to ask if they had records of devastating cat viruses during 2004, but found nothing out of the ordinary. So disease was ruled out - if that had been the case there would have been dead cats found close to where they lived. The fact that no newspaper reported anything of that nature should have been enough, but I needed to make sure.

Mystery of missing cats

CATS are going missing in suspicious circumstances in Bridlington, the RSPCA has warned.

There has been a spate of dubious incidents reported to the charity, including one resident who had lost a cat and then suffered the same fate again after moving to a new home.

Cat rehoming officer Mary Gray said: "The summer months are always dodgy but in the last two months I have had about 20 reports of cats missing.

"Some of them will have just gone walkabout and I know a couple have been run over but there are quite a few missing in odd circumstances. A lot of missing cats have lovely colours – white, grey or ginger.

"In most cases it has happened at night. There is no hot-spot area, it is happening all over the town."

The RSPCA has urged cat owners to take steps to help prevent the misery caused by losing a pet.

Mrs Gray said: "People should micro-chip their cats, collars can come off, and keep cats inside when it gets dark. Cats don't like it but they will get used to it.

"And cat owners should be very wary."

Blackout

HIGH winds caused overhead power lines to short out leaving homes without electricity for more than four hours.

At least one property in Water Lane and another in Bridlington Road, Flamborough were affected shortly after 11.15pm on Sunday.

Bridlington firefighters were called out after a report from householders in Bridlington Road that electricity was arcing between overhead power lines which had been blown together.

Engineers from power suppliers YEDL turned out to repair the faults and power was restored by 3.15am on Monday.

Body in the Harbour

On Thursday November 4th 2004 the Bridlington Free Press reported a man's body had been recovered from Bridlington Harbour on Sunday October 31st.

43-year-old Kenneth Michael Bottom had been visiting the town for the annual National Scooter Rally. It was not known how he came to be in the water, but discovery of his body was reported to the Harbour Master's Office around 8.30am on the Sunday and Bridlington lifeboat rescuers recovered his body a short time later.

There was no evidence to suggest Mr Bottom had been the victim of a crime and when he was found he still had his wallet and other possessions with him. Although it said there were no suspicious circumstances, the investigation that followed stated his death was being treated as unexplained. The Free Press article had reported that Mr Bottom's body had been found in the harbour, but that is incorrect. His body was just outside the harbour, close to the harbour quay.

I spoke at length to one of the lifeboat crew who recovered the body. He told me he could not remember seeing any suspicious marks but did say the body was fully clothed. He also said Mr Bottom's hands were clasped with his fingers interlocked, like someone would if they were praying. I suspect this may have more to do with the cold temperature of the water. The lifeboat crew member also said he remembered seeing a large bag of apples floating next to the body, which was an odd thing to note and may not be connected in any way. He just pointed it out, telling me that certain things stick in the mind.

Scooterist's body found in harbour

A MAN whose body was found in Bridlington Harbour had been in town for a scooter rally.

Kenneth Michael Bottom's corpse was discovered in the water on Sunday morning and an investigation into his death is underway.

"We are treating it as an unexplained death.

"There are no suspicious circumstances, but the thrust of the police investigation is how he came to be in the water," said Insp Steve Page, of Humberside Police.

Mr Bottom, who was 43 and lived in Boroughbridge, in North Yorkshire, was described as "an avid scooter rider" who had travelled to Bridlington for the rally, which was held at Leisure World and The Spa.

The body was first seen in the water at around 8:30am and harbourmaster Chris Wright contacted the coastguard.

"The police were informed and Bridlington lifeboat was launched to recover the body.

"The harbour was sealed off so police officers could look for places where the victim may have gone into the water.

It is not thought Mr Bottom

Police cordoned off the North Pier for a time on Sunday. (PA0444-25a)

had been the victim of a robbery because he still had his wallet and possessions with him.

He was formally identified on Monday and a Home Office post-mortem examination was due to be carried out yesterday.

Police are appealing for anyone who saw Mr Bottom going into the water or witnessed him while he was in the water to contact them on 672222.

His death is the second sea tragedy in Bridlington within three weeks.

Bridlington mother-of-three Deborah Kendrick drowned after going into the sea on the North beach following a night out.

96

The Disappearance of John Deakin

Four days after the death of Kenneth Bottom, it was reported that a man had vanished just three miles up the coast at Flamborough. I wrote about the disappearance of John Deakin in TP1 as part of my initial research into the missing men of Bempton.

John Deakin went missing on Thursday November 4th 2004. His disappearance came as a massive shock to his family and friends and has never been explained. Deakin was described as someone who loved his life and lived it to the full. In the words of his widow, *"It was as if he'd vanished off the face of the earth"*- a phrase which has been echoed by others who have lost loved ones around this area. Despite extensive searches, no trace of John Deakin has ever been found. His last known whereabouts were very close to where the 22-year-old man was said to have jumped to his death two months earlier on August 24th.

The final news item about Deakin's disappearance appeared in the Bridlington Free Press on December 9th stating that the search had now been scaled down. The article mentioned that Deakin's walking boots, walking stick and his uneaten sandwiches were still inside his car when he was first reported missing. Does this mean that he never even began his walk? Could he really have just vanished?

Coastal search for missing man

POLICE from three forces joined three coastguards units and a lifeboat crew to search for a man who has been missing for a week.

Officers are increasingly anxious to trace John Deakin after his car, containing his walking stick, boots and uneaten sandwiches was found at Flamborough Head.

A search involving officers from Humberside Police and South Yorkshire Police and a police helicopter was launched over the weekend.

Coastguard units from Speeton, Flamborough and Bridlington also took part and Flamborough Lifeboat launched for 40 minutes last Saturday afternoon.

On Monday, North Yorkshire Police joined in as the search was extended towards Reighton, following reports Mr Deakin may have been in the village last Thursday, the day he went missing from his home in Stannington, Sheffield.

His blue Renault Laguna was later found at Flamborough Head, but at the time the Free Press went to print, there had been no sightings of Mr Deakin.

The 53-year-old is said to be a keen walker who has never gone missing before, he is 5ft 6ins tall, of medium build, with brown eyes and black hair which is thinning on top.

He wears glasses and was last seen dressed in a navy jumper, grey fleece top and dark trousers.

Anyone who may have seen Mr Deakin should contact South Yorkshire Police on 0114 296 4804.

Throughout this period the deaths of domestic cats were also reported. On Saturday December 18th, two cats died in the space of 24 hours after their owner found one of them in distress. The first was treated for horrific internal injuries, perhaps the result of a road accident, but a short time later the owner's second cat was found to be suffering similar symptoms. Neither of the two animals survived. The report suggested that both cats had been in contact with something highly toxic. The article also mentioned a third cat had been found with teeth missing.

October Power Cuts

These occurrences, however unlikely, seemed to be revealing a pattern. So, following the unlikely trail, I was not surprised to read that 900 homes had lost power around Bempton Lane in the same timeframe as the two men had gone missing. In fact, this was less than two days from when Kenneth Bottom was found in Bridlington Harbour. The short article stated that an electricity pole supporting overhead power lines at the top of Bempton Lane had fallen at 11am on Friday October 29th. The Free Press covered the story on the same page they reported the discovery of the body in Bridlington harbour.

900 homes lose power

MORE than 900 homes in Bridlington were without electricity last Friday after a electricity pole fell over.

The pole at the top of Bempton Lane fell at 11am, bringing down the electricity cable.

Most of the homes were without power for an hour between noon and 1pm while Yorkshire Electricity Distribution Limited put up new overhead lines. Police closed the road while the work was being carried out.

I doubt this unlikely type of scenario could ever be replicated. I cannot prove that any one of these unusual events are related to the other, but I think it would be a mistake to say that a pattern in these events was not beginning to form. It seems to go against the grain to even read reports about power outages and missing cats, on the same pages as something so sensitive and tragic as someone vanishing or losing their life.

I need to make it clear that these unusual happenings would not have been my first choice for a storyline. It is not my intention to create a mystery where none exists - far from it. These events are so far apart in relation to one another that they were not something I ever expected to find. But I have nothing that links them directly, A to B, except the fact that they are happening - and this truth must override our lack of understanding why.

It is frustrating that I cannot prove they are anything more than a repetitive sequence of events, even though I believe something cold and calculating could be at work. I say this because whatever is responsible, appears to have the ability to do whatever it wants without detection. Therefore it can be declared impossible in a world that wants hard facts and solid proof. But if whatever is responsible lives outside of current human understanding, that proof may never be found. If these unusual happenings had come together just once, it would have been an interesting set of circumstances. However, these unusual events are grouped together and they happen at random times, sometimes with months and years between them. This has to mean something, even if no clues are left behind. The sheer fact that they appear to repeat in similar patterns, suggests that something more than coincidence is at work.

I have said previously that spikes in animal deaths and disappearances are rare, but why cats? Why not dogs, or other family pets. Livestock have been known to vanish over the years from remote areas, but without any natural predators in the UK it is hard to say what is responsible. Rustling has been blamed for the majority of these cases – in fact I suspect rustling is to blame 99% of the time. But it does not explain sheep that vanish from fields far away from access roads or the carcasses of wild deer found with incisions that look like they have had medical procedures. In the future I will check with farmers in the area, whether the key dates of missing people, cats and power cuts coincide in any way with missing or damaged livestock.

Between August 2nd and August 13th 2004 there were twelve cats reported missing, dead or displaced in the Bridlington Free Press newspaper. In one report from Monday August 2nd, a group of seven unrecognised cats were found in a distressed condition. No one had any idea who they belonged to or how they just suddenly appeared that morning. Despite appeals, no owners ever came forward to claim them.

It occurs to me, that whatever is responsible for these events does so in a cold, unnatural way. Perhaps this is another clue? Could the phenomena's apparent lack of human emotion and understanding indicate that we are dealing with something non-human? It most often strikes in isolated places, hitting its target hard and leaving no clues other than location as key. Whatever is responsible could be invisible and airborne. How else could it evade detection and be so far ahead of the game? Whatever the answer, it is clear that we are not equipped to tackle this mystery, otherwise we would find better explanations than the ones currently on offer.

Considering all these variables creates a knowing, but not having the tools to describe the knowing is incredibly frustrating - so much so that at times I have been close to throwing my laptop at the wall.

Surprise Big Cat Sighting

As if all of this was not confusing enough, another odd report appeared on October 21st 2004. Two men from Bridlington claimed they saw a huge black panther, in a field just a few miles out of Bridlington. I should place this account in a chapter devoted to big cat sightings, but due to the high strangeness of the events of 2004, I have to include it here. The article describes how the two men were driving to work one morning and saw the huge panther crawling along the edge of a field towards some hay bales. They stopped the car and watched it in amazement. One of the men thought about going to the nearby farmhouse to warn the owners, but said they were too scared to get out of the car. This was a daylight sighting and both men were convinced of what they saw.

As far as I am aware this was the only local sighting of a big cat reported in 2004. Unless these men were lying, it is another example of high strangeness that suddenly impacted on a pair of witnesses and left no other clues. Nothing was seen or heard of the animal after this sighting. I believe the big cat was real and for a time, it existed in the real that we know, the real we can touch and can understand. But it's entrance into our sphere of existence was so short-lived, that nothing but one surreal sighting was ever recorded.

I am not suggesting this big cat could be responsible for any of the events described above. I only include this account as an example of high strangeness, because it is an animal we all know exists. In it's natural habitat the rarely seen panther has vast jungles and forests in which to hunt and roam. Yet in the UK, a country the size of a postage stamp, we have random sightings of a creature that should not appear in farmer's fields. Could the sudden appearance and disappearance of this animal be indirectly connected with the other equally unexplainable events of 2004?

Brid men spot wild 'panther'

TWO Bridlington men spotted what they believed to be a black panther crawling across a field near Filey.

Alex Ethington and Matthew Traves, both 25 years old, were on their way to work at Infotone in Eastfield when they saw the creature on farm land near to the A165, just outside Filey.

Mr Ethington of Grasmere Grove said:

By Jodie Beecroft

"We went past a round-about and saw it crawling towards a load of hay bales in a field on the left-hand side of the road."

The pair pulled up and watched the animal crawl behind a farmhouse. They said they were going to tell the owner, but they did not want to get out of their car.

Mr Traves of Willow Drive said: "It was like one of those big black cats you see on wildlife programmes on the TV.

"It was really low to the ground like it was stalking.

"I know it wasn't a dog, it was a wild animal. I nearly crashed the car because I was so shocked."

Many people have spotted panther-like animals in the Scarborough area over the years. The most recent was in 2001 when a creature was believed to have attacked a lamb.

There are a number of theories about the sightings, but no-one knows for sure what these black cat creatures are and what they are doing roaming the countryside.

101

Reflections on the Missing Men

In TP1 I wrote a lot about the missing men of Bempton and the surrounding area - and as macabre as it may sound, I expect to be writing about more in the future. During my research I found the UK website 'Missing People' featured many of these missing men. It is an excellent resource to help locate missing people from all around the UK.

The site allows users to select the region they wish to search. When I used the site recently I selected the 'Yorkshire and Humberside' option. The page displayed thirty-nine photographs of local people who had all vanished without trace, spanning a 24-year period between 1992 to 2016. Of those listed, five of the men vanished in close proximity to RAF Bempton. The site shows where each person lived, but the location of their last known sighting is not listed. The list does not include those who disappeared and were later found dead in unusual circumstances.

One slight improvement I think could help those who use this important resource, would be the addition of the last known location each missing person was seen. I contacted Missing People to ask why this information was not specified on their site and emphasised that this detail is just as important as where a person lived. And since I thought there was a pattern to some of these disappearances, I asked if they realised at least seven of the missing men had vanished from the Bempton area alone. I include their response below, not as a criticism, but because it indicates a gap in the valuable information that *could* be included, to help those searching for missing person in their lists.

"Dear Paul, thank you for your email. When you last got in touch, we suggested you consider making contact with the National Missing Persons Bureau. While we publicise appeals for missing persons in conjunction with the police, we do not have all the details relating to a missing incident. Consequently it might be more appropriate to approach the National Missing Persons Bureau as they may take a more analytical approach to incidents of missing people and pattern identification."

I believe my research into the missing men of Bempton highlights a pattern in the disappearances. I wonder if other areas around the UK would reveal similar patterns if the location a person went missing from was also available. Location is key, but with this important information missing, does it mean that the resources are inadequate?

Strangeness in 2006

UFO Terrifies Young Driver

This first-hand account was shared with me a few years ago by a young farmer named Luke from Flamborough. His close encounter with a UFO occurred early in 2006, and it is another excellent example of just how unique this area can be.

Luke told me he had recently passed his driving test and liked to practice his new skills by cruising around the nearby town of Bridlington and the back roads of Bempton and surrounding villages. Usually with a few of his mates in the car, he would spend time around town talking with girls and enjoying the new found freedom that his car gave. The closest estimate he could give for a date was either February or March 2006. He is quite sure of the year, because he was driving his first car at the time and had not owned it long when he had the UFO encounter.

Luke told me he had been driving some friends around Bridlington and the neighbouring villages for most of the evening. It was getting late so they decided it was time to head home. The route they took out of town was up Bempton Lane and the plan was to cut across Short Lane and head back to Flamborough. (In 1992, the junction of Short Lane and Bempton Lane is where Raymond Johnston was suspected to have been hit by an off-road vehicle, later to be found dead over a mile away at Windmill Farm). Luke told me it must have been after 1am when they took the right turn onto Short Lane. Everything would have been in darkness at that late hour and his car was the only thing moving. Or so they thought.

They were all in high spirits after a good night with friends and they were all having a laugh and enjoying the drive. Luke explained what happened as they continued along the single track lane towards home;

"We were just coming to the sharp bend, about half a mile from the junction, when something sliver flashed in front of us. I mean it went straight across the road in front of the car and it was only ten or twelve feet off the ground. We all said what the f**k was that? I stopped the car but it had gone. We all saw it though; it had lights and it was bright and fast. We were all yelling what was that - did you see that? Our faces

were all pressed against the windows. But it wasn't fear, it was amazement and shock at what we had just seen flash in front of us."

My conversation with Luke was a chance encounter. I was in the area looking for information about a big cat sighting, so I imagine my surprise when he said, *"No, I haven't seen or heard anything about the cat, but I have seen a UFO."* He agreed to tell me his story and even allowed me to record what he had to say.

"After the excitement passed I started the car and we continued on towards Flamborough. We were about a quarter of a mile from the junction of Short Lane when the thing came back. It was like a wasp, it was so fast as it flashed over the car. It was up in the sky, but not that high. We were all shocked and our eyes were everywhere trying to catch sight of this thing, it was huge and silver. We were close to the junction at the end of Short Lane and the next thing it was in front of us above the road. I slowed to a stop. It was the most amazing thing to see, I have never seen anything like it before or since. I would say it was a space ship. It's hard to explain what it was like, but it seemed to be slowly turning and as it turned we could see silver and yellow and blue lights - like panels of light sliding from one colour to another.

That's the best I can do to describe it. It was turning very slowly and as it turned, it was getting lower. We were all feeling a bit frightened, we thought it was going to land. It got very close to the surface of the road, and then just before it touched the road it shot into the air at the most incredible speed and was gone. One moment we were looking at something that would fit better in a science fiction movie, the next, everything was normal. Well not quite normal because it scared us to death, I mean we s**t ourselves. I put my foot to the floor and got us all home in record time."

I thanked Luke for sharing his UFO story. I have since tried to reignite our conversation in an effort to get more details, but my attempts have fallen on deaf ears. I'm not sure why this happens with witnesses, but I am grateful for what I was told.

The Deer Butcherers

It is interesting that Short Lane in Bempton should be connected to so many unexplained happenings. It featured again in another Bridlington Free Press report from 2006. This article described how a mutilated deer had been discovered on Short Lane on Wednesday February 15th. I remember people talking about this incident in 2006, but recall there were definitely more deer found than those in the report. There was talk of carcasses being discovered in a similar condition at Bempton and at Danes Dyke.

Whoever or whatever did this was not interested in the prime meat of the animal, because none of that was taken - which is strange in itself. These were strange deer hunters indeed, who went to the trouble of removing parts of the animal, with almost medical precision, but left the meat behind.

The fact the animal's flesh had been removed in such an unusual way caused confusion. So what exactly happened to these unfortunate animals? On March 2nd the Free Press took the unusual step of printing a second article in an appeal for information about the mutilations. In that report they revealed a second deer had been found at Wold Gate around the same time the first carcass had been found on Short Lane.

It is clear to me that poachers were not responsible for these acts of animal mutilation. Deer are fast and elusive creatures that require stealth and skill to track and kill. There was no mention of a suspected cause of death, only that the flesh had been removed from the bone in an unusual way. I cannot see why skilled poachers would skin an animal, pare the meat from the bone in an unusual way by the roadside and then just leave it behind. Whatever killed these unfortunate animals did not do it for their meat.

Butchered deer carcass found

A MUTILATED deer carcass, has been found dumped on the grass verge of a country lane.

The animal had been partly skinned and its legs had been removed and meat looked like it had been sliced from the bone.

A passer-by told the Free Press they had noticed the remains in Short Lane, off Bempton Lane, in Bridlington, yesterday morning.

Our staff contacted the RSPCA and a wildlife crime officer with Bridlington police.

Police hunt for deer butcherers

POLICE are hunting the culprits who butchered two roe deer in Bridlington.

The carcasses of both animals were discovered last month.

Both had been skinned, or partially skinned, and butchered and police believe they were killed for their meat.

One carcass was found in Short Lane at Bempton.

It had been butchered for meat but unusually most of the meat was left.

The other was in Woldgate, between Boynton and Bridlington. It was in a stream and its head and feet were missing.

The police wildlife crime officer is investigating and anyone who knows anything about either incident, or who may have seen anything suspicious in those areas, is asked to phone Bridlington police on 0845 6060222.

Missing Man

February 2006 saw further unusual events begin to unfold around the area. The first I found was a report in the Bridlington Free Press on the discovery of a body below Reighton cliffs, just five miles along the coast from Bempton. Malcolm Ireland was reported missing from his home on Thursday evening February 23rd. His widow said he was a kind and caring man who very much enjoyed his life. Yet his body was found five days later at around 11.30am on Monday February 27th. There were no suspicious circumstances surrounding the 65-year-old's death.

The report stated it was not clear how he came to be at Reighton four days later. Information on events during time leading up to and after his death is vague. I only include this report here as it coincides with other strange occurrences around the same time. The first interesting coincidence I found was that Mr Ireland lived at Queensgate, very close to where Jimmy Gorman had lived. The two disappearances are almost three years apart and have no direct connection that I know of, besides sharing this location.

I looked into this case while writing TP1 but found very little information other than newspaper reports. However, working on Jimmy Gorman's disappearance opened my eyes to other unusual happenings, so I decided to take a second look. I realise that a location does not necessarily link two disappearances directly, and nothing I have written here is proof that one is directly connected to the other. They just sit alongside each other in an uneasy silence, screaming for answers that no one seems to have. I looked back over my notes for anything I might have missed during my original research; missing cats were the last thing I would have imagined finding. Who would be looking for such things?

It was a long time before I noticed the newspapers were reporting the disappearances and deaths of cats around the dates that people were vanishing. When I began considering that there might be a possible link, 2006 did not disappoint me. Finding reports of missing cats and power cuts in those newspapers, along with the strange animal mutilations, felt nothing less than sinister.

Young Man Vanishes

29-year-old Gavin Wilson was reported missing just 15 miles up the coast at Scarborough. Gavin went missing on Monday February 27th and was said to have been feeling upset over a minor disagreement at work, but his disappearance was totally out of character.

His father John has never given up the search for his son and has worked tirelessly to keep his unexplained disappearance high profile. However, despite all their efforts Gavin appears to have vanished off the face of the Earth. Better known as Bob to his friends, Gavin was a keen rambler who loved to walk along the clifftops. His father said they don't have a clue what happened to him and it is unbearable not knowing.

The following report was published in the Scarborough Evening News in February 2008, two years after Gavin's disappearance;

"Gavin Wilson, 29, disappeared in February 2006 and has not been seen since – despite the efforts of police, family and friends. His father, John Wilson, said this week his son's disappearance is still 'very baffling'. He said the BBC was planning to put out a daily programme each morning during April and Gavin would be featured in one of them. In the meantime, Mr Wilson, a hospital maintenance assistant, is still continuing his efforts to raise money for the British charity 'Missing People' in the hope his son will turn up one day.

Mr Wilson, who works at Cross Lane Hospital, has organised a charity quiz and supper at the Valley Bar in Valley Road this Sunday between 5pm and 7pm. His bid to contact his son was previously raised in a BBC3 series entitled 'Runaways'. Mr Wilson said, 'It still surprises me in this day and age that someone can just disappear off the face of the Earth and as yet hasn't been found. It would be fantastic to hear from Gavin to know he's safe and well. I have been on his favourite walks, including one towards Ravenscar. His bank account has still not been touched. It is all very baffling and worrying.'

Recently, Mr Wilson handed over a cheque for £460 after organising a raffle of 100 Belgian beers with the help of his local pub. And last year he raised £750 by organising a quiz. This year he also persuaded the pub to run a weekly bonus ball with 39% of the proceeds going to 'Missing People'.

Gavin, who was 29 when he disappeared, lived alone in a flat in Esplanade Gardens. He was last seen on February 27 2006 and since then his father has been striving to raise the profile of his missing son. Gavin is 6ft tall and slim, with collar-length dark-brown hair. He speaks with a Yorkshire accent and was known by the nickname Bob. Police said he was known to frequent pubs in the Ramshill area of Scarborough and liked to walk long distances, particularly on the clifftops. After Gavin disappeared his parents and friends put up posters around the town and on local buses. The former Pindar School student had been working at St Helen's Nursing Home in Avenue Victoria.

These cases of tragic disappearances are all unique and deserving of our upmost respect. There is nothing I can write that will make these events connect to each other in any way we can recognise, but after all of my research it is evident to me that something links them all.

If the only thing I reveal is a pattern of events, it is at least a start. A link in the chain is missing and I fear, like all missing links, the ones that matter will never be found. All I can do is highlight possible connections. My research may run against the grain of public opinion and the official line, but I feel that sometimes our thinking has to be steered onto a different road. One that might ultimately open our eyes to new truths.

More Dead Cats

On Wednesday March 8th 2006 two cats belonging to the same family at Burton Agnes, died of suspected poisoning within days of each other. The village is less than two miles away from Woldgate in Bridlington where, a few weeks earlier, a deer carcass was found mutilated in an unusual manner. The Bridlington Free Press reported that they believe the cats had been poisoned. Although no definite conclusions were made, a vet from the Priory Clinic in Bridlington suspected poison to have caused the deaths. Reading between the lines, I think it is clear they did not established this as fact.

The deaths of these cats may have no bearing on any of the other mysteries in the area - they may simply have been the victims of some cruel individual. But I find it odd that people with callous intent towards these animals appear to be active around the times that people vanish. The people I spoke with at the RSPCA remember some of these incidents involving animal mutilations and the cat disappearances. They told me that no one had any idea what was going on.

Strange Gold Light Over Bridlington

The following UFO report is a sighting of my own from April 16th 2006. It has been archived on my old ILF-UFO website since I closed the site down in 2013. I think it is an interesting account that adds to the mix of strange events in East Yorkshire in this unusual year.

"At around 11.45pm on Sunday night I opened my back door and gave our dog a shout. It had been a long weekend with many late nights and I was ready for some rest. I stood in the darkness for a while watching the dog and thinking about how the weekend had gone. I cannot explain why or how, but I sensed something and looked up into the sky.

It was very dark with low cloud cover, but I could see an orange light and a dark oval shape within the cloud. It was hard to make out, but I could definitely see something. Whether it was below cloud or above it, I could not tell, but I quickly went inside and picked up my Olympus C-70 Zoom camera.

I took the first picture right away, then walked down the garden a little and took another. I captured a streak of bright light on my second photograph. The light was stationery, in or behind the cloud. No noise could be heard and there was no wind.
I have to say it was strange to 'know' there was an object of some sort in the sky. It stayed in the same position, but the streak of light is all I managed to capture, then the object vanished..."

I am so pleased I wrote about that sighting back in 2006. I'm not sure why I looked up into the sky when I did, but I know what I saw. It resembled a piece of burning coal that glowed in different areas – areas that were invisible until the faint glow of orange highlighted their edges. It made no sound, so would have gone completely unnoticed if I had not looked up when I did. There was no inner voice compelling me to look up, but I am pleased that I did.

Body Found

On April 27th 2006 the Bridlington Free Press reported the body of a woman had been found on the beach below Danes Dyke and Sewerby. The body was found on Thursday April 20th and later identified as that of 66-year-old Doreen Horobin. The article states that the body was found at the foot of the hundred foot cliffs by a member of the public, who alerted the police. The inquest was opened and adjourned and there were no suspicious circumstances. An appeal followed, for witnesses who might have seen the lady in the area.

I thought about the wording of the article for a moment. By stating that the body was *found at the foot of the cliffs* immediately places an image in the mind of someone falling. This may well have been the case, but it does not say that.

Divers Search for Missing Man

The April 13th edition of the Bridlington Free Press ran an half-page story asking for help to trace a missing man. Ian Hobson disappeared from his home in Rotherham on April 3rd 2006. His abandoned car was found in Bridlington town on Wednesday April 5th. The police said it was totally out of character for Mr Hobson to do this. Acting Sergeant Andy Cockburn of Rotherham police said, *"He appears to have vanished off the face of the Earth."*

Although police conducted extensive searches in and around Bridlington harbour, working in conjunction with specialist divers, they could find nothing to suggest Ian Hobson had ever been there. He simply vanished without leaving a single clue.

Three weeks later, on Thursday May 4th, Bridlington Free Press reported that a police underwater search team, out on exercises in the harbour, had discovered a body around 11am on Thursday April 27th. Although the body was not formally identified, it was thought to be that of Ian Hobson. The article states that the body was found in a place that divers had previously searched, yet nothing was found in the first search.

On May 11th the newspaper reported that the body had officially been identified, but curiously, to add more confusion to the tragedy, they stated the body had been spotted by a member of the public on the 27th and was recovered sometime later by officers. Yet what I find strange, is that in the previous week's edition it was reported that divers on routine exercise had made the discovery.

Divers in search for missing man

By Thom Kennedy

thom.kennedy@ynltd.co.uk

N underwater search team has been touring Bridlington harbour in search r a man who went missing from his me in Rotherham last month.

Ian Hobson disappeared from his ome in Upper Haugh, in Rotherham, on pril 3, and his car was found in ridlington a few days afterwards.

He was spotted in Scarborough before riving in Bridlington, probably on pril 5. He is known to have previous mily connections in the town.

His Rover car was found abandoned in ince Street on Wednesday, April 5. It was issued with a parking ticket, but e traffic warden grew suspicious when saw it unattended in the same place e following day.

His aunt Jean Hobson, of Rhodena venue, Bridlington, issued a desperate peal for his return.

She said: "Auntie Jean and Uncle thur would give you space to come d talk to us.

"If you didn't want us to tell anybody won't.

"We are just worried, we want to know y he's disappeared.

Missing ... Ian Hobson

"We really do want him to come back."

Mr Hobson is white, between 5ft10in and 6ft, has thinning grey hair and a grey moustache.

He was wearing black trousers, a black kagoul, and a black t-shirt bearing a faded Half Price Ink motif. He speaks with a Yorkshire accent.

Police have described Mr Hobson's disappearance as "totally out of character", heightening concerns for the 50-year-old.

Acting Sgt Andy Cockburn, of Rotherham Police, said: "He appears to have disappeared off the face of the earth.

"Previous to this he has never gone missing and has no history of problems.

"He is the most regular bloke you can imagine – a proper, decent family guy.

"His disappearance is completely out of the blue.

"His wife is crawling up the walls with worry. She is devastated.

"We want him to get in touch with us or his wife and would tell him there is nothing that can't be sorted."

A search was launched in and around Bridlington harbour on Monday morning, but proved fruitless.

Police have urged hotel and guest-house owners in the town to come forward if they see anything.

The town's CCTV footage and hospitals have been checked, resulting in one possible sighting of Mr Hobson in King Street.

Anybody with information should contact Rotherham police on (01709) 832147.

112

Harbour body identified

THE body found in Bridlington harbour a fortnight ago has been identified as that of missing Rotherham man Ian Hobson.

He went missing from his home in Upper Haugh, Rotherham, on April 3, and a few days later his car was spotted in Prince Street, Bridlington.

Police had conducted a previous search of Bridlington harbour, but on that occasion found nothing. His body was spotted by a member of the public on April 27, and it was recovered by officers.

Lightning causes power black-outs

MONDAY night's storm left a number of homes in the Bridlington area without power.

One of the worst areas affected was Thwing, where the power went off at 4pm and did not come back on again until 10am on Tuesday.

A total of 83 premises in Bridlington were also without power from 8.40pm on Monday to 5.35am on Tuesday.

The rest of the town seemed to escape the worst and for many the power cut lasted 20 minutes.

One of the businesses affected was The Falling Stone, in Thwing, which had to close on Monday night and lost £200-worth of stock because it could not be refridgerated.

Tesco and Morrisons supermarkets in Bridlington also suffered when their systems went down as a result of the storm.

A spokesman for Tesco said: "The tills and the lights went off and the customers had to go outside."

A spokesman for YEDL said: "Engineers worked through the night to locate sections of our overhead network damaged by lightning.

"As the safety of our staff is paramount, restoration work was interrupted as they were stood down on two occasions while further storms passed through the areas they were working in.

"Direct hits by lightning on transformers on top of our poles caused the majority of the damage."

Power Blackouts 2006

The power cuts that that appear to accompany these tragedies could be nothing more than coincidence and I cannot see what connection they might have - but they do happen when things of an unusual nature occur in this area. So for that reason they are documented here.

On Tuesday May 2nd 2006 there was a 45-minute power blackout on Carnaby Industrial Estate near Wilsthorpe, south of Bridlington. Then between Monday June 12th and Tuesday June 13th there was a power outage in Bridlington and surrounding areas. The cause was reported to have been lightning bolts, which damaged transformers on top of poles, after direct hits. I realise that the weather is a law unto itself, but I find it amazing that these incidents seem to occur in conjunction with other events – and all of them highly unusual. Missing people are an everyday occurrence throughout the world. Power cuts happen on a daily basis. Cats die and disappear. But do do all these things follow a similar pattern that encompasses them to within days and weeks of each other?

East Yorkshire is a dot on the map, in a small world which hangs in the vast gargantua that is everything. I think anything is possible and the only restriction that limits us, as human beings, is our own minds. I have invested so much thought into the questions 'why' and 'how' and I still have no clue. I know there is something which is always just out of touch from what we call reality. It is something so surreal, so obscure, it evades attempts to capture evidence. To the world it is non-existent and the events of high strangeness are blameless - but the search continues.

Part Two:
The Wilsthorpe Incident

I spent a great deal of time wondering where to start with this story, because the September 2009 incident at Wilsthorpe is a strange series of events, which is more involved than I could have imagined.

For me it began in May 2014 with a story shared by an elderly couple that was nothing short of sensational. It was an event that would have fitted perfectly into a science fiction movie. At the time I struggled to believe what I was told and I left it out of TP1 for that very reason. Yet parts of this story had been there all along, like seeds of truth that were planted, just waiting for the right combination of words to bring them to the light. In a way, I could say that I knew the ending before I realised I had a beginning.

Merlins over Bridlington

First, I want to share a personal encounter with helicopters over my home in 2009. At the time, I had no idea I would be including this sighting as part of an amazing UFO account eight years later.

I cannot think why two military helicopters would be circling our home on the afternoon of September 18th 2009, but that is exactly what happened. At least one of the choppers had its rear loading ramp half open and for some reason the men inside were observing me. The two helicopters circled several times and from the flashes I observed from inside them, I believe I was being filmed and photographed.

When I filmed them I had no idea there would be a connection to a major UFO incident. How could I? It was another five years before I had even a hint that anything unusual had taken place at Wilsthorpe. So far it has taken me seven years to connect all the accounts - mine and those of the people who have been bold enough to submit them. Together I believe they tell an amazing story that, if true, stands with the great UFO incidents of our time.

Around the time I filmed the helicopters, the area of East and North Yorkshire was experiencing a peak in UFO activity. My old ILF-UFO website recorded many reports up to and beyond September 2009, but back then I knew nothing of the incredible event that took place in Wilsthorpe. It was not until May 2014 that the story really began to unfold. Before then, everything was just quietly waiting on my archived webpages for me to find.

116

I operated ILF-UFO.co.uk from 2002 until 2013 and closed the site down due to family and work commitments, which were preventing me from devoting to it the time it deserved. ILF-UFO proved to be a highly successful site but it was also very time consuming. Back then I had massive work commitments that took priority over most things. This is not an excuse, but under different circumstances I might have realised the true extent of what was happening.

Thankfully, the force that is the internet somehow archived many pages from my old website - which is good for me because, as a searchable record, it backs up my claims of multiple UFO sightings connected to the Wilsthorpe incident. I do not have the knowledge to change an archived website, but the connecting reports and emails, as originally documented in 2009, are still there for all to see. They are dated, archived and set in internet stone, as proof of my words. Back then, I was unwittingly documenting sightings and reports online which add great weight to this sensational story. The foundations of the Wilsthorpe incident were already in place , I just didn't know it at the time. It was another five years before I realised their importance.

In the same month I filmed the two Merlin helicopters over our home in 2009, the military arrived at Wilsthorpe. During this period the skies were alive with activity. I also filmed a Typhoon fighter aircraft ripping through the sky above our home that day. I have never before seen military helicopters or fighter jets so low over the roof tops. I cannot say if my sighting is directly linked to the Wilsthorpe incident, but the timing is right. I also found proof in a published article of the arrival of helicopters, one afternoon in September, at South Shore, Wilsthorpe.

Nothing I put forward can prove with any certainty that the Wilsthorpe UFO incident occurred as reported. All I can do is build the evidence for and against the case. For some people, I realise that no amount of evidence will ever be enough, but I am not writing this book to please those people. I have no physical evidence to share, but this does not mean that the events of September 2009 are any less true. What is true, is that the phenomena hits us full between the eyes every time it presents itself, then slips back into the outer nowhere.

Before getting into the primary elements of the story I first need to provide a background of events leading up to them. The three accounts that follow were uploaded onto the ILF-UFO website as they were reported to me back in 2009. I cannot stress enough that these historic reports remain unchanged since that time. The words, times and dates can all be checked. It would be wrong for the sceptics to dismiss these sightings. They help to tell a story, one that is only just beginning to make sense years later. The first report is a sighting of my own, which I witnessed along with Steve Ashbridge on the Yorkshire Wolds in February 2009.

Banner from my archived website

ILF-UFO Archive:
Large Blue UFO - February 4th 2009

"It was approximately 10.55pm. The sky was very overcast and the conditions were freezing, with snow and ice on all the fields and roads. We arrived at about 8.30pm and did think from the beginning that it would be an uneventful night due to the poor visibility. The conditions on the Wolds have been quite bad over the past few weeks.

The cloud cover was quite low and appeared to circle the surrounding area - and if you looked straight up, stars and planes could be seen. About 500 metres into the distance is a farm on the left-hand side of the road. Beyond that is a small area of woodland which belongs to the farm. We have spoken to the farmer several times during our visits and exchanged contact numbers. The farmer and his family had their very own close encounter many years ago and were not at all surprised by my interest in the area.

The trees are about 30ft high and, from where we were sitting, they gave us a good reference point. To the right and many miles into the distance is RAF Staxton Wold. I have to say that Steve saw the object first and from the few seconds of him seeing it, to shouting out in excitement for me to turn around, it all lasted no more that 10 seconds at most. Steve says that out of nowhere a huge blue oblong-shaped light appeared above the trees. He said, at that first moment it appeared to be as big as a bus. It was flat at the bottom and curved down at the front. It was travelling very slowly and getting smaller with each passing second. When I turned and saw it myself, it was still quite large and looked pale blue in colour.

We had no idea of its distance, but due to its great size we think it was within a mile of us. This is however only speculation, as the weather conditions did not allow me to be more accurate. The object just dissolved into the cloud and I did think we would see it as it passed over Staxton Wold, but we saw nothing more. We can definitely say that it was in the air, since the tree line has no high land behind it.

Despite this being a brief sighting I do regard it as very interesting due to the huge size and colour of the object. Another point is that everything was in total silence. There were no cars, no aircraft noise, nothing."

Something I could not have known at the time of our sighting, was that we were standing at the location of the Easterby UFO sighting, less than quarter of a mile from the area of the Cottam Wood UFO sighting. I documented both of these sightings in TP1. So again, location is key.

Sketch by Steve Ashbridge of the large blue object over the trees.

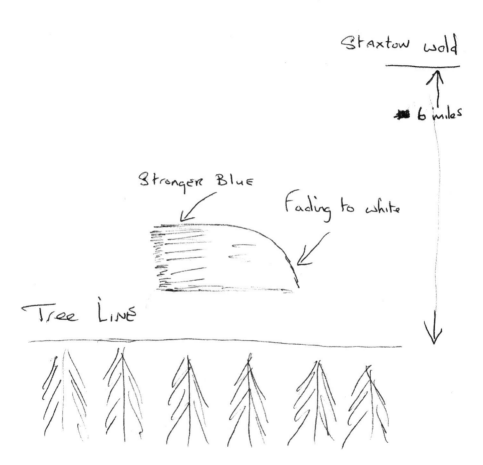

ILF-UFO Archive:
Wolds UFO - February 16th 2009

"Large amount of footage taken, including a helicopter flying at tree level from the Staxton area towards the object. The helicopter covered over 10 miles to reach the glowing object. The gold light simply vanished as the helicopter closed in. Two more helicopters arrived in same area from the opposite direction - which would have been Humberside."

The brief account on my website was just one of many, but the area was so active in 2009 that lots of sightings went undocumented. This entry reminds me that low-flying helicopters also became a common sight after the lightforms first appeared. The lights themselves usually appeared in an instant and vanished just as quickly as they came. I remember adding this account to the site because it was a little more interesting. Interesting because the light was still present as the helicopter closed in. Usually, whenever Steve Ashbridge and I saw the lightforms, helicopters or planes arrived in the area a short time later. We were always in no doubt that they seemed to looking for the lights.

I remember talking about the helicopters and the lightforms with Clifford Spencer, the owner of Springdale Farm in nearby Rudston. His son, then in his early twenties, had spoken with me about seeing them on more than one occasion. Clifford told me about the time he was out walking early one morning and being startled by an apache helicopter that suddenly appeared from the other side of a hedgerow. It is impossible to say why it was there but something about the area was obviously interesting them. The farm had no prior warning that helicopters would be low flying around the fields.

Looking back it seems clear now that the military were very interested in the area and the lightform activity. For a military presence to be around so soon after the lightforms appeared must mean they could somehow track or predict their arrival - and if an individual like myself is able to gather as much information as I have, I just wonder what official agencies have managed to document. In most instances the affected areas are never more than ten to twenty miles distant from RAF Staxton Wold. Although a reply letter I received from the base on November 16th 2010 suggests that the facility does not have the ability to detect objects in such close proximity.

I am in no position to dispute such claims, but a Bridlington Free Press news clipping from 1974 makes for interesting reading. The article states that the radar at Staxton Wold *could* detect anything in any given direction for 240 miles and was able to detect something the size of a golf ball coated in copper within a 50-mile radius. It was written 35 years ago, so imagine the improvements made since then.

ILF-UFO Archive:
Huge Airship-shaped Object - March 17th 2009

*"Two fishermen reported seeing a large object out to sea whilst digging
for bait on Bridlington's south beach, near Wilsthorpe...they say the
object remained in the same position for a considerable time. A boat
came around the headland from Flamborough and it appeared very
small compared to the grey object in the distance. This was mid-
afternoon and the sky was relatively clear. I'm sure if these men saw
this then others must have seen it also. It is hard to say what it could
have been with such a vague description, unless anyone can offer more
information."*

I learned nothing more about this unusual sighting. I do know that the
two witnesses are not the same local fishermen who used to work
around Bridlington Harbour and digging bait for a living. These men
were on the beach at the time of the sighting just trying to save
themselves some money by digging their own fishing bait. Because this
report is dated Tuesday March 17th, I have been able to accurately date
the following report, which fortunately came my way on Saturday March
21st 2009, after an overheard conversation.

Right Place, Right Time

One of the strangest accounts I ever collected in 2009, or anytime for that matter, was from two men in their early 20s while I was shopping with my wife in Bridlington town centre. It was pure chance that I actually found myself close enough to overhear their conversation. It began when I heard one of them speaking enthusiastically about something I would never have expected to hear on a busy street.

It was Saturday March 21st; the only day of the week I went into town. My wife and I were out shopping, slowly making our way up the high street. We were walking behind two young men who I didn't know, although I recognised one of them from the local motor spares shop. I had never spoken to either of them before in my life. Like everyone else on that Saturday morning, I was just involved in doing my own thing. That was until I heard one of them say something that instantly caught my attention. *"The small ones were coming out of the mothership..."*

The word *mothership* is not one I ever use, but I knew it was a UFO-related term, so I stepped up the pace and got a little closer. I was intrigued and wanted to eavesdrop on their conversation. I could not believe what came next. I heard one of the men tell his friend about a giant UFO he had seen off Flamborough Head just days before. I turned to my wife, who had no idea what I was up to, but from the look I gave her she knew that something had caught my interest. I showed her my hand and silently said, *"five minutes"*, then I continued to follow the two men, trying to catch their conversation.

One of them had definitely used the term *mothership*. *"We were in the car at Thornwick Bay and this giant mothership was over the sea,"* I heard one of them say. *"It was huge. Never seen anything like it. It had this band of yellow lights round it - round the middle. We all saw it and smaller ones were coming in and out of it and others were going into it."*

It sounded like he was describing something from a science fiction movie instead of something real, but I still wanted to learn more. His friend was replying with the odd yes and no, which allowed his pal to tell the story uninterrupted, but he didn't seem as interested in the story as I was. I followed them for a few hundred metres and eavesdropped for a little longer, before finally making myself known to them.

I must have seemed like a stalker at first, but I could not let such a rare opportunity pass without asking a few questions. I explained that I had overheard them talking about a UFO and then quickly told them about my website. I was hoping they might be impressed, but to be honest, they seemed uninterested. They were more surprised that I had been listening to them talking, which I suppose is not surprising. In the awkward moments that followed, I attempted to ask them a few questions. My persistence paid off when one of them suddenly said,

"If we had not seen the lights around it we wouldn't have even known it was there. It was dark and the lights gave it away. It had a shape above and below them, a big shape. Smaller glowing spheres or lights were coming out of it and other lights were going back to it. The lights were yellow, maybe orange and they were quite small compared to the big one. It was hard to take in what we were seeing. A few of us had gone for a drive up to Flamborough, that's when we saw it; it was just before midnight."

This and the previous report sound incredible, but I have always tried to steer clear of fantasy-type reports. Although they may take my mind to places I never thought I would go, I think some researchers prefer them purely for attention. They use creative names like Pleiadian and Draconian for the craft or their occupants, but I have no clue about any of these things. I am more interested in discovering the how and why about them. I believe anything is possible; the memories I have of the alien beings I saw as a child leave me in no doubt about that. Even if all they left me with were memories of fear-filled nights and the frustration of 'knowing' - but not knowing why.

Many of the reports from 2009 seem incredible and by themselves might not be taken seriously, no matter how credible the witness. They still deserve to be acknowledged and be given serious consideration. My gut feeling about these last two accounts told me something significant did occur - unless all the witnesses I spoke with were liars, but I do not believe that for one second.

So was this the beginning of a build-up towards a major UFO event in September 2009? Knowing what I now know and with all the reports coming in, I would have to say yes. As the weeks passed, the activity along the coast was steadily growing, but at the time, Steve and I were still documenting the lightforms seen around the Yorkshire Wolds.

ILF-UFO Archive:
Lightforms and Helicopters – April 29th 2009

"First of all - and I need to say this - Chinese lantern theorists, please go elsewhere with your ideas. For at least two years now, I have been saying that the East Yorkshire UFOs I have been filming on the Wolds are nothing to do with Chinese lanterns. I have reports of sightings out at sea and on the remote Yorkshire Wolds - and I keep asking myself 'why the Wolds?' They never seem to fly from anywhere in particular. It is as though they are breaking through from somewhere else.

Usually, before a sighting, we see a small flash of light, then sometime after, the object appears. The time span can be anything from ten minutes to an hour after the initial flash. This sighting from April 29th was no different. They do not seem to stick to any set time; they appear during daylight hours as well as at night. Although the bulk of my footage is recorded in the evenings, because this is when I have the most time to spare. The weather conditions don't seem to cause any problems for these objects. They seem to emit light all around them, bright enough to light up any clouds that may be in close proximity. They do seem to have an awareness of what is happening on the ground below, because many times I have observed that an approaching car will cause them to fade away, only to reappear when the car has passed.

The reason I know they are silent, even though we often observe them from a distance, is because helicopters can clearly be heard well in advance of us seeing them. (I do not think they are military, but I do think the military are aware of them.) Many times after a sighting the helicopters will appear. I once reported that a Chinook helicopter had landed in a field, just a short distance from where we were observing and it shut down. This was unnerving, knowing that a short distance away they were also there in the darkness, watching. The objects always seem to be one step ahead, which adds to my theory that they have an awareness. ILF = Intelligent Light Form."

I have asked myself many times why that Chinook landed so closely to where my wife and I were skywatching that night. At first I thought it wanted to observe the objects as we did, but now I am not so sure. Intimidation may have been a factor. The downwash of air from the huge helicopter scared my wife, because it actually shook the vehicle we were sitting in.

To the best of my knowledge no one else has ever spent time trying to film all this unusual activity before me. I was also highlighting it to the world for the first time through my ILF-UFO website. The activity of 2009 continued to build with people from all around the area reporting strange aerial activity.

ILF-UFO Archive:
Bright Red UFO off Flamborough Head – May 10th 2009

"At 4.30am on May 10th Simon Esberger saw a bright red UFO off Flamborough Head. He described the object as being three times larger than a star and says it hovered below the clouds for ten to fifteen minutes. He is sure that it would have been observed by boats out on the horizon at the time. Simon was walking his dog on Bridlington sea front when he saw the object. He was looking towards Flamborough Head when he noticed the bright red ball of light to the right of Flamborough lighthouse. He says the object was definitely out at sea and even though this was in the early hours of the morning, he is sure that others must have seen it."

ILF-UFO Archive:
Large UFO at Riverside, Driffield – May 16th 2009

"I had an interesting telephone conversation today (May 19th 2009) with a couple who both witnessed a huge UFO over Driffield on Saturday night (May 16th 2009). They told me the object was spherical and appeared low in the sky at about 10.30pm. It seemed to be hovering over Riverside 'close to the mast'...and although the weather conditions were very wet and windy, the object was steady and unmoving.

It was deep red and appeared to be on fire within itself. My first thought was a Chinese lantern, but the couple dismissed that saying the object was huge. I next suggested a hot air balloon, but they said it was nothing like a balloon. (I actually find it hard to believe a hot air balloon would be in the air at 10.30pm in those weather conditions, but I had to ask). When they pulled up and got out of their car to get a better look, the object rose to cloud height, hovered a few seconds and then shot up vertical at incredible speed. Its light could be seen flashing through the clouds. I have contacted the Driffield Times but have not had a reply so far. It will be interesting to hear if any more sightings come to light. An object of this size must have been seen by others in the area."

ILF-UFO Archive:
Second UFO at Riverside, Driffield – May 19th 2009

Below is another witness report from the same location as the previous sighting at Riverside. I am sure this group of friends all saw the same object, but from another viewpoint. Even the locations are very close to each other.

"I live in Driffield and on the night of May 19th 2009 my partner and myself were at my mother's house for a BBQ. At approximately 10.30pm my partner, myself and seven other witnesses all saw a spherical-shaped craft glide silently over the house. It then shot off into the abyss. After a lengthy debate about what it could have been, the craft returned, but this time it passed over the garden until it suddenly disappeared."

Driffield is only twelve miles away from Bridlington and the other locations mentioned are between the two towns. The amount of activity at this time is self-evident. However, I received lots of additional reports of sightings that never made it to the website due to work commitments. I kept in touch with the couple who saw this returning UFO and they later provided me with additional details of their sighting.

"The object was at least twenty metres in diameter, if not more. It did appear as though it was on fire, so I presumed that it was a Chinese lantern at first - until it made manoeuvres opposite to the wind direction. Therefore it was not being carried by the wind; but rather a mechanical device, I would like to assume. The flight path was in a north to south direction when it first appeared. The second time, it had a lower altitude but an identical direction and seemed to glide much slower. The pictures on your main webpage of the glowing red UFO are scarily similar to what we all encountered. Furthermore, the object we saw was bright orangey/red. It glided and didn't make a sound. Five of the seven witnesses with me believe that it was a craft of some sort. The others had considerably more to drink than the rest of us at this point and believed that it was nothing that couldn't be explained. Although later, when I pestered them separately for their individual accounts, not one of them could explain it to me in logical terms.

One thing I did notice was, the first time the object passed overhead it seemed to climb in altitude at considerable speed and then disappear.

The second time, it seemed to lose altitude and slowly disappear behind the far side of a neighbour's house. I went out into the street to see if the UFO was still there, but it had disappeared completely."

ILF-UFO Archive:
Large Glowing Lights, Bridlington - May 25th 2009

On May 25th 2009 four separate witnesses saw large lights hanging in the sky at around 12.20am. They were described as the size of dustbin-lids and as bright as halogen floodlights.

It was a star-filled night when Alan Norrie noticed a large glowing ball of white light from his kitchen window. He opened his back door and stood there watching it in amazement, then shouted his wife Shirley to come and look. At first she thought it was a searchlight from a police helicopter. Alan told me it was about the same size, except that this object was totally silent and quite close. After a few minutes the light moved over to the right and gathered pace. Alan thought it was heading towards Grindale, north-west of Bridlington. He was so taken by what he saw that he called the local radio station who interviewed him about it the next day.

At the same time Maggie Masters and her teenage daughter were observing the same object, from the garden of their home in St. Johns Avenue, Bridlington. Their description is the same except they saw *two* large glowing lights. I have since spoken to both pairs of witnesses, who do not know each other. But these were not the only witnesses to see something unusual on May 25th. Nicola Sinclair [no relation] was able to photograph a bright red ball of light as it passed over her home on Mount Drive in Bridlington. The Free Press newspaper also reported that the Baines family from Flamborough had contacted them to report a red object hovering over the sea on the same day. The article included the account of another witness, who had been out walking his dog when he saw a single ball of red light hanging below clouds.

At some point we have to stop looking for rational explanations for these things and accept them for what they are. Most, if not all, of the local UFO sightings reported in 2009 have no simple explanation, but because they cannot be understood, should we say that they never happened?

Next page: article showing Nicola Sinclair's UFO photograph.

Mystery over UFO sightings

By Steven Hugill

steven.hugill@yrnltd.co.uk

THE saying that the truth is out there could be about to take on a new meaning in the area after a string of mysterious sightings in the sky.

Suspicious bright lights dotting the night sky above Bridlington and Flamborough throughout May drew curious members of the public to contact the Free Press in an attempt to get to the bottom of the strange events.

Alan Norrie, of Field Road, Bridlington, was one who witnessed the most recent example – on Monday, May 25 – of a large glowing light shining brightly before quickly disappearing.

He said: "I went into the kitchen and looked out of the window into the back garden and noticed there were a lot of stars in the sky.

"Then I saw a really bright light flashing and all of a sudden it moved.

"It looked like a really bright halogen light shining

Is this a UFO? The red light captured on camera above Bridlington by Nicole Sinclair.

"Then all of a sudden it moved to the right and disappeared behind the houses.

"I used to scoff at things like this, but it was really strange."

More intriguing activity in the skies was captured by Nicole Sinclair, who photographed a red object above her home in Mount Crescent.

Nicole, 14, who witnessed the strange light, said she is convinced the light is a UFO and added she had sent the picture to Calendar News.

She said: "I saw lights that were red in colour and they were going really quickly across the sky.

131

ILF-UFO Archive:
Jet Rocks the Boat, Bridlington – July 1st 2009

"A fisherman and his crew were off the Bridlington coast and claim they saw a jet, no more than 30ft off the surface of the sea, pursuing a red object. The man, who does not wish to be named, said he had never been so frightened in all his life as the jet aircraft ripped through the sky above him. The incident happened at 1.30pm on July 1st 2009."

This brief entry from my website conjures up mental images of an incredible encounter out at sea, with what turned out to be a Typhoon fighter aircraft. It also confirms that many strange things were in our airspace around that time. I have since spoken with the fisherman on numerous occasions and he still talks about the day the RAF Typhoon passed over their boat. Each time he relays the account, his voice still carries a mixture of fear and excitement about it.

"We were netting and next thing we saw was like red thing shoot past, but before the red thing shot past we had a jet blast over us and we thought they were using us as a marker. Then next thing this red thing came belting past and another jet came and it went up and round and followed the red thing. They both shot straight out to sea and disappeared. We were about six miles out off Wilsthorpe."

Whatever this red object was, it never disturbed the boat as it streaked past them overhead. Although the jet did cause the small trawler to rock so violently in the water that, for a moment, the crew thought they were going to capsize. The fisherman says that for a few seconds it was an extremely terrifying experience. At the time, they were in their family-owned trawler, named *'Our Grace'*, between Bridlington and Barmston, just south of Flamborough Head. This places them around six miles off shore from Wilsthorpe. The fisherman claims that the red object was shaped like a pencil and was illuminated. This is what he said about the military presence when I caught up with him in November 2016.

"After we saw that red thing being chased by the jet, we noticed there was a lot of military activity going on. This was around the same time those helicopters landed on the beach up at South Shore. Don't know where they came from, we were about six miles off shore that day and they flew over the top of us towards land. They came from out at sea, maybe they were off an aircraft carrier? Very strange, if you ask me.

And that red thing, I have never seen anything as fast in all my life and it was silent. Its scary knowing something that big could pass us at speed. We would never have known it was there if not for the jet chasing it. But the jet had no chance, it left them standing. If it was man made then I wonder why it's not being used to fight wars. It made that jet look slow."

As I continued to collate information, I realised that this trawlerman's account was one of many that seemed to be tipping the balance in favour of something extraordinary happening around Wilsthorpe. I remember thinking at the time that these lights out at sea had to be linked to the lightforms seen inland. Back in 2009 Steve Ashbridge and I missed many of the amazing sightings that were reported over the sea, because we were concentrating on the East Yorkshire Wolds area. Over the previous two years Wolds farmers had contacted me about unexplained activity they had seen. I had also been documenting my own sightings there. So the Wolds proved to be a hotbed of activity, but I was not surprised to also have reports coming in from along the coast.

I have also noted that the coastal lights are somehow different to the Wolds lightforms, which makes me wonder if that difference perhaps relates to them coming from the sea? I do not necessarily mean this literally, but those lights seen over the sea appear different in their vibrancy and richness of colour, to those lights usually reported over the Wolds and elsewhere. Maybe they are the exact same objects and it is only the differing conditions, both over land and over water, that make them appear different? This is pure speculation on my part.

Can we really be expected to believe all of these sightings were simply misidentifications? As far as I am aware none of the witnesses who contacted my website during 2009 knew each other. The only connection they had was their UFO sightings and their locations. Some witnesses did not even live in the immediate area, but they still felt the need to contact me after being so amazed by what they had seen.

The following report is a typical example of what has been seen inland; in this case, six miles inland and twelve miles south of Wilsthorpe. The objects sound very similar to what we have seen off the coast of Bempton and Speeton as recently as January 2017.

Impression of jet chasing UFO past trawler.

ILF-UFO Archive:
Lights Over Brandesburton – July 25th 2009

"Hi Paul,
I just wanted to tell you about something I saw last night at
Brandesburton. But I need to tell you what my two friends saw first.
They were driving home and were in Brandesburton, last night around
10.30pm, when they saw 7 orange lights in the sky - travelling towards
them in formation...when I saw them there were only 3 lights. The lights
I saw were stationary and they were spaced out evenly and horizontally.
There was also no noise. Neither were they a brilliant light, they just
looked like 3 very large orange light bulbs. They stayed there for around
30 seconds before gradually fading away. I have seen many things in the
night sky but have never seen anything like that! I would be interested
to know if anyone else has seen anything.
Regards Sue"

The fact these witnesses saw lights travelling in such a formation
reminded me of another sighting by a retired fisherman, who described
seeing six red balls of light over the sea, which were travelling in just
the same way. (This account is included after the next chapter.) Whilst
researching the events surrounding the Wilsthorpe incident I tried to
contact the witness named Sue, but was unsuccessful. I wish I had also
been able to talk with Sue's friends about their sighting.

For East and North Yorkshire I think 2009 was just strange full stop. But
unexplained aerial phenomena was not the only thing being reported to
my website in 2009. One of the most unusual were the reports of white
noise that came from an amateur radio enthusiast. Its part in all this
may be nothing more than coincidence, but I still think it has to be
documented. It may be of interest to future researchers, even if I have
no clue why I feel it might be relevant as I write at this moment; 4.26pm
on April 9th 2017.

White Noise

Although the white noise phenomenon was reported to my website throughout the latter part of 2009, I admit that I never actually gave it a great deal of thought at the time. The following account is the only documentation I have of this incident and I may be looking for a UFO connection that does not exist, but looking back on all the unusual activity in the affected area at the time, I do find the white noise interesting.

I remember there was lots of local electrical interference; if that's the right word. Via our CCTV we saw frustrated drivers out on the street having problems with their vehicles. We discovered that their car remotes would not lock or open. At times, I had to press the key fob for my own vehicle many times before it would open or lock. The neighbours put it down to someone having a strong Wi-Fi signal.

Below is an extract from an email I received from a Bridlington man who still lives in the town. It is clear he has some knowledge of radio frequencies and certainly realised there was a problem in 2009.

ILF-UFO Archive:
The White Noise Problem – August 5th 2009

"Hi Paul, as a radio ham from 1997 I have had a lot of experience setting up antenna and working stations on all the ham bands. But since about 18 months back, on what hams call 80 metres (that is 3.000MHz to 3.799mhz) I have what sounds like white noise to a high degree. It wipes out all incoming signals and outgoing, so that part of the band has become useless. Other parts of the ham bands are having this noise creep in at times. Ofcom (the Office of Communications) *have sent two investigators who deal with this type of thing, but they cannot find out where it is coming from. It appears that it's just a Bridlington thing and is found in all parts of Bridlington. What it is we do not know. Any other hams who have any thoughts contact Paul, then I will contact them."*

I spoke with this amateur radio enthusiast many times. He told me the white noise problem was getting worse and he had never known anything like it before. The only other information I have on this phenomenon is taken from a personal email to the radio enthusiast from Ofcom, sent during their own investigating into the white noise.

Email received: August 12th 2009 17:47 GMT
*"Following our earlier conversation, I wish to confirm that I am closing
this investigation. I found the interference complaint is due to your
receiver/installation sensitivity, resolving extremely low signals near to
the equipment noise floor.*
*For information, I did identify two items close to your installation,
radiating noise on 80m; however when switched off your "interference"
continued. Driving throughout Bridlington I found, as you did, a
constant low level of mains type noise again, just above the receiver
noise floor.*
*If you require or have any further information please contact me
quoting the reference..."*

The radio enthusiast told me,
*"Suddenly Paul, they were closing the investigation. It was very odd.
Have they been told to go away and leave it alone?"*

However, this interference did not stop until sometime after 2009. My
contact conducted many tests on his equipment, including changing
major components, but he was unable to resolve the problem. I learned
that other radio enthusiasts in the area were experiencing similar
problems. Then, for no apparent reason, the problem resolved itself in
early 2010. My contact remains convinced that something highly
unusual was responsible for the problems.

The May 27th edition of the Bridlington Free Press carried a complaint
from a frustrated Bridlington resident, regarding bad interference
received on his TV. This was following other similar complaints.

*"In response to Steve Embleton's letter about bad TV reception, I have
spent a small fortune on the latest digital aerial, internal boosters,
digital TV, etc. Many of my neighbours are having problems too. I also
would like to know if people on the south side are going to be able to
watch Channel 5, Setanta Sports and many other channels...as at the
moment the service we are receiving is nothing short of a joke."*
Mr G.S Plunton, via text, South Shore Holiday Village, Wilsthorpe.

This was just one of numerous complaints about electrical interference
in the area during 2009. It is interesting that Mr Plunton writes in from
South Shore at Wilsthorpe.

Scarborough Evening News Reports

A few miles up the coast from Bridlington, around Muston and Scarborough, unexplained activity was beginning to build. During 2009 the Scarborough Evening News carried accounts from holidaymakers and locals who wrote in about the strange aerial activity they were witnessing. I am unable to reproduce the original articles here, since the only microfilm viewer in Scarborough library is in need of repair. Thankfully, library staff allowed me to take photos from the screen.

The first reports were of a 'black triangle' seen over the sea towards Flamborough, on Friday June 12th. The object was described in precise detail and said to be moving across the sky at approximately 80 miles an hour. On Friday July 3rd four people reported seeing three spheres of red light travelling towards them, while they were near the historic Bridlington Spa complex. They watched in shock as the glowing red spheres suddenly changed direction and headed out over the sea.

On Saturday July 18th at approximately 11pm, a Scarborough resident reported seeing lights of all colours above an area of high ground called Oliver's Mount. They went on to say the lights appeared to be chasing each other. On July 20th another local witness reported seeing an egg-shaped object over South Bay in Scarborough. He stated the object had blue lights on its sides. The distance between Wilsthorpe and these two locations is less than seventeen miles, as the crow flies. On the same day, a silver circular object with orange and red lights was seen by a motorist travelling along the A165, Scarborough to Hull road. He saw the UFO on his left as it travelled at tree height, before it changed course and crossed in front of his car.

On July 31st another Scarborough resident reported seeing a large 'black cloud' that appeared to have lights all around its perimeter. The object was seen over Oliver's Mount, one of the highest points around for miles. On August 4th 2009 the Scarborough Evening News reported that while Barry Liles and his wife were travelling back to their caravan by taxi, they saw a large white object with two bright lights. They estimated it was two and a half times the size of an average caravan and only fifty feet above the ground. The couple described the object as being 'monstrous' in size, as it hung in silence over the rooftops. The taxi driver was so frightened that she did not want to drive back to Filey.

Did you see the Muston UFO?

by Ian Duncan ian.duncan@ynltd.co.uk

A HOLIDAYMAKER is today asking readers if they also spotted anything unusual hovering in the sky above Muston earlier this month.

It is just one of a spate of unidentified flying object sightings across the Scarborough area in recent months.

Barry Liles, 60, and his wife were travelling by taxi back to their touring caravan in the village when they saw a large white object at least 50ft above the ground

He said it had two bright lights and he estimated that it was about two and a half times the size of an average caravan.

"We wound the window down but there was no noise," he added.

The sighting was at 11pm on Tuesday August 4, when he was returning from a Chinese meal with his wife and the taxi driver had just pulled up at a crossroads on the edge of Muston.

Mr Liles said he had visited the area for a number of years but this was the first time he had seen anything unusual in the night sky.

The Barnsley resident said: "It was above the roofs of the buildings there. There were two lights, red and amber, and they were shining quite brightly.

"We were a bit surprised. It looked flat and made of white shiny plastic. It stayed there for what seemed like an eternity but it was probably only seconds."

He added that he reported the matter to Filey Police but they had received no other sightings. He said: "It'd be most reassuring to me if somebody else saw it. It was most definitely not an optical illusion. I've been going to Muston for years, so I know the area."

The Flares That Never Were

I find it hard to believe that so many people could have misidentified what they reported in these accounts. The chances that all these sightings were mistaken observations just seem so slim. Whatever they were, I would say these descriptions definitely rule out Chinese lanterns, unless of course they can now morph into silver spheres, black triangles or clouds with lights around them. At the same time, just eleven miles up the coast from Wilsthorpe, residents in and around the village of Muston were also reporting unexplained lights in the sky.

On Thursday September 17th 2009 Scarborough coastguards were called out after members of the public reported seeing red 'flares' in the sky over the North Bay beach in Scarborough. It was later reported that these flares were a false alarm.

I really love reports of the 'flares that never were' because, apart from their initial appearance, explanations for their cause are rarely given. The cold truth is, the media rarely have any clue, besides the witness descriptions of these lights over the sea. Any explanation has to fit with what is considered possible, no matter how ridiculous that explanation might sound. Perhaps one day an emergency callout log might read; *"After an extensive search of the area nothing could be found. No ships or aircraft were reported missing or in distress. We have no rational explanation for what could have been responsible for the mystery lights. Therefore we have to conclude with the strong possibility that these lights were the, as yet unexplained, phenomena known as ILFs."*

On August 29th 2009 an unexplained orange light was seen in the sky over the old Scarborough coastal road, approximately twelve miles from Wilsthorpe. Holidaymakers from Widnes, Amanda Gwilliam and her husband, reported seeing the orange light in the sky while returning to their campsite in Filey. They were travelling from Scarborough along the old coast road when Mrs Gwilliam spotted an oval-shaped orange glow in the sky, just after 9pm. Mr Gwilliam said, *"I pulled onto the pavement just above Cayton Bay. It was like an orange glowing fire, oval-shaped and it was high and travelling quite fast. We watched it fly overhead then out to sea, where it climbed and then disappeared."*

I can say in hindsight, that it appears each of these reports were building up to what I now consider would become the main event at

Wilsthorpe. At the time I did not know what that event was, but the evidence continued to accumulate.

The first piece of the puzzle to be put in place has to be location; every UFO sighting seemed to be close to the coast. In the above report we even have holidaymakers going out of their way to report something unexplained - but why shouldn't they report their sighting? Surely the last thing on their mind would be getting involved with local news to report strange lights in the sky. I can only think that whatever they saw must have looked so surreal that they felt compelled to report it.

For me, the fact that seasoned trawlermen were also reporting unexplained objects at the time, stamp the events with even more credibility. I cannot imagine so many experienced trawlermen mistaking something ordinary for something paranormal. Much the same can be said about the reports from local rock anglers, who have all, at one time or another, seen the lightforms. One or two of these men also work on oil rigs for a living; they are familiar with distress flares and aircraft navigation lights, but they had no idea what the lights were in 2009 off the East and North Yorkshire coast.

Once again location is key and this tiny strip of land on the edge of the North Sea does not disappoint. It is almost as though we are allowed to see the objects, but visual contact is usually where the experience begins and ends and the witness is left with no more than an imprint on the mind, that no words can adequately describe.

On very rare occasions something more than a simple visual sighting is reported. Here it is worth adding that with these closer encounters, an element of fear usually accompanies the experience. I do not know whether this fear is a warning to witnesses or if they are sensing something almost primal. The fear of this unknown can be overwhelming, but as discussed in TP1, I believe there is a real inter-mind connection between object and witness. Maybe the mindset of the witness actually creates the outcome of a sighting, but are these lightforms friend or foe - or are they completely indifferent?

In 2009 many people reported sightings that defied explanation, including the local fishermen, who rarely share things outside of their own circle. Encouraging any of this close-knit group to break rank and share information will never be an easy task, so a single random report is always of interest. The fact that several of these men contacted me to say they had seen the lightforms made suggestions they had seen Chinese lanterns difficult to accept.

I pointed out in TP1 that these unexplained lights have also been attributed to flares, meteorites or weather balloons. Lifeboats were often launched after such reports, yet on many occasions a vessel in distress was never located, which must rule out the flare theory, and to confuse meteorites with flares is ridiculous to my mind. Yet when all else fails, in the absence of anything else, these are the explanations given.

Old lifeboat logs held with the Royal National Lifeboat Institution reveal that many of these phantom flare callouts record that nothing is ever found. No one looks any further or seems bothered to ask why there are so many that remain unexplained? A few examples of false alarm reports follow, taken from the Bridlington Free Press and Scarborough Evening News between 1952 and 2009.

Following pages: articles highlighting the flares that never were.

Flares sighted

Red flares off Flamborough Head on Monday evening caused Flamborough lifeboat to launch. It was recalled nearly an hour later — the flares were from aircraft on exercises.

Flares but lifeboat draws blank

Bridlington lifeboat searched during the night after a report of red flares at sea. They found nothing and returned at 3 a.m. yesterday morning. This is the fifth report of such flares along the North East Coast in the past fortnight, and lifeboats have found nothing.

Theories being considered are that flares have been stolen and are being let off; or that people are mistaking meteorites or lightning for flares in misty conditions.

The first recorded rain for some weeks fell on Bridlington yesterday at the end of 24 hours two-hundredths of an inch of rain had been recorded, and is believed to have been the result of dense fog and heavy dew.

Alert on flares over bay

SCARBOROUGH coastguards were called out last night after reports of red flares.

A team were called to the North Bay area after a member of the public reported the sighting at 9.20pm. A coastguard spokesperson said it was a false alarm with good intent.

MYSTERY FLARES ALERT LIFEBOAT: ALL-NIGHT SEARCH

Bridlington lifeboat joined the Humber lifeboat in an all-night search which ended in mystery flares being unsolved on Monday morning. At 10.30 p.m. on Sunday the coaster Achilles reported to Humber Radio that they had seen green and yellow rockets or flares to the south of them while they were steaming 10 miles off Flamborough Head.

Humber radio then contacted the Flamborough coastguards, and after hearing of three other sightings of the mysterious flares, one from a lightship, another from the game warden at Spurn Point, and the third from the Withernsea police, District Officer Coastguard J. E. Levitt alerted the Bridlington and Humber lifeboats.

The boats were launched before midnight and halving the area between Bridlington and the Humber, they made an intensive search which lasted until 4 a.m. on Monday, when they were recalled.

The Bridlington lifeboat Coxswain, Mr. John King, said: "We sailed 15 miles east of Bridlington. It was bitterly cold and there was a big swell, but it was a very fine night and if there had have been a boat in distress we would have had a very good chance of seeing it. When we were recalled at 4 a.m., we were off Withernsea and only a mile away from the Humber lifeboat."

Mr. King said he remembered the lifeboat being called out about five years ago after mysterious green flares had been seen, and on that occasion it turned out to be Polish and East German trawlers signalling to each other.

The lifeboat arrived back in Bridlington at 7.30 a.m.

Some Bridlington fishermen who were at sea in the area say that the flares were definitely caused by French or Polish trawlers signalling for their store ship to attend them.

Another theory is that the flares were made by meteorites entering the earth's atmosphere.

Green flares are normally connected with aeroplanes that are about to ditch into the sea, but no aircraft were reported in the area.

During the search two naval fisheries patrol vessels gave assistance.

Lifeboat Launched For Mystery Flares

Visitors at Thornwick Bay on Friday evening last week reported to Flamborough coastguards that they thought they had seen two red flares or lights in the sky, north of Flamborough Head. At the request of the coastguards the Flamborough lifeboat, with coxswain Richard Cowling at the helm, was launched.

A two-hour search was made of the area, but nothing was found and the lifeboat returned to North Landing. Commented Mr. Cowling: "The sea was calm and the visibility good."

Several members of the launching crew of Flamborough lifeboat were taking part in a cricket match at Flamborough when the maroons were fired. They dropped everything and hurried to North Landing where, still wearing their cricket whites, they launched the lifeboat.

The rest of the team carried on until the others returned. Flamborough won the match.

The Evidence Builds

The increase in local UFO sightings in 2009 is highlighted in an online report for unexplained aerial phenomena issued by the Ministry of Defence. It is a real eye-opener with many sightings explained away with the recurring theme of Chinese lanterns. While some could have been attributed to these floating lanterns, it is clear that many were not. Some of the objects described in the report are similar to those seen along our coastline. Many accounts come from qualified observers, whose occupations require a trained familiarity with all types of aerial activity; air traffic controllers, pilots, retired military personal and police officers. They all reported unexplained objects in 2009.

If I had not received the call from an elderly couple in May 2014 I am sure none of this research would ever have come to light. Their account was the vital key that connected all the other reports. Seven years ago I simply did not have the time, but perhaps some things are meant to be, because now I *had* the time to fit the pieces of the jigsaw together and watch the picture form. Individually these accounts are weak and the regurgitated explanations issued by the media and the authorities usually keep a lid on the situation - but as a collective they become a combination that is hard to discredit.

It is important to note that I am not alleging a cover-up here. With respect, I think the Maritime and Coastguard Agency and the RNLI are as brainwashed as the public. I am sure people higher up the food chain understand the scale of this. However, because no one ever gets close to the truth, official bodies only dish out the required explanations. The groundwork has been done over decades. Mass training of minds through the media ensures that very few people want to talk openly about UFOs or the paranormal. Even people in power believe their own lies, because the masking of truth comes from much higher up. It is easy to suppress anyone who dares to step over the line. Belief, en masse, in this subject's non-existence, has been drilled into our minds since birth. This will continue as long as the phenomena holds onto its secrets.

My research will not cure the blanket of blindness that people experience when they read or encounter the unsolvable. The smothering of our senses is a drip-fed process that no amount of proof can change. All I can do with the events of 2009 is present a reasonable argument. It is not proof that I am right; however, I think it stands on firmer ground than meteorites, flares and unusual atmospherics. For a government body to say they have no idea what these objects are, would register a massive fail. To come out and say they suspected it was a highly unusual phenomenon without providing an explanation would put them on the same level as the public; which is in fact correct, but they would never admit to being clueless.

I hope I have presented enough information so far, to make a case that something was happening around Wilsthorpe, something more plausible than mere misidentification. And still the sightings continued to occur.

ILF-UFO Archive:
Six Red Balls of Light – late August 2009

"A retired fisherman, who owns a small boat in Bridlington harbour, described to me what he saw at around 2am in late August. He decided it would be a good idea to check his boat was secure during the high tide. It was a clear night and weather conditions were good. From his location on the harbour he saw six strange lights in a straight line, in the sky off Flamborough Head. They were quite big and low over the horizon. He could tell they were low because they appeared to be at the same height as the clifftops, which stood out from the headland. He watched the line of lights as they began to move rapidly away from Flamborough Head and travel down the coast in a matter of seconds."

He later told me the lights stopped just off the coast, near Hornsea. From there they shot up vertically, hovered for a few seconds below the cloud base then disappeared.

I sometimes try to imagine what might be inside these spheres of light. We each have our own opinions about them, but I think we have to stop calling them 'visitors', because we don't know if that's what they are.

What if they are simply intelligent lights, working and interacting with the intelligence that controls the physical-looking craft? What if they are able to influence our emotions and morph into anything they want us to perceive? The combination of scenarios is mind-numbing and endless. Each report seems incredible and we can choose to believe they all have a perfectly rational explanation or we can choose to believe they are something more – something not created by the human mind.

That, in part, is the major obstacle in our path; and one the scientific community can neither answer nor explain. It is in denial, at least in public - and the public believe what they are told.

The fisherman reported his sighting to me in late August 2009. He has also described seeing them a few times *after* this initial sighting, in an area off the coast between Bempton and Hornsea. The inland sightings also occur between these two locations and Wilsthorpe is situated between them. So do the sheer volume of reports from 2009 load the dice in favour of the Wilsthorpe UFO incident being genuine? As my investigations continued, events began to gather pace.

Impression of the fisherman's sighting from Bridlington Harbour

Eileen Hopson: The Barmston Sightings

Eileen Hopson lived in Barmston with her husband Eddie in a beautiful picture-postcard cottage half a mile from the beach. Eddie Hopson is a well-known and respected accountant in the area and Eileen had recently retired, after working many years alongside her husband in the family business. Barmston is a small village less than four miles away from Wilsthorpe. It has just one road in and out, which is under one mile long from start to finish, and is lined on either side with cottages and old farm buildings. To the back of these homes is nothing but fields and open country.

I remember receiving Eileen's phone call after she had found my contact details online. She was keen to find out if anyone had reported seeing anything strange in the area. When I told her that many UFOs had been reported in recent months the phone went silent for a few moments, until she said, *"I saw something unusual land in the fields over towards Wilsthorpe a few nights ago."*

I asked Eileen for more information and an awkward spell of silence followed, then she said, *"can we talk about this face to face?"*
It was obvious to me that she did not feel comfortable discussing her experience over the phone and asked if I would come and see her to discuss it. I was keen to speak with her as soon as possible, because she had told me that something had actually landed in fields near to her home. So after gathering the necessary details, I agreed to visit the next day with my friend Steve Ashbridge.

The Hopson's home overlooks open fields that stretch to the Wolds, with uninterrupted views along the coast towards Bridlington. From their back garden at night it is possible to see the single streetlight that stands on the A615 roundabout at Wilsthorpe, and through the upstairs windows even more can be seen. Other than this, the skies are free of light pollution.

Our first meeting with Eileen was strange. I arrived armed with a few questions and expected to hear her talk about the objects that landed in the nearby fields just days before, but it soon became clear that something else had happened in the weeks leading up to this. After a few pleasantries Eileen explained that she first wanted to tell us about another sighting she had a few weeks earlier. I wasn't about to argue, since first-hand accounts are gold to a researcher.

My first impressions of Eileen were that she was a warm and genuine lady who simply wanted to talk with someone about what she had seen - someone who would not just roll their eyes and dismiss her story as nonsense. As we listened, Steve and I could tell that whatever had happened had troubled her.

Eileen began to explain what she had seen, then led us to the upstairs of the cottage. She told us she had been looking through the bathroom window at the time of her sighting; since there are no other houses overlooking the Hopson's home, the glass in their bathroom window is clear. Eileen said that it was sometime after 3.00am, possibly between the 13th and 15th of September 2009, when she had got out of bed and gone into the bathroom. She looked out of the window; the sky was clear and crisp that night, so she had a clear view across the open fields towards Woldgate. Then, to the far right, something caught her eye - and in all the years she had lived in the cottage, it was something Eileen had never seen before.

In the distance, quite low in the sky, was a large ring of orange/yellow lights over the open fields. Eileen was able pinpoint their location because she could also see the familiar streetlight on the traffic roundabout at Wilsthorpe. She said she watched them for about five minutes before returning to bed. But something about the lights troubled her and few minutes later she found herself walking back along the landing to have another look. The lights were still there, but now they seem closer and lower to the ground - and she thinks they were slowly turning.

As I listened to Eileen's description I wondered if she had witnessed the same object described as a mother ship, by the young man in my overheard conversation a few weeks earlier. I asked if she could tell whether the lights were independent of each other or if she thought they were part of one huge connected circle.
"It is hard to describe them Paul. I want to say it was one big circle, but I don't think that's what it was. If you can picture a pearl necklace, but yellow and orange, that's what it was like. I remember they were paler on the outside. Yes that's right, pale yellow - the darker bit was

definitely on the inside and was deep orange, almost red. So they could have actually all been separate ones. Do you see what I mean? I think they were separate, but I just don't know"

Eileen obviously could not say with any certainty. All she knew was that it or they were not like anything she had ever seen before. She added that they also felt somehow eerie and so unsettling that she did not sleep well after seeing them. *"I didn't like how they made me feel. I told Ed, but he just said it was the streetlight on the roundabout. He didn't even want to look."*

An impression of Eileen's first sighting from the bathroom of her home

Eileen could not give me an exact date for this sighting, but due to the timing of her second sighting, she believes it must have been sometime in mid-September. If she had not had her second sighting I doubt I would have even learned of this one. After her experience, Eileen says she spent a while considering what to do. She spoke about it with her husband Eddie several times, but he had no interest in anything of this nature and was quite dismissive.

He was convinced she had only seen the light from Wilsthorpe roundabout and no amount of talking was going to change his mind. Eileen knew that was not the case, but if it was that simple then why had she never observed it this way in all the years they had lived there? She felt annoyed, because she was certain the lights were something very special - something that could not be explained away as a simple streetlight in the centre of a roundabout.
" I wouldn't mind, but I could even see the glow from the roundabout light, so I know it wasn't that. And it just felt altogether weird."

These lights over Wilsthorpe troubled Eileen for days. She said that on more than one occasion, both day and night, she found herself looking through the window in the direction they had appeared.
"I think they knew I was looking at them Paul. I don't know why and I don't know how, but this should not have bothered me the way it did."

Then Eileen began to describe her second sighting - the one she had originally contacted me to discuss. Directing our eyes away from the location she had seen the circle of lights, she began to tell us about the objects she had seen land in the fields days before.

"They landed in the fields Paul, just over there. I was in the garden."
Her outstretched arm pointed to the open fields in the distance; directly behind them was Wilsthorpe beach.
"I watched them hovering for a while, then they slowly came down. They looked strange; like upside down ice-cream cones. And they glowed orange to yellow, um...I don't know if they glowed; they might have been pulsing light, like a heartbeat. I'm not sure how to describe them, because they were not like anything I had seen before. But they were bright, not very big, but very bright."

The two stories jumped back and forth in her mind, as she told us various bits from each. At times it was hard to untangle one from the other, but by the time Steve and I left, we were in no doubt that Eileen Hopson had seen something highly unusual.

She wanted to show us the approximate area where the objects had landed, so we spent the whole afternoon with her. We visited the field where she said they came down and we stood in the approximate place beneath where the circle of lights had hovered. Both locations are within a short walk of each other. I would love to say we found landing marks in the earth or some other unexplained trace, but we found nothing.

What I like about this story and the others that were reported in 2009, is that they were documented. As previously stated, I closed my ILF-UFO website sometime in 2013, with no knowledge of the Wilsthorpe incident until May 2014, but these reports are all still there, exactly as I recorded them in 2009. Below is Eileen's account in full, recorded exactly as it appeared on my website - which can still be found if the correct words are entered into a search engine.

ILF-UFO Archive:
Orange Objects seen from Barmston - October 11th 2009

"Two orange cone-shaped objects were seen at around 8.30pm on Sunday evening; that's the 11th October 2009. [The witness] went on to tell me that they were quite large and were pointed at the top. She viewed them from her cottage in Barmston, which has outstanding views over Fraisthorpe and Wilsthorpe. [The witness] thinks the objects were midway between the two locations and she believes they came down in the fields. She only saw one object initially, but a few minutes later another one appeared. The second one looked smaller and not as bright. This could have been due to it being further away.

This latest sighting seems to back up sightings and reports published in the Bridlington Free Press earlier in the week. The descriptions are very similar. I also have a report from several weeks ago, from the same location. I have passed part of that account to Gary Heseltine, who runs the police UFO database. Information about the sighting is slowly coming out. I spent a few hours last evening [12th October 2009] observing the area with my friend Peter, but we saw nothing out of the ordinary in the sky. The only thing of slight interest was a police scientific investigations van, which was tucked away on a side road in the darkness. Seemed an odd place to be."

On October 18th 2009 I returned to Barmston to talk with Eileen Hopson and her husband Eddie. Eileen was having flashbacks and they were clearly bothering her.
"I'm certain about what I saw Paul. I even thought something was in the bedroom watching me the other night - it's ever since I saw them. I just can't get it out of my mind. I think they knew I was watching. I have not seen anything in the room, it's just a feeling I get, and I keep waking up between three and four a.m. It has even changed the way I sleep and I cannot stop looking out of the bathroom window during the night. I wish I had never seen anything."

Eileen's story always remained the same, the only addition was that she now found herself regularly standing at the bathroom window to look out over the fields. I wish I could have helped her more.

I recorded my visit to Eileen on the 18th on my website at the time;
"Update 18.10.09 - Went back to Barmston today with Steve Ashbridge and we spoke again Eileen to these objects. We all stood overlooking the area and now have a good idea where the objects came down."

Eileen Hopson died in October 2014. In January 2017 I spoke with her daughter Samantha, who said, *"Mum told me about what she saw Paul. It really got to her. At the time it was all she talked about. I remember you coming to talk with her, she really appreciated it."*

A Police Presence and a Strange Car

My archived webpages are an invaluable source of evidence, which let readers know that I was actually documenting these UFO sightings in 2009, as they were happening - and they are invaluable now in light of what I was told in 2014. Looking back at the pages a few things stand out that seemed quite insignificant in 2009. At the time, I recorded them as observations more than anything of importance.

While out with my friend Peter Masters, I remember we saw *two* police scientific investigations vans. One was off the road behind some trees, but I remember it was in total darkness and there was no one inside it. We were midway between Wilsthorpe and Barmston, overlooking fields, roughly the area of Eileen's sightings. We were parked there to observe the location and maybe see some UFOs ourselves, but I wonder why I missed such an obvious clue at the time? There had been multiple UFO sightings and now there was a police presence *and* scientific investigation vans in the affected area. Maybe this was just another coincidence, but looking back, I don't think so.

We saw the first scientific investigation van earlier that evening at Woldgate, but thought very little about it at the time. When we parked up behind the second van one thing I do remember, was that it had a kind of rounded hatch on the roof. It was made from dark glass or perspex and was about the size of half a football. I wondered what it could have been for, perhaps it was some kind of camera, but no one appeared to be around. Perhaps they were in the back of the vehicle monitoring the surroundings. Maybe they were out in the fields.

I remember that night back in 2009 being quite uneventful. It was a very foggy night, but our chances of seeing anything unexplained in those conditions must have been high for us to go out there in the first place. We had gone up to Woldgate first because we thought that would offer better views of the entire coastline. This was where we had seen the first scientific investigation van. However, the fog ruled out our idea of seeing anything, so we were soon heading back towards Wilsthorpe.

As we travelled towards the location we later found the second van, I remember we saw only one car on the road. There is an isolated bungalow just before the turn-off we needed and due to the terrible weather conditions, I made the mistake of turning my van into the entrance of that property. It is set back from the road and very private, but I immediately realised I had taken a wrong turn and put the van into reverse. I glanced into my side mirror and was amazed to see the same car we had seen earlier. I am sure it had followed us all the way from Woldgate, but it had now stopped behind us at the entrance of the bungalow. I reversed out onto the road and we left. At the time one of us commented, *'What are the chances that the only car on the road wanted to go to the same bungalow?'*

My van only has side mirrors, so I lost sight of the car as we drove away. We thought the car belonged to the owners of the property and as we left we assumed it then entered the drive of the bungalow, but I am not sure. I found it quite embarrassing at the time and remember commenting to Peter that when we turned into the entrance of their home we must have unnerved them. Minutes later we were at our observation area where we discovered the second police scientific investigations van.

Now, as I look back at this sequence of events, I wonder if the car *had* actually been following us all the way from Woldgate. I was the only person in the world at the time who was documenting these UFO sightings as they were happening, so had I unknowingly attracted some attention?

ILF-UFO Archive:
PCSO Talks of UFO Encounter, Fraisthorpe – October 2009

"I really hope I get the facts on this sighting."

I am so pleased that my archived website contains this brief reference to a UFO sighting by a Police Community Support Officer in Fraisthorpe. Back in 2009 I passed this information on to Gary Heseltine - the former police detective who runs successful UFO conferences in the UK and is editor of UFO Truth Magazine. Mr Heseltine never replied to my email in 2009 but it is archived and remains as proof of the story.

I remember writing in TP1 that it is sometimes only when we look back at past events that the real picture begins to form. Quite what the picture is I do not know, but what are the odds of all these unusual events occurring in such a small area of East Yorkshire and in the same timeframe? I suppose the sceptics would say, *'it is all just coincidence. You don't have any real proof, not real proof.'*

I wonder if they would say that if the argument was loaded in their favour? I believe that if such an overwhelming set of circumstances presented itself to suggest that nothing had happened at Wilsthorpe, the sceptics and debunkers would use it like a club to beat home their point. Thankfully, this is not the case and I have yet to hear an argument against my research thus far.

I sent the PCSO's report to Gary Heseltine because I felt he was better placed to deal with it. It appears I was wrong. Maybe if I had gathered more information to send with the report it would have been followed up, but then that would have meant doing the job myself.

I stopped giving away my hard-earned research many years ago, after realising there was no shortage of people willing to sit back and let me do all the work. I remember once reading a news article with the headline 'On The Trail of the UFOs'; accompanied by the author's name. It was good research, except that my own name was not even mentioned, yet I was the one who had done all the work. I am not suggesting that this is the case here, but lessons were learned.

The PCSO's Sighting

I received the following details of the PCSOs sighting on October 1st 2009. The event had actually occurred two weeks before this, which puts it right in the hot zone of reported activity.

It was night on the A165 road as the officer drove from Barmston towards Bridlington. As he approached Fraisthorpe, another car heading in the opposite direction began to slow, then came to a stop and its headlights dimmed and went out. This particular stretch of road is not a good place to stop a vehicle at night, as it is unlit and is renowned for speeding. The PCSO slowed down with the intention of assisting the other driver if needed.

Suddenly he became aware of a large, black triangular-shaped object rising from the fields at the other side of the hedgerow. It is not known if the object had actually been on the ground, landed or whether it had been moving around the field, but as it lifted higher into the air the other car's headlights came on again and the engine started. The black triangle then slowly moved over the fields towards the sea. Something had clearly affected the engine or electrics of the oncoming car as it passed or got close to the triangle. But, from what I am told, it did not affect the PCSOs car, so if the object was responsible we have to assume it had to be very close to have such an effect.

Second Sighting on the A165 – Sept 2009

I have another account of an object described by a police officer, ironically from the same stretch of road [A165] between Barmston and Fraisthorpe, which also happened mid-September 2009. It is only because of my dogged perseverance that I managed to get a few details of what happened from the officer involved. He was so reluctant to talk that it took weeks of messaging back and forth before we actually met. This is what I was told;

"I was on the A165 driving towards Bridlington when it happened. I remember I had just passed the pizza restaurant at Barmston when everything started to go black. It was like some huge dark shadow was passing over the car. The lights dimmed on the car and it slowed, I'm not sure if it stopped. It was all so strange. I looked out of the driver's side window and could see a huge dark shape slowly moving towards the coast. I have no idea what it was. I could not see any lights or anything, but it was very low in the sky."

Fraisthorpe is only a few miles from Wilsthorpe and both communities are very small. There are just sixteen seafront apartments at Wilsthorpe and less than twenty homes at Fraisthorpe, including farms, so to have of such an abundance of witnessed UFO sightings is highly unusual.

ILF-UFO Archive:
Sonic Boom over East Yorkshire – September 11th 2009

"Contact ILF-UFO if you heard this"

This one line reference is all there was on my website to document an unusual sound heard by residents of Bridlington, including myself. It was a huge explosion that rang out during the day and sounded like a sonic boom. It is interesting to note that no official body stepped forward to accept responsibility for it or to provide an explanation.

I remember people commenting on the explosive sound and thought the local radio stations would have reported it as a news item, but there was nothing. It was not even mentioned in the local newspapers the following week. I often wonder why that might have been, because it was certainly heard by enough people and so loud that it seemed to shake the ground. So it remains a mystery, until someone comes forward with new information.

ILF-UFO Archive:
Euro Fighter over Bridlington Rooftops – October 11th 2009

The skies around East Yorkshire roared to the sounds of low flying military jets, when a fighter plane and another aircraft flew over homes in Bridlington in October 2009. I was able to film these aircraft and the images shown are frame captures from the footage. Although they were not dated when I shared them on the original ILF-UFO webpage, I recorded the footage on October 11th 2009. So far I have been unable to identify the aircraft in the second image, although I believe it is a drone. It clearly had something beneath it as it flew, which did not appear to be attached.

The footage and photographs of these aircraft in no way proves any UFO incident. However, the aircraft activity around this time was incredibly intense and to have fighter jets flying so low over the rooftops was quite an experience for sight and sound. I have never seen them so low before or since that day.

Next page: screen captures from my footage of a fighter jet and 'drone'.

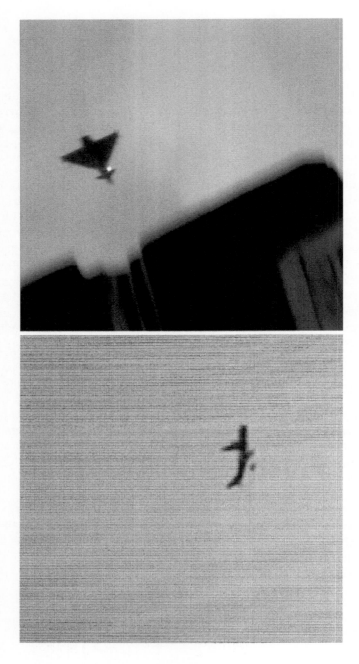

The Search for an Answer

As a collective the evidence I have presented so far, to me, seems overwhelming, but I still realise I have proof of nothing, which is so frustrating. If this evidence was for anything other than UFOs I think it would be accepted as proof. At the end of the day, the multiple UFO reports could all be classed as misidentification and whatever was happening at Wilsthorpe and surrounding areas could, in fact, be nothing more than the ramblings over active minds. Do we believe that? I don't for one second - unless a huge interconnected web of witnesses from all around the area got together to create a hoax. A hoax that took almost seven years to come to fruition.

I think a major part of my writing is an attempt to put over an argument in defence of witnesses. They have no proof other than what is stored in their heads and nothing in the world can be drawn upon to compare with what they have seen. It is an attempt to show that many of the encounters are as real as everything else we see and experience. The only difference in these cases is, they leave witnesses with nothing but a confused mind and no way to explain what they have experienced. Perhaps in the future, techniques and machines might be developed that can actually read people's minds. Something along the lines of a super-advanced lie detector, that could actually show images of the things witnesses are attempting to describe. That would certainly be a breakthrough and a type of proof that could not be ignored.

Despite my very high work load in 2009 I was still able to talk with many witnesses, although at the time I did not capitalise on the true extent of what was unfolding. The build-up of activity leading up to September 2009 included; unusual aircraft activity, spheres of light, cone-shaped objects and black triangles. Other websites and newspapers were also receiving reports of UFO activity around East and North Yorkshire, and across the country in Liverpool and its surrounding areas. The official explanation for the majority of the Liverpool UFOs was that they were nothing more than Chinese lanterns. I have read many of these reports, including one account from a police officer in Liverpool, who described seeing a black triangle - which look nothing like Chinese lanterns.

In December 2009 the Ministry of Defence officially closed their UFO desk, which had operated for over thirty years, despite a surge in reported sightings. According to the BBC News website;

"Documents from the National Archives reveal the last cases to be dealt with by the Ministry of Defence's UFO department...the UFO desk was closed because it served "no defence purpose" and was taking staff away from "more valuable defence-related activities", newly released files show."

Until January 2010 the MOD's own website stated,
"as of 1 December 2009 the dedicated UFO hotline answer-phone service and e-mail address will be withdrawn."
The webpage containing this statement has since been removed and can only be found by searching the archives.

I am not suggesting the Wilsthorpe incident was in any way responsible for the MODs decision, but I cannot believe the military no longer have an interest in UFOs. Here is a reply I received from RAF Staxton Wold on December 7th 2010, which may confirm this. It is their response to a letter asking about a significant UFO sighting, which happened close to the base. This reply came a full year after the MOD announced that it was closing down their UFO desk.

"The T102 radar which we operate at RRH Staxton Wold is designed primarily as long range radar. I am not at liberty to discuss in detail its detection parameters; however, I can inform you that the UFO described would have been close to RRH Staxton Wold for the radar to produce what we call a "plot". Therefore we would not have been able to track it on our systems.
I have forwarded your letter to RAF Leeming Flight Operations. They along with the other Main Operating Bases around the UK collate UFO in an attempt to provide an explanation to these sightings.
I am sorry I could not be of any assistance."
Yours sincerely...
Station Commander
RRH Staxton Wold

This letter has never been published, until now. I think it is a little bit of UFO gold for researchers like myself. I believe staff at RAF Staxton Wold did not realise the significance of their reply to those of us who are interested in sightings of unexplained aerial phenomena. Of course, it does not prove that UFOs are real, but it does indicate that the MOD were still taking an interest in them by December 2010 - despite officially closing their UFO desk on December 1st 2009.

Remote Radar Head
Staxton Wold
Royal Air Force
FYLINGDALES
PICKERING
North Yorkshire
YO18 7NT

16 Nov 2010

RESPONSE ████████████████████████ **- DATED 07 DEC 2010**

The T102 radar which we operate at RRH Staxton Wold is designed primarily as long range radar I am not at liberty to discuss in detail its detection parameters; however, I can inform you that the UFO described would have been to close to RRH Staxton Wold for the radar to produce what we call a "plot". Therefore we would not have been able to track it on our systems.

I have forwarded your letter to RAF Leeming Flight Operations. They along with the other Main Operating Bases around the UK collate UFO sighting in an attempt to provide an explanation to these sightings.

I am sorry that I could not be of any assistance.

Yours sincerely,

Station Commander
RRH Staxton Wold

164

Building the Gun

I have heard people talk about finding the 'smoking gun' - a truth that could catapult the subject of UFOs into the mainstream. I was armed with such a massive amount of information, but without a trigger or specific direction to aim, the stories I had collected remained dormant for over five years. That was until May 2014. I was midway through writing TP1 when I received a phone call from an elderly lady in Wilsthorpe. She said she had something to tell me, something that would be the most incredible thing I would ever hear - and the most amazing thing she had ever seen or experienced in her life.

The lady lived with her husband in one of sixteen apartments at Wilsthorpe; these are four beachfront properties, each divided into four individual flats with unobstructed views over the North Sea. They were built in 1935 and have remained relatively unchanged since that time. During the war they were requisitioned by the MOD. Directly behind the flats are two unoccupied farm houses and a small campsite owned and used exclusively by the Royal Yorkshire Yacht Club. Directly behind that is half a mile of open fields - the location of Eileen Hopson's sightings - which run parallel to the A165 road from Bridlington to Hull.

I have changed the names of the witnesses in this account to protect their anonymity, but have kept the details of the story as close to the truth as possible. When I spoke to 'June' on the phone, I asked her if she knew of any other residents who had seen the same things she and her husband 'Ron' had seen that night. I got the impression that she actually seemed annoyed that only herself and her husband had seen them.

Some of the apartments were unoccupied at the time of the sighting, but I did visit the location to meet June and to ask other residents if they saw or heard anything unusual. None of those I spoke to saw anything resembling the 30 to 40 boomerang-shaped objects over the sea that June described to me - but they do remember her talking about it for weeks afterwards.

Four of the residents remember seeing army personnel on the beach, but they assumed they were there for a routine military exercise. One of them suggested that the army would not have been looking at the beach at that time of night, but did remember seeing lots of lights. I wondered how they could have seen this from indoors, but I was informed that since there is no one overlooking these particular homes, residents rarely close their curtains or blinds.

One resident, real name Mick Baxter, who lives in one of the apartments, told me he remembered June talking about unusual lights she saw over the sea. He remembers she asked if he had seen them too, but admitted he had not seen anything out of the ordinary. Perhaps this is not surprising in Mick's case, as he is a taxi driver and is out most evenings into the early hours.

There were just twelve people residing in the sixteen flats on the night of June's sighting, so the odds of more people seeing anything so late at night must have been quite low. None of this makes June and Ron's story any less true, but I discovered there were other witnesses to back up much of what they told me.

In fact, June and Ron's experience would have remained nothing more than a fantastic story if not for a chance conversation I had in 2016 with Martin Roberts from Bridlington. Martin had a story to share that made it possible for me to connect June and Ron's sighting to the reports recorded on my ILF-UFO website. It was the final link in a chain of unexplained phenomena that began early in 2009 and continued to build until the night of June and Rons incredible sighting.

Recent photo of the flats overlooking the sea at Wilsthorpe.

Triangles Over and Into the Sea

It was during my 2016 research into the disappearance of Tornado aircraft ZE732 that I learned of a UFO sighting which almost mirrored June and Ron's story from 2014. Even the location was the same; all I needed now was a date. So far everything had been hidden in plain sight; the historic reports I had from 2009, June and Ron's sighting - all of it. The first hints there had been an incident at Wilsthorpe was during one of my many visits to the harbour.

Bridlington Harbour is full of interesting characters who have spent their lives working out at sea and around the coast. It is a hard way to make a living and the men who do have grown hard to the harsh conditions and unnatural working hours. They are also unaccustomed to talking with strangers about what they have seen and experienced, so encouraging these men to share their experiences is never easy. Even though I have friends on the harbour who are highly respected and who consider me a friend, this still does not give me a free pass to information.

Martin Roberts is one man who has worked on the harbour for many years and his knowledge of the sea and surrounding coastline are second to none. He owns and runs the bait shop on the harbour top, which sells all manner of sea angling paraphernalia, but the mainstay of his business is fishing bait. I initially went to speak with Martin about his own UFO sighting, which he'd had as a young man some fifty years earlier. During our conversation he happened to mention two men who used to work for him as bait diggers. Martin told me they had seen dark triangular-shaped objects entering the sea off South Shore. I was amazed and intrigued to hear this, so I asked if he could remember when it happened.

"I am not exactly sure when Paul. It would be a few years ago now, maybe five or six. I remember they were down towards South Shore, bait digging at Wilsthorpe. There had been some really big tides. They saw 'em twice - once in the daytime and then the next night as well. That's when the Army lads got 'em."

Army lads? What did he mean *'the army lads got them?'* Even before he said another word I knew this might connect to June and Ron's sighting, so I asked what he meant.

"I mean, my lads went to dig bait at low water up at Wilsthorpe and

before they knew it, they were surrounded by soldiers with guns. They were going to arrest them. It was serious. These guys weren't messing around. They wanted to know what they were doing, where they were going and who they worked for. They got interrogated on the beach and were asked all sorts of things. They scared the s**t out of them. It was serious stuff."

It sounded like Martin was saying his men were stopped at gun point. *"Yes that's exactly what I am saying Paul and they weren't nice about it either. They explained that they were bait diggers and were there to dig for fishing bait. That's what they do. They have to dig at low tide, so that's why they were there. Well, one of the army guys said to them, "Listen mate if you are not off this beach by the time I turn around you'll be going nowhere." They were scared to death Paul. They were going to arrest them. The soldier said, "we will take you away and you will not be seen again if you don't get off this beach now."*

I asked Martin if he was sure this happened at Wilsthorpe, *"Yes I am sure. It was opposite those beachfront flats on the clifftop. My lads gave the soldiers a bit of backchat at first, because they just wanted to dig for bait; they just wanted to earn some money. But they soon shut their gobs when they realised the soldiers weren't messing about. They really were scared to death. This was serious and frightening. The soldiers must have seen the light from my lad's torches from a long way off and were just waiting for them. The lads said they just seemed to appear out of nowhere and surround them."*

I asked Martin how many soldiers were there and if they said any more. *"They didn't see loads of 'em at first - just the ones with guns who were questioning them. But the lads hung around after they had been ordered off the beach. They stayed near the clifftop. They were pi**ed off and wanted to see what was happening, so after a while they crept up to the edge of the cliff and had a look. They said the beach was swarming with men. Soldiers. Not just a handful, bloody loads and loads of them - from the shoreline to the top of the beach.*

They said some of them had headlights on and were holding things that looked like metal detectors; he said he thought they were looking for something. I know they weren't lying about what they saw because they came back empty-handed and they were really shook up and frightened. At first I thought they had sold the bait behind my back and ripped me off. But when they told me about what had happened with the army on the beach, I knew they were telling the truth. I reckon it had something to do with them triangle things they saw going into the sea."

Martin said the two bait-diggers had told him they saw triangular-shaped objects that actually went under the surface of the sea - one at night and one in daylight. They described the objects as being more wedge-shaped than perfect triangles, but on both occasions the objects were completely silent. They said they were black in colour and apparently seamless. They did not see any windows in them or anything resembling a door and the one they saw at night had no lights at all.

Martin said that the soldiers on the beach had also stopped a dog walker who was out early that morning. They told him, in no uncertain terms, that he had to leave the beach and when he asked why, he received a similar response as the bait diggers. It is fair to assume these were the same soldiers who ordered the bait diggers off the beach. I have so far failed to trace this man, but my research is on-going.

I knew at this point that June and Ron's story and Martin's account from the two bait diggers had to be from the same time. So now I had four people describing very similar events around Wilsthorpe, but I still had no date. All Martin could say was that he thought it was five or six years ago and it could have been sometime during September. He said this is because the big night tides are in September and they provide the best conditions for digging bait at Wilsthorpe.

I continued to gather information, trying to build a picture of what had happened at South Shore beach at Wilsthorpe. I now had the potential month these events had occurred, but I still needed to identify the year and I wanted something on paper to tie them both together.

I learned that some members of the Royal Yorkshire Yacht Club remembered that the military had been on the beach. Several years ago one member named Kevin Porter was working in the nearby boat compound when the army arrived quite out of the blue. I was told that for a few days the beach was completely out of bounds. If the Yacht Club had already been informed of a possible military exercise, then they never passed it on to the men in the boat compound. Kevin said it all happened very quickly. The first they knew about it was when the helicopters arrived. This is pure speculation on my part, but if the Yacht Club had been informed and had not told their members because it had to remain a secret, surely they should have at least stopped them using the compound on the actual day of the military exercise?

As part of my investigations I made a Freedom of Information request to the MOD. Their email response stated that a top secret military exercise had taken place at Wilsthorpe from the beach extending out to sea. Now I am in no position to dispute the official explanation for this military presence at Wilsthorpe, but I do think the UFO accounts I received tell a slightly different story.

Maybe this is just a coincidence, because when the evidence is stacked up all we can do is stand back and evaluate. After all, what would be the point of telling a lie? The powers that be say these events were part of a top secret military exercise. This suggests that all the people I have interviewed must have misidentified or imagined what they saw. Unless they were just subject to mass hallucinations?

Part Three:
The Wilsthorpe Incident Is Born

A Spectacular UFO Sighting

Out of all the research I have amassed surrounding incidents in the Wilsthorpe area, this next story has caused the most impact. Even though it may only be a fraction of something much bigger, it is the crucial link that enabled me to piece everything together.

It has been difficult to know how best to reveal each part of the story so far. The reports I have already shared identify the year and give clues to the coming climax in activity at Wilsthorpe. They give a background of events during 2009, so I placed them first in the book for that reason. Martin Roberts' story came my way later, in 2016, but it was the magnet that pulled them all into place.

The following recollections were kindly shared with me in May 2014 by June and Ron of Wilsthorpe. I have tried to keep their account as accurate as possible, but if it sounds fantastic, then I have done my job. Because if June and her husband Ron actually saw what they claim to have seen in September 2009, it was nothing less than spectacular.

This is the first conversation I had with June and Ron, in their own words:

"I saw them just before I went to bed one evening Paul. It was four or five years ago. I went into the porch to turn off the outside light, but it was already off. It's a light that's shared between the four flats here and whoever puts it on usually puts it off. I don't normally bother to switch it off if I have not put it on. But for some reason I cannot explain, I went into the porch. I have asked myself why I did that loads of times since."

'Why you did what June?'
"Why I went into the porch Paul. I don't know why, well not without a good reason. I found myself in the porch and realised the light was already off. I looked up and down the coast wondering why it seemed so light and remember thinking something must have been happening further up the coast. So I just turned and walked towards the living room. But then a voice said go back and have another look."

'You heard someone speaking, inside or outside your home June?'
"I heard the voice inside my head. It said 'go back and have another look'. I did exactly that and I looked again, I just looked a little bit

higher and that's when we saw them, the lights above the sea.
I stood there for a few seconds thinking 'I don't believe what I am
looking at'. My jaw just dropped; I had never seen anything like it in my
life before. There were loads of them all in a big circle. That's when I
shouted Ron to come and look; he was just about to go to bed. We were
both going to bed, but for some reason I was drawn to the porch. He
came right away. He knew something was wrong, I'm shouting 'Ron!
Ron! Come and look at this, you're not going to believe this'.

Well he came running through and when I showed him he just said, 'Oh
my God, what the bloody hell is that? It's like a Christmas tree.' We both
stood watching them for a few minutes in shock. We really did feel
shocked, we didn't know what they were, you see. Then Ron became a
bit scared and said he was going to bed and that's exactly what he did.
He went to bed and put his head under the pillow because they
frightened him so much. I didn't - I stood there and watched them for
almost an hour."

Real Spaceships

'I asked Ron why he felt so unsettled by what he saw.'
"I just did Paul and I don't know why. I suppose it was because I had
never seen anything like it before. They were so bright, like Christmas
tree lights. I didn't want them to see me that's for sure. I knew as soon
as I saw them it was something I should not have been seeing. I mean
they were spaceships - real space ships - and it looked like they were
taking something from the sea. June stayed though. She was amazed."

'What did you see June that was so amazing?'
"Spaceships, just like Ron says. That's what I'm telling you. Lots of them
all lit up in a big circle over the sea. "

Her delivery of the word spaceships was loud and fast. I assumed that
when she described seeing more than one light over the sea, there were
maybe four or five. At this point I had not formed an image of my own
for what was clearly imprinted in June's mind. I tried to explain that
lights had been reported off the coast for many years. However, when I
asked for clarification, it soon became clear that my reports of lights
were nothing compared to what the couple saw.

'So you both saw them over the sea? What were they, balls of light? Is that what you are saying, you saw a few lights out at sea?'

"No not just lights. If all we saw was lights I would not have even bothered to contact you. There were loads of them, all glowing blue and white in a big circle. These were more than just lights, ask Ron. They were spaceships, loads of 'em."

At this point in our conversation it became clear to me that June had wanted to get the story off her chest for some time - and I still had no idea what she saw. 'How many did you see?' I could sense the urgency in her words and I could not help myself, I just wanted to know.

'How many lights did you see June?'

"That's what am coming to. There was at least thirty, maybe even forty, all in a big circle. And they weren't that far out either, because I could see them easy without binoculars. They were glowing blue and white and looked like boomerangs. As soon as Ron realised what they were he was off to bed. They bloody scared him to death. I just stood there mesmerized, there were so many of them. They were in a circle and were shooting lasers or what looked like lightning, onto the water. There were lasers or lights darting about in all directions onto the sea. And the sea, 'oh my god...' the sea beneath them was boiling and steaming with activity. It was splashing and bubbling in a pale white and blue light. It looked like something out of a science fiction film. I could not take my eyes off them. I stood in the darkness of our porch watching them for almost an hour."

'Can you remember if it was high or low tide?'

"I think the tide was coming in. I'm not exactly sure, but I don't think it was high tide. I wasn't thinking about the tide if I'm honest. I could not take my eyes off the spaceships."

I think anyone who has lived on the coast for a number of years would be able to estimate how far away something was from their home and considering the height of the tides at the time June didn't seem to think it was high tide. I asked if she managed to take any pictures, or if she felt the urge to call any of their immediate neighbours.

"No I never thought about anything except what I could see happening in front of me. I wasn't moving from that spot. Ron had gone to bed scared. Even if I had a camera I would not have took a picture - no way.

The last thing I wanted to do was draw attention to myself. If you had seen them you would know what I mean.
There were so many of them. I don't know what they would have done if they knew I was watching them, but then again, I don't know why I went into the porch. So maybe they did know I was there. It was just strange. I never took my eyes off them and don't mind admitting I was a bit - not scared exactly – I think I was more amazed really. Because I don't think I should have been watching them."

June explained that these spaceships were all independent of one another and were not very big. I asked her about their shape, because since she said they looked like boomerangs, I assumed she had meant they were triangular.

"They were like small boomerangs, all of them the same and curved. I suppose they might have been triangle-shaped, but I could only see two sides lit up, so I don't know. That's why I said boomerang-shaped. They glowed pale to dark blue and I don't think they were that big - maybe twelve to fifteen feet. I can't be sure but they seemed to be in pairs. It's hard to describe them. I have never seen anything like it in my life, they were amazing."

I have to confess that I now feel a little guilty for not doing more with June and Ron's story when I was first contacted. But at the time, it really did sound too incredible to be true. This is part of the reason why I have shared all of the archived ILF-UFO reports first. I had to build a picture strange enough to retell June and Ron's story. I remember asking them several times for an approximate distance they thought the objects were from where they were standing. The objects must have been quite close to be able to see such detail. I didn't want to sound as though I did not believe them, but I had never heard anything like it, I wanted to be sure.

Ron told me,
"They were over the sea, all in a big circle. The first thing I thought was that they looked like a giant Christmas tree. It sounds daft I know, but they just looked so strange. They cannot have been that far out because we could see them so clearly. They might even have had windows, I don't know now. They were like blue and white glass. I think they were near the low water mark although it was not low water. I think the tide was coming in.

"It's no good asking Ron, he went and put his head under the pillow when he realised what they were."

I asked June what she meant by saying 'realised what they were'?

"Well they were spaceships, that's what I mean. You had to be there and see them to understand. It feels strange talking about it, even now I cannot quite believe it. To this day I cannot understand why I went back to look a second time. I mean, I would not normally do that but the voice said 'have another look'."

The view out to sea, as seen from June and Ron's home at Wilsthorpe.

June paused mid sentence, it was as though the next words hit the back of her teeth and stopped. She looked at me and I could tell she wanted to say more, but at the same time seemed unsure whether she should. I already suspected what she was about to say. In my mind I could see the face of Eileen Hopson on the day she described the circle of lights to me and Steve. It seemed ironic that both these ladies were describing something from the same location, from around the same date.

"Something told me to go and look, do you know what I'm saying? I've never done that before for any reason, not walked back into the porch for no reason. But this night, of all nights, something said go back and look again. And they were there. Spaceships over the sea. I will never forget them as long as I live."

This event was so surreal that at one point I actually told June that she was very brave to even speak about her sighting. Relating what she saw with her husband must have been difficult, I could understand that. She had told everyone close to her and got nothing back, except mild ridicule. On the other hand I have had a lifetime of questions and soul searching that I never shared until I was in my late forties. Now here I was asking this lady questions about things that seemed to have turned her head inside-out. They had both been witnesses to something that may never have been seen before. Thinking of June's own description of these objects as *spaceships* is where many of the problems originate. After seeing something that is alien to all we know and understand, it flips understanding and belief of what is real onto its head.

First of all we question our own minds; if we cannot understand it, how can we expect anyone else to believe what we have seen? This is real mind trauma. It becomes even worse if you are with others during such an encounter or experience, if their reaction is the polar opposite. Some people are so ingrained and focused by the way media has conditioned them to think, so that shutting the experience out invariably outweighs the truth. End result, they refuse to talk. So the frustration is doubled when a person with a more open mind reaches out for confirmation of the unbelievable and gets none. Ron chose to go to the bedroom and put his head under the pillow, which was how he dealt with the visual and mental overload in what he saw. En masse we may believe we are the height of intelligence, but encounters such as these leave a person in no doubt about our place.

Seeing a genuine UFO is a visual experience that can be as confusing as trying to understand another language. They are seen and we have the experience, but that experience cannot be fully processed because of the huge gap between the phenomena and our perception of their reality. Our understanding of them has not evolved to the point of fully comprehending them. If there was a shift towards accepting these events of high strangeness as real, they might be easier to deal with.

In fact, we have to forget about understanding; acceptance has to be the first step. We are all conditioned to look for the most logical answer. But if it is a genuine event of high strangeness an answer that is considered normal will not exist. Usually the first stage is telling a few close friends and family, because by then all a person wants is a little understanding and maybe an answer. After a while that becomes a painful, tiring process. How can anyone understand what you are telling them if you cannot understand it yourself? Trying to explain the unexplainable with the tools we have is simply impossible. I take my hat off to people like June and her husband Ron. In the end, most people become reluctant to even talk, the constant sniggers and verbal abuse are simply not worth the effort. This is why I knew, after listening to June, sharing the events of 2009 that their experience was real.

The beach at Wilsthorpe is long and flat and local fishermen tell me it is possible to walk out to a considerable distance, even at high tide. For that reason I was keen to get an approximate distance, so I asked June again how far out to sea she thought these objects had been.
"I don't think they could have been more than 800ft from the shore, I could see them easily without binoculars and they were quite low. I bet they were less than 100ft over the sea. The water was boiling and splashing with activity, I could see it clear as day. All these lights were shooting down and bouncing off the water. The sea looked like it was full of fish, I don't know how else to explain it. It was alive below them and they were all just hanging there in a massive circle, all glowing in blue and white light. It was exciting, but at the same time a little unnerving, like I was seeing something I was not allowed to see."

I knew that military helicopters would eventually be blamed for what June and Ron claimed to have witnessed that night, so I asked if, at any point, they had heard any sounds outside. I was sure that after standing in the porch for almost one hour, she would have heard something if there was anything to hear.

"We could not hear anything, not a whisper and we would have heard it. That's one of the things of living here; no roads, no sounds from anything. After Ron had gone to bed I watched them from our porch in total silence. I kept as still as I could and never took my eyes off them. It was ten past eleven when I first saw them and the last ones left just before midnight. They could have been there a long time before we saw them. Another strange thing, we closed our curtains that night but never normally do that. I still don't know why I went into the porch to look. I'm pleased I did, but now I cannot stop thinking about it."

When interviewing people about their sightings I treat each and every conversation as though it is the last one we will have. In the past, some people have contacted me to share their story, then refused to talk a second time. So I will sometimes ask a question more than once to try and get as much out of the conversation as possible. Glancing at my notes I asked June to explain what she meant by 'the last ones left'.

"Well they were in a circle, but like I said before, they also seemed to be in pairs; two and a small gap then another two. But even though the sea was boiling mad, they did not move about or anything. I tried to count them but it was hard because they were pulsing all kinds of blues and whites. It was impossible. I still say there were between 30 and 40 of them though. After I had been standing there about half an hour, two of them sort of went up into the air. They went up at an angle, slow at first, then really fast and vanished. Then a short time later another two did the same. I don't think they did it in any order, but each time two left, the circle closed. I wish I had counted them now, but I just watched. I did not know what would happen next."

'Did the objects travel up the coast towards Flamborough or down towards Hull?'
"They went away at an angle, but they were going up at the same time. They just went out of sight very fast. If they went anywhere else I would have seen. They were very bright. And even though they were separate, they were perfectly in time with each other. Just before midnight the last two slowly lifted a little higher and then shot straight up becoming nothing more than dots of light. I got up close to the glass in the porch door and looked up, but they had gone. That was it! I never saw them again, but I will never forget them as long as I live."

The Red Bikes

The memory of the blue and white boomerangs played on June's mind. When she told all her friends, none of them seemed that interested and Ron just wanted to distance himself from the experience. In the end, June was left to deal with the confusion alone, which is not unusual for UFO witnesses. I felt especially sorry for her because the experience had shattered her view of the world.

I visited June And Ron again, in late April 2017, to hear about another unusual incident June had experienced back in September 2009, just a few weeks after she saw the boomerangs.

"After I had seen them I used to go outside in the evening. No one was ever around and there were no lights or anything. I would just sit there watching. You never know, they might have come back. Ron never sat outside with me. You wouldn't get him looking for them things. I mean, he knew what he had seen, but there was no way he wanted to see them again, they scared him. But I could not get them out of my head and one night, about two or three weeks later I saw something else.

In its own way it was just as strange as the boomerangs, but different. I don't know how else to explain it. It was just strange. Even though I didn't know what the boomerangs were, I could see them clearly. But this was peculiar because I'm not sure why I thought they were bikes. I just sat there and I thought to myself, 'who's on pushbikes at this time of night?' They all just appeared in a line, on the path at the bottom of the gardens. They were higher than the fence, so I realise now they couldn't have been bicycle lights, but that's what I thought when I saw them. Isn't that strange? Why did I think that?

The cliff top path is uneven, it goes up and down, and these lights were perfectly straight. A row of red lights; twelve I think. And another light but for some reason I cannot remember its colour. I just thought, 'why are all those bikes there at this time of night?'"

We will never know for sure what June saw that night in late September 2009, but after visiting the location, as she retold the story, I cannot see how the lights she saw could have been bicycles. Before this interview, I had spoken with June about the boomerang-shaped UFOs she saw with Ron. What she told me next changed everything.

Impression of the object with red lights that June described as 'red bikes'.

Soldiers on the Beach

I remember feeling really unsure about what to do with June's account of the boomerangs over the sea. Our conversation was just about to come to an end when she said, *"The next day they were everywhere, all over the beach."*

Her words made no sense and for a moment they spoiled any interest I had in what sounded like a scene from 'close encounters'.
I had to asked the question, *"What do you mean June? Did they come back in the daytime, the boomerang objects? I thought you said that was the last time you saw them."* After a slight pause she replied.
"No, the army. The army came, lots of them. All over, they were up and down all day and night. They arrived in helicopters - big helicopters and landed on the beach down there."

June pointed towards an area of beach just in front of the old boat compound near the Royal Yorkshire Yacht Club.
"They were everywhere. Soldiers walking up and down, up and down; you could tell they were looking for something. It went on all night and they used powerful lights to look at the sea. They were just like those lights they used during the war. They were in the sky and on the sea all night. I knew they were looking for the spaceships, I just knew. But they had no chance - not a chance of catching one of those things."

As incredible as their story was I realise that at the time these accounts were the only proof I had that an out-of-this-world encounter took place at Wilsthorpe. Unless I uncovered more information about it I could not publish such a sensational story. This does not mean I didn't believe them; I had a gut feeling they had witnessed something very strange, but gut feelings are not the same as multiple witnesses accounts. However, there were key elements within their story that would later tie in with other information I had from 2009, but it was not until 2016 that this information snapped into place. The day that Martin Roberts told about the army ordering his bait diggers off the beach was the day I realised that Ron and June's story had to be told. Once I learned the year it had occurred, all of the archived reports came into play and all the important pieces of the puzzle suddenly began to connect. I am so thankful the pages of my old website were archived.

But what was so special about Wilsthorpe and the surrounding area in 2009. It is a small stretch of barren land on the East Yorkshire coast, a place with no more than 20 homes, some not even occupied all year round. It does boast a small chalet complex where holidaymakers come to spend the summer, but this is a considerable distance from the area in question. From where June and Ron saw the UFOs there are only 16 homes overlooking the North Sea. A dead-end single track road is the only way to the flats and it has no street lighting. I think 'very isolated' would be a good way to describe it. In the summer it is a little known natural beauty spot on the East Yorkshire coast, but I would go as far as to say that in September, it is bleak and isolated.

Nothing was easy about investigating this case. June and Ron contacted me in May 2014 after the Bridlington Free Press had printed an article for me explaining I was writing a book and wanted people to contact me with interesting and unusual stories. Their story sounded spectacular but it had no dates to connect it to anything I had previously documented. The UFO reports from 2009 seemed very distant and I had no reason to associate them with this story. It was Martin Roberts who narrowed down the years for me with his account of the bait diggers, thus giving me a fighting chance of finding a date - but I did not find out about that story until 2016.

Ron and June thought the incident happened four or five years before I interviewed them but, although I was fascinated by what they told me, I felt I could do nothing with it unless new information came to light. To contact me the way they did took great courage and I could see no other reason for doing so, other than to get it off their chests. In truth it was June who really needed to talk about it because of the way it had affected her. I believed them, but I needed more information to take it any further. This subject is already so full of opportunists, who would not hesitate to destroy a person's credibility and in 2014 I was not willing to risk writing about Wilsthorpe for that reason. It would take another two years before more information surfaced - information in the form of the bait digger's account. Those sightings, combined with my own website reports, had all been waiting for their moment.

Other people did have things to add. Kevin Porter, the yacht club member, was up at South Shore working on his boat on the afternoon some of the helicopters arrived. He was with a few other men at the time and they were close to the beach. He told me it was quite an incredible sight to see. Some of his group began taking photographs of the helicopters, as they skimmed the coastline and settled just a few hundred yards away. Once again I could not pin Kevin down to a specific date, but he did say he thought it was September. He thought it was around the time some work was being done on a new boat compound. He also told me that soldiers from the helicopters had made the men erase their photographs from their phones and they were told to leave the boat compound.

I was now gathering small bits of information that might possibly lead me to a date. So far, no one could be specific. The closest I had got was that it had occurred four or five years ago. This tied in with Martin Roberts who said he believed it happened in September, because of the big night tides at the time. Kevin remembered it was September, but neither could remember the year. I guessed I might learn the date if I found out when the work on the boat compound was completed. But now I had accounts from multiple witnesses to a military presence in the month of September, four or five years earlier. Somewhere between 2008 and 2010 was a good enough place to start searching.

The story was left to settle amongst the mountain of information I had already acquired while working on TP1. I knew June and her husband had seen something unusual and Martin Roberts' account reaffirmed this. I spoke with June several times over a one month period and her story remained the same each time. I talk with Martin to this present day and his recall of what happened has not changed. Armed with a few key bits of information, I decided it was time to visit Bridlington Library. Their archives contain lots of information and the staff there are always very helpful. I was sure that documentation from 2008 to 2010 would be there. My first job was to discover when work commenced and ended on the South Shore boat compound.

On arrival at the library I was told by Sarah, the head librarian, that all papers for 2010 had been sent away to be put onto microfilm. I crossed my fingers hoping that 2010 was not the year and loaded the 2008 microfilm rolls onto the viewer. A slow search from January to December revealed nothing. The only interesting thing about 2008 was that I found nothing of interest. This was in itself unusual; perhaps I will look into that in future. It is not the only year to have been uneventful and they too may one day reveal a pattern. One that might in time show us when a window of unexplained activity is due to open. But that would have to wait, for now Wilsthorpe was the target.

A few days later I was back among the microfilm archive, armed with four reels dated 2009. Some may think I am a little dull when I say I actually enjoy skimming through the old papers. You just never know what you are going to find and the archive for 2009 was not about to disappoint me.

Some events from that year opened up other avenues of research, which are unconnected to this particular story. This was when I began to notice reports about cats going missing around the area. It was quite peculiar when the printed copies were laid out and studied. I also noted that the power blackouts and reports of missing cats occurred within the same timeframes. I still have no idea if any of these events are directly connected to the other, but an hour or so later my eyes settled on the front page of the Bridlington Free Press dated September 24th 2009. All appeared quite normal until I saw what was printed on page 31.

Visitors Catch Glimpse of Lynx?

Upon reading this headline I immediately thought I had found another report of a big cat sighting, but as I have already said, I just never know what I will find which is why I love the archives. Big cat stories intrigue me so I began to read the text. This would be well worth the time I had invested searching the archive. However, to my amazement it went on to describe how people in Bridlington had caught sight of two Lynx helicopters and two Chinooks arriving at South Shore at Wilsthorpe on September 15th 2009. Incredible! Eureka! I now had the date I had been looking for. Just when I thought I would have to wait until the 2010 papers returned back to the library on microfilm, this appeared.

This had to be the date I was looking for; it was the closest thing to an official date I was going to find. My years of searching the archives had never revealed a military presence on the beaches around East or North Yorkshire before this. But here was proof that the military did arrive a short time after the UFOs had been seen. It may not have tied the military presence to an incredible UFO account, but it did place many pieces of the jigsaw firmly on the table.

The article stated that helicopters 'swooped' into South Shore at Wilsthorpe. This confirmed Kevin Porter's recollection of the Chinooks landing close to where he was working in the boat compound. In my mind I could hear June talking about the day the army arrived on the beach. The short article described how visitors could be forgiven for thinking they were in a war zone, when a fleet of army helicopters landed at shore for a training exercise at 4pm on Tuesday the 15th.

Free Press, Thursday, September 24, 2009

Visitors catch glimpse of Lynx

VISITORS to Bridlington's South Beach could have been forgiven for thinking they were entering a warzone last week when a fleet of Army helicopters swooped onto the shore. A crowd of up to 50 people gathered to watch the impressive sight of four helicopters – two Chinooks and two Lynxs – circle the skies before landing on the beach for a training exercise at around 4pm last Tuesday.

A few days after finding the article, I visited the RNLI station. I showed the member of staff at the station what I had found and asked if he knew anything about this 'top secret' military exercise from September 2009. He said that as far as he was aware, they knew nothing about it. Although he did remember seeing the helicopters arrive, adding that he had just collected one of his children from school and they rushed to the seafront to watch them go up the coast towards Wilsthorpe. So from that conversation I knew the lifeboat station had not been informed of a large scale military exercise. If they had, it was not passed on to the only full-time member of staff at the station.

I have since spoken with an officer from the Maritime Coastguard Agency who informed me they know months in advance of any military exercises that are going to take place. The officer I spoke with smiled and said he could not comment on the information I was asking about. His smile may have meant nothing, but I think if they *had* been informed they would have told the lifeboat station about it to avoid any confusion. I know from talking to lifeboat men and from reading articles over the years, that the relevant authorities are not always informed of a military exercise. The amount of times that lifeboats are called out to investigate unexplained lights at sea, which are later explained as a military exercise, seem to contradict the coastguard's words.

Flares alert lifeboat crew

Bridlington lifeboat crew were alerted late on Saturday night after Humber coastguards reported flares close inshore just south of Hornsea.

A police patrol car joined coastguard Land-Rovers in a search of the area before it was established that the flares had been part of an Army exercise.

Lifeboat secretary, Mr. A. Dick, said: "It was after midnight before I was able to tell the crew they were not needed. The Army had notified the police of the exercise, but had stated that flares would not be used."

SECOND FLARE COMPLAINT, AND GALE DUTIES FOR LIFEBOAT

Bridlington lifeboat secretary Mr Arthur Dick has complained to R.N.L.I. headquarters about the use of Ministry of Defence flares off Bridlington without warning to local coastguards. The lifeboat recently spent two hours searching the bay, the second launch this year caused by unannounced use of flares.

Coastguards were alerted last week, after red and green flares were seen five miles out, but it was later discovered that they came from an aircraft on exercise.

Mr. Dick has complained to lifeboat headquarters who say they will take the matter up with the Ministry of Defence.

"This sort of thing does happen periodically and it is something which we do want to stamp out," said an R.N.L.I. spokesman in London. "I'm sure that when Mr. Dick's letter is received we will take it up with the Ministry and normally we either receive an apology or they say that the coastguards were informed of the exercise."

Earlier this year the lifeboat was called out after flares were reported off Atwick. Army cadets were responsible, and the R.N.L.I. later received an apology from the Army.

Bridlington lifeboat was launched twice in this week's gales to escort local fishing boats into the harbour

A call for assistance in very rough seas was received on Monday from the keel boat Guide Us

In almost similar conditions next day the lifeboat went to escort the coble Margaret Ann which appeared in difficulties off Hornsea.

The coble was the only Bridlington boat to leave Harbour after a gale force 10 forecast; it was sighted after a search between Spurn and Flamborough by coastguards using Land-Rovers. The lifeboat was out for three hours.

187

I often wonder if the military fail to inform the MCA about manoeuvres over the sea, because at times they have to scramble jets at short notice. Anything suddenly entering UK airspace would need investigation and it would not always be possible to inform the relevant bodies, until after the event. For that reason an 'after the event' staple explanation would be needed. A 'military exercise out at sea' would cover most enquiries.

The military activity of September 2009 was said to be top secret - so secret that they arrived during the day. Their presence must have been considered sensitive or the men at the boat compound would not have been ordered to erase the photographs they took of the helicopters as they arrived. It still puzzles me why Merlin helicopters would be circling my home as they did, they were clearly observing me. I don't know if it is normal practice to fly low over built-up areas with the loading ramps down. Maybe it was something to do with my website being the only place in the world documenting all of the local unexplained activity? Or was I just being paranoid and all this was just a series of coincidences?

Once the story of UFOs over Wilsthorpe began to gather pace, my next job was to untangle the many reports I had received at various times over the seven year period between 2009 and 2016. Maybe this secret military exercise just happened to coincide with the UFO sightings in the months leading up to and beyond the middle of September.

June and Ron's amazing story did tie in with the bait digger's incredible account. It also validated Eileen Hopson's two sightings and all of the others, including the PCSOs strange account from Fraisthorpe. The inside of my head was pinging with information that jumped from one scenario to the other. My brain felt like a knotted ball of string; sometimes I thought I had found another clue, only to find, after picking at the truth, it had been a wasted effort.

I ran so many things backwards and forwards in my mind.
1. Could it be pure coincidence that a large-scale top secret military exercise took place in close proximity to where the UFOs were seen?

2. Could the said UFOs have been a prop, staged by the military to gauge public reaction? The newspaper article stated that over fifty people gathered to watch the helicopters arrive. Fifty people is hardly a town full. The article was only two paragraphs, each containing five lines, so if that was the case it was an epic fail.

3. Multiple objects were seen by people who have no connection to each other. Not only that, but at the same time, the military conducted a top secret exercise that involved them arriving in full public view at 4pm in the afternoon. I wonder what the odds would be of these events coming together by chance. For me the answer every time is 'not a chance'.

4. Had a build-up in UFO activity been taking place around the area to such an extent, that military observation/involvement took place. Was that the reason there were Merlin's were over our home and was ILF-UFO highlighting the activity.

Readers may agree or disagree with any or all of the above. I don't have the answer, I wish I did. Some things seem to unfold in sequences; I first noted this during my work on TP1. One strange event appears to be the tripwire causing a domino effect that produces a whole series of even stranger events. Each one is highly unusual, but when put together as a collection they fall into the abyss that is high strangeness. I realised many years ago that proving the existence of UFOs is virtually impossible, hence this book's title Beyond The Thinking Mind.

My main focus is to find more unexplained events around the same timeframe as, what is considered to be, the major event. If they can be found and they are 'off the scale' of anything considered normal, the case becomes harder for the sceptics and debunkers to dismantle. In short, I try to stack the illogical alongside the logical and let readers make up their own mind. I hope this helps to explain why I shared the archived ILF-UFO reports first. I had to first share the build-up of events, even though they had lain dormant for so many years. It was not until I had identified the year as 2009 that the old reports became relevant.

I think it is highly likely that June and Ron saw the glowing boomerangs at the same time that the bait diggers saw their black triangular-shaped objects entering the sea. I think the military presence confirms this. It connects the two and the Bridlington Free Press article date-stamps these events with Tuesday, September 15th 2009.

Very few people are better placed to see anything unusual from the beaches other than bait diggers, mainly because they work there all year round. The two men employed by Martin Roberts saw their first triangular UFO in daylight, very close to the beachfront flats at

Wilsthorpe. They described the object as being large, black and silent and they saw it actually enter the water without disturbing it. Martin Roberts pointed out something else that was odd in this account; that the sea is so shallow at South Shore. So it would make more sense to say these UFOs entered the sea further out, where it was deeper. But this was not what I was told and I will not change the details to make the story more plausible. Eileen Hopson would also have been watching the objects around the same time, my ILF-UFO website confirms this. How or why they chose that particular location is another mystery.

The military presence witnessed after these sightings is not in doubt. Whether we believe their arrival is pure coincidence or something more is for the individual to decide. Kevin Porter of the yacht club remembers the soldiers being around for a number of days and residents who were in the flats at the time remember the military activity. They also remember June and Ron talking about seeing something very strange, because the day after their sighting June had told their neighbour Frank. Frank has since confirmed to me that June did tell him all about seeing the spaceships over the sea.

Once I had all the information in place, including the dates, I put together this short FOI request to the MOD asking for information relating to a military presence around Wilsthorpe in 2009.

To the Chief Information Officer, MOD:
"Dear Sir or Madam,
I am requesting any information held about a military exercise (or any other military activity) that took place in or around Wilsthorpe on the East Yorkshire coast between September 15th and 18th 2009.
Please acknowledge receipt of this request, I look forward to receiving the information in the near future.
Yours faithfully,
Paul Sinclair"

I think my request was polite and to the point. I did not mention June and Ron's sighting or any unexplained lights. After the standard response time of twenty days had passed and without even receiving an acknowledgment, I decided to follow this up with a phone call. To my surprise the person I spoke to that day seemed to be expecting my call. He knew who I was, even though I had only given my first name - which I think is quite remarkable.

He was apologetic and assured me that my request would be dealt with. His said it had just been overlooked, so I politely accepted this and reminded him they should have responded to my request by October 31st. The days passed and I still heard nothing after my simple request for information. So on November 11th, thirty-two days after my original request, I contacted them again. At this point the only confirmation I had that they were dealing with it, was the verbal acknowledgment that came during the phone conversation. I sent this short follow-up enquiry:

To the Chief Information Officer, MOD:
"Dear Sir or Madam,
I submitted an FOI request on October 11th, requesting information about military activity in or around the Wilsthorpe area of East Yorkshire, on the dates of the 15th, 16th, 17th and 18th of September. I phoned a few weeks ago to inquire why I had not received any correspondence from yourselves as it had gone over 20 days. I was told that you knew about the request and the staff within the department had overlooked it. I am respectfully asking if you have any information regarding my FOI request.
Yours faithfully,
Paul Sinclair"

I am not sure why they took so long to respond but *forty-six* days after my initial request, the long awaited reply came.

OpsDir-parlibusiness@mod.uk via mod.uk
"Dear Mr Sinclair,
please see attached response to your FOI request.
Regards,
Operations Directorate - Ministry of Defence"

I did not know what their reply would consist of, but after taking more than twice as long as usual to respond, I thought it might have at least been a little more interesting.

Ministry
of Defence

Ministry of Defence
Main Building
Whitehall
London SW1A 2HB
United Kingdom

Ref: FOI2016/09440

Telephone [MOD]: 02072189000
E-mail: OpsDir-SC@mod.uk

Mr Paul Sinclair
Flat 1 14 Blackburn Avenue
BRIDLINGTON
East Yorkshire
YO15 2ES

25 November 2016

Dear Mr Paul Sinclair,

Thank you for your email of 11th October 2016 requesting the following information:

I am requesting any information held about a military exercise (or any other military activity) that took place in or around Wilsthorpe on the East Yorkshire coast between the dates of 15th and 18th September 2009.

I am treating your correspondence as a request for information under the Freedom of Information Act 2000 (FOIA). A search for the information has now been completed within the Ministry of Defence, and I can confirm that information in scope of your request is held. An extract of this information is below:

- The exercise on 15th to 18th September 2009 was one of a number carried out on a regular basis by our armed forces as part of their on-going commitment to the defence of the UK.

- While MOD training areas are most often used for training they do not always contain the features required for certain activities. In these cases alternative locations are sought and used with the agreement of landowners where relevant.

- No live ammunition was used on the exercise. Exercising troops were issued with 'blank' simulated ammunition which mimics the sound of firing without any projectile exiting the weapons.

- Any explosions heard were controlled detonations of simulated munitions to assist the exercise.

However, some details of the information you have requested falls entirely within the scope of the qualified exemptions provided for at Section 26 (Defence) of the FOIA and has been withheld. Section 26(1)(b) has been applied to some of the information held because it would reveal considerable detail about Defence's exercise programme and capabilities, which would increase

At least they *had* confirmed the military presence, so that was another piece of the puzzle in place. The mention of 'simulated ammunition' and 'controlled detonations' surprised me, as none of the witnesses I interviewed ever mentioned hearing any sound at the time. I cannot say they are wrong - all I can do is stack the information on either side of the scale, then stand back and observe. After searching the archives and speaking with residents at Wilsthorpe and the surrounding areas, not one person has told me they heard the sound of guns or simulated explosions during that time or at any other time. I thought about the FOI reply for a while. They took forty-six days to reply and the response was not enlightening at all, so on Wednesday December 21st I decided to ask a few more questions.

To the Operations Directorate, MOD:
"Dear sir/madam,
thank you for the reply to my FOI request sent October 11th asking for information about military activity during September 2009. You reply was helpful, however I ask the question; if this was a top secret military exercise, as you imply, why arrive in the afternoon and land Lynx and Chinook helicopters on a public beach in full public view?
The Bridlington RNLI was unaware of any military exercise and I am told the Royal Yacht Club, whose slipway was used to access the beach from the road, were also unaware. Your reply makes reference to any guns heard being dummy rounds and any explosions heard being from simulated munitions. Yet no one reported hearing any guns or explosions and the helicopters and military personnel were on the beach in front of 16 private flats that overlook the sea at Wilsthorpe.
Regards, Paul Sinclair"

Below is the reply I received on Thursday January 5th 2017;

"Dear Mr. Sinclair,
thank you for your email dated 21 December following our response to your Freedom of Information request.
For the reasons outlined in the formal FOI response it is not possible to provide further clarity to your questions.
Regards,
Operations Directorate - Ministry of Defence."

Over the months and years that follow I am sure that more information will come to light about the Wilsthorpe incident. I hope after reading the information I have shared, readers might think there is more to the story. I feel sure that the evidence is overwhelming in support of genuine UFO activity. If some prefer to believe the military presence occurred quite by chance, then that is fine. I cannot prove otherwise and will not attempt to. If those in power choose to remain tight-lipped, there is nothing that any number of FOI requests can do to change this.

The Liverpool Link

During the latter part of my investigations, while searching for further UFO-related activity from 2009, additional information came to light. I discovered there had been a rise in sightings in the North-West of England, with Liverpool in particular appearing to have had more than its share of activity at that time.

I discovered the following account in MOD files available online. It is an interesting report by a police officer from Liverpool, which may link with events at Wilsthorpe.

Reported sighting in Formby, Merseyside - September 25th 2009
"An off-duty police officer PC Steve Miles observed a silent triangular-shaped UFO that made no noise and had no navigation lights. He was certain it wasn't an aircraft, as it passed over the skies of Formby in Merseyside. A week earlier the Press had reported that a member of the public had seen a similar object."

Admittedly the police officer who saw this triangular object was on the other side of the country; some 120 miles away as the crow flies, but it is nevertheless, an interesting sighting. His description of the object seems very similar to those witnessed by the bait diggers at Wilsthorpe and by the PCSO at Fraisthorpe. Another coincidence maybe, but when I did a little more research into the report it appears the area around Liverpool was also having a huge amount of unexplained sightings.

I wonder how long it would have taken such an object to get from point A to point B? Due to the date of the sighting and the credibility of the witness the possibility of this being connected has to be considered. It is also worth pointing out that the Liverpool sightings received quite a bit of media coverage at the time. I recall Chinese lanterns being used as an explanation for many of the reports. The bait diggers saw the triangular UFOs a week prior to this sighting and described them as being black with no navigation lights or windows and the PCSO at Fraisthorpe described something similar. For those who believe this is coincidence, then this case is closed – and that goes for all the reports from 2009, which must also be classified as misidentification and inaccurate reporting and research.

Help from Mr X

Over the years I have become acquainted with a few former lifeboatmen and coastguards. I even have a collection of reported sightings from a former lighthouse keeper. Many of these people have now retired. For those who think outside of the fixed mindset these are never good career options and for that reason many of the reports I receive come years after the event.

I was given this next piece of the puzzle from one such person during 2017. In the past we have spoken about many things and this person has been helpful on more than one occasion, particularly when I was looking into the Tornado crashes of ZE723 and ZA610. Our conversations usually touched on the unexplained, but sometimes months would pass without any further contact and I would never push for information. Sometime early into 2017 I received a phone call, the caller told me of some information that would be of interest. I put the phone on loudspeaker and took down the following notes as we spoke. For ease of reading and to maintain anonymity I will refer to this person as 'X'

"Hello Paul? It's 'X' here. Just thought I'd give you a call see how you're doing. Did you get any further with that stuff you were looking into around Wilsthorpe?"

After a few pleasantries X began to tell me something about the events of September 2009.
"Whatever it is that those witnesses were telling you Paul, let me just say this, I don't think they were lying. Now I am not sure what was happening but it was not normal, I can tell you that for sure. I am in no position to say what or who was responsible, but I would say most of the people who told you about the things they saw were probably telling the truth. Something happened that they do not want made public."

I said that I would be submitting a few FIO requests in the future and that's where we left our conversation. X knew the approximate dates because I had previously talked about Ron and June's experience. I also mentioned the PCSO's encounter with the triangle over Fraisthorpe, but that was where we left things. A few days passed and I received a second call from X. What I heard next was a big surprise.

"Paul after we last spoke I decided to ask a few questions, pull a few strings and see if I could find out anything. I am interested in this. After I had seen all the evidence you had gathered and the stuff on your old website I could not help myself. I think you might have stumbled onto something that was supposed to remain hidden, I really do. You better be careful. I was told that a lot of the information around the dates you were looking at had been put into protected archive. So for that reason not much could be seen - but that tells me something important happened to place so much secrecy around it."

Protected archive? This suggests something that has to remain hidden and if it is in the interests of national security I would strongly agree. I would never advocate searching for anything illegally, but what if it contained UFO-related information? What if some of the reports that came to my website in 2009 were mixed in with the information or at the very least, information that confirmed what I had shared on the old site. Would that be considered so sensitive that it had to be placed in a protected archive? These are UFOs after all, which are of no interest to our government, right? A quick look back at the RAF Staxton Wold response letter earlier in the book would suggest otherwise.

I wondered if placing information into a protected archive was a recent thing? Could that have been the reason why my first FOI request took forty-six days to come back to me; more than double the time it should have taken? It still puzzles me why, when I phoned to enquire about that FOI request, the man I spoke to seemed instantly aware of who I was. These are all questions that will remain unanswered. Perhaps if they were answered, it would prove that many of the events reported in 2009 were in fact true. My friend X told me there was another bit of information I would find of interest.

"One bit of information that will interest you Paul fits in with the information you already have. It surprised me if I am honest. It's a transcript from a 999 call that came in around the time you were receiving all those reports. It was a night-time call from someone who lived close to the chalets at South Shore."

When I heard this I instantly thought of June and Ron. It had to be June who had made this 999 [emergency] call, although she made no mention of making such a call when we spoke.

" I cannot give an exact location Paul and the names have been redacted. But the caller was taken seriously. They described seeing three globes of orange light travelling down the coast towards Wilsthorpe. They wondered if they could be flares of some kind. It does not sound like that was the case Paul, because next thing was that two more [lights] were [seen] travelling up the coast from the opposite direction.

Now this next bit is even more interesting and made my eyebrows raise up. Paul, you told me about people seeing those black triangles over the sea? That's what most of this Wilsthorpe stuff is about right? Well this caller goes on to say that the flares [orange spheres] looked like they were going to meet up with something hovering over the sea. This is the bit that will interest you and made me raise my eyebrows, apparently both sets of lights were travelling towards something that looks like a black yacht sail over the sea. The name has been redacted Paul, but that's how it reads. You're onto something mate, not sure what, but you have found something. Be careful Paul."

I was amazed to hear this. It did tie in with everything I had found and been told previously. The 999 caller could not have been June. Her description of the objects was different. but no less amazing. A black yacht sail? This was a triangle over the sea by any other name. And the orange globes of light travelling towards it from opposite directions has to rule out flares - it certainly rules out Chinese lanterns!
When I last spoke with X I explained that the response letter I received after my FOI request stated that all relevant authorities would have been informed about a military exercise. X said there was no information to indicate if this was true or false. The information X shared was the kind I needed to hear after spending so long looking for clues.

The Military Presence

The military presence was key to dating what I felt were the most important events. The bait diggers' black triangle sightings were over a two day period on September 14th and 15th 2009. They told Martin Roberts they had seen it twice and on both occasions it had entered the sea off Wilsthorpe. June and Ron's sighting of the boomerangs had to be on the 14th because June is certain the army arrived the next day which was the 15th. This ties in with the bait diggers, who told Martin that the army removed them from the beach. The Bridlington Free Press article confirmed that the helicopters arrived on the 15th. Add to this Eileen Hopson's incredible account within the same timeframe and considering the archived reports throughout 2009 and we have a good case for the Wilsthorpe UFO incident.

Someone made a call made to the emergency services and described seeing spheres of light moving towards a black 'yacht sail' object over the sea. This fact proves there was another first-hand witness living close by - someone who, for the moment, remains elusive and silent.

Any sighting, if genuine, warrants attention, but I think the Wilsthorpe case and all its associated reports exceed all others. If we accept that the witness accounts are true, then the possibilities are endless. But what was so important about East Yorkshire in 2009? Something wanted or allowed the intelligence behind the UFOs to show themselves to so many people - but what was it?

Could a gateway of some kind exist in this area; an entrance to another dimension? If triangular-shaped objects entered the sea where it is too shallow to conceal anything, where did they go? I would think that if the bait diggers made up that story, they would have at least agreed to say the objects disappeared in water deep enough to conceal a large object.

I began to wonder if this technology was so far ahead of our own understanding, that if used in these areas of high strangeness, they might use it to pass from our world to theirs whenever they choose. A theory is hardly proof, but they only ever leave us with a visual imprint and a location to go on. I spent many hours talking with Martin, asking and re-asking the same questions. Did he recall his men saying anything about lights on the objects or hearing a sound as they entered the sea?

"No lights or sounds were ever mentioned Paul - and I would have remembered, because they talked about nothing else for weeks after they had seen the bloody things. And that's another thing; the water is too shallow where them things went in. They should have crashed. It's just not deep enough. So where did they go?"

Martin believes his men when they say they saw the black triangle at Wilsthorpe during low tide. He says it must have been approaching low tide, otherwise there would have been no point in them being on the beach in the first place. They dig for bait at low tide, because the tides dictate their work pattern, both night and day.

He explained to me how shallow this area of sea actually is; "The sea is very shallow off Wilsthorpe even at high tide. With chest-high waders you could walk for a considerable distance out into the sea, before you got into water any deeper than chest height. That's why those things going into the water, where they did, was even stranger. I mean, where did they go? They should have been able to see them in the water, even at low tide. It does not make any sense to me. But then again, why would it? These things were nothing man-made."

Martin's observations are interesting on many levels; he puts faith in the detailed accounts of his men, he even considers the objects are not manmade, but he still struggles with what he considers to be possible.

So is he right and the triangular-shaped objects actually entered the water much further out than low tide? I am not suggesting this is what I believe, but how they could slip below the surface in water that is not deep enough to conceal them? The men had already told an unbelievable story, then made it even harder to accept by saying the objects vanished in shallow water - but these are not the first reports of dark objects entering the sea close to this location. In TP1 I wrote about the crash of Tornado ZE732. During my research into this tragedy, I learned that local fishermen saw black triangular-shaped objects entering the water.

Martin remarked that if the object entered the water at mid-tide it would have been *fully* visible at low tide, due to how shallow the water was. So for that reason he thinks they may have entered the sea further out than the low water. I have to stress that this was his own theory. I think it is an excellent example of a very human attempt at trying to make something fit into what is believed to be the only possibility.

He had already explained that these were big tides, which meant, at low water the sea went out further than normal. This throws confusion onto June and Ron's sighting of the boomerangs. June said they were close because she could see them clearly without binoculars. Yet, during our conversations, she never mentioned seeing the objects enter the sea.

I wondered whether the tides themselves could have actually played some part in the appearance of these UFOs. The intelligence behind them is currently beyond our understanding, but we can speculate that it must have already known the best conditions and times to do the things it needed to do.

For example, June's husband Ron believed the UFOs were taking something from the sea. So I wonder if we worked with information relating to tide times, it might even be possible to predict future sightings, no matter how random. This would involve searching through archives for similar historical incidents. We would need to look for patterns that show a build-up of activity along with indications of the prime conditions when these objects are seen.

An impossible task for one researcher to do alone, but as a collective it may be possible. I think an object that is capable of making a controlled entry into the North Sea would be more than capable of moving below its surface with ease. For that reason I would not expect it to be visible at low tide or at any other time, before or after.

I will never fall into the trap of thinking that everything we experience has to fit into current human understanding - and this sighting was outside of that perimeter. We just have to accept that, for some unknown reason, the area around Wilsthorpe is the place they chose. But there has to be a reason why unexplained objects are seen entering and leaving the sea along this stretch of coastline. Perhaps in this research we should extend the theory of prime conditions and add additional key locations to our search? The odds may be great but at least we could narrow down the variables by concentrating on the prime locations.

The bait diggers estimated the size of the black triangles to be no more than 30ft long by 20ft wide. They said they displayed no visible means of propulsion, did not appear to have windows and were just seamless solid black triangles. If it was a failed experimental aircraft, this does not explain how they saw it more than once and it does not explain the glowing boomerangs witnessed by June and Ron - which have to be linked to the objects seen by the 999 caller.

We have to remember this is a public beach, but at no time did anyone report seeing any military warning signs advising people to stay away. There were no Ministry of Defence signs displayed on the road down to the beach either. This is something to consider when reflecting on the reply I received to my FOI request in October 2016, which said, *"locations are sought with the agreement of landowners"*; implying that people who may be affected by the exercise had been informed. The response also stated that *"troops were issued with 'blank' simulated ammunition"* and *"any explosions heard"* were *"simulated"*.

Through my interviews with some members of the Royal Yorkshire Yacht Club I learned there were some restrictions. Those I interviewed told me they were barred from going near the beach and even told to keep away from their own clubhouse. They explained they had been camping on their own land, near to an abandoned farmhouse, on the day the army arrived. And although the Yacht Club had been informed the day before that the military would be arriving, it seems this message had not been passed on to their members. Those I spoke with told me the army's arrival was totally unexpected, because they knew nothing about it.

One of the members told me he saw two military wagons arrive with a jeep and they used the slipway from the beach to get onto the field where the clubhouse is situated. He said that one of the wagons was loaded with electrical equipment and it was reversed up to the door of the wooden clubhouse and unloaded. He watched as their clubhouse was taken over and used as an operations room by the military.

He told me that soldiers came to the gates that cross the slipway and told them no one could enter. They were barred from going near the beach and barred from going anywhere near their own clubhouse, which is positioned right next to the beachfront flats overlooking the sea. He said, *"It was all hush hush. They did not want anyone to know they were there."* He said he believed that they came without notice because something had landed or had come down in the water.

Next page: recent photo of yacht club member's wooden clubhouse.

Dean Dealtry's Sighting

I still find it amazing that so much information can emerge from one area. In February 2017 I was ready to close the story of the Wilsthorpe incident and move on to another part of the book, when another interesting piece of the puzzle appeared that I knew had to be included.

I received a report of strange activity over Wilsthorpe from a former security guard named Dean Dealtry, who worked for many years at Bridlington Links Golf Club.

In 2009 I had not met Dean, but knew of his keen interest in UFOs through a work colleague who knew him very well. I heard about the things Dean regularly saw while he worked his night shifts at the golf club. Because of Dean's interest in UFOs, his job gave him the perfect opportunity to view the night skies, which he did every day regardless of weather conditions, whilst getting paid in the process. He even had his own YouTube channel with clips of many unexplained lights and unusual aircraft that he was able to catch on camera in the area.

Dean knew of my own interests and was keen to find out what I had been observing. In 2017 he asked to join me on a skywatch, so we arranged to go up to Bempton Cliffs. That night we spent several hours talking about the lightforms seen over the sea. Dean asked if I intended to write another book after TP1 and I told him I was almost finished the second book. Then I began to tell him about the story I was currently working on; the incident at Wilsthorpe.

I was surprised to learn that in 2009 Dean had actually been able to film some night-time manoeuvres involving helicopters over Wilsthorpe. Almost seven years later the significance of what he saw would become another piece of the puzzle that formed the Wilsthorpe incident.

Bridlington Links Golf Course is situated next to Danes Dyke, between Bridlington and Flamborough, just four miles from Wilsthorpe. It has amazing views up and down the coast and Wilsthorpe can easily be seen, even on a dark overcast night. Just behind Wilsthorpe, a few miles further down the coast, are wind turbines close to the village of Leven. The bright red lights on the top of the turbines gave Dean the perfect reference point for what he filmed in September 2009.

I told him about the black triangular-shaped UFOs and about June and Ron's sighting of the boomerangs. When I mentioned the helicopters he interrupted, *"Paul I saw them. I saw the helicopters mate. Gunships, like the ones we saw over the Wolds last year."*

When I met up with Dean a second time I showed him the Bridlington Free Press article that described the two Chinooks and two Lynx helicopters seen by the public. Dean insisted that the two he saw were gunships, because they had rockets or gun attachments on either side. The newspapers had never made any reference to the Merlin helicopters I filmed directly over my own home, so I could not argue with him about what he said. If he said they were gunships, then that's what they probably were.

"I remember seeing them going up the coast Paul. It was in the afternoon, because I remember coming out of my flat to watch them. More had already passed over, so it's possible I missed the Chinooks, but the ones I saw were definitely gunships. I have no idea what type of helicopters though. "

It is impossible to say whether the helicopters Dean described to me were armed with live ammunition or not, but he seemed sure about what he saw.

"I filmed the helicopters over Wilsthorpe with my Yukon Ranger night vision camera Paul, and guess what? I caught two balls of light in the same footage just above them. I never saw the balls of light at the time, but they are definitely there on the footage. I uploaded it onto my YouTube channel and other people soon took an interest. It was some keen-eyed enthusiast going through the film with a fine-tooth comb who first discovered the balls of light.
They were right too. Because once it had been broken down, frame-by-frame, the objects above the helicopters were there to see. I still have the footage. Sometime after that my Youtube channel got closed down. I'm not saying that was the reason, because I have no idea why they closed it. I never thought it could have anything to do with the helicopter footage until now. Paul, that YouTube channel was monetized and it had literally hundreds of thousands of hits, but it got closed down without any reason I can think of."

When Dean's information was placed alongside the other reports I had gathered, the end result was a catalogue of unexplained events that no one understood or realised at the time. They were linked by so many clues, but also isolated, by the distance we often put between ourselves and the unexplained. Of course, if this was something more acceptable to our understanding, then I am sure many more people would have reported these things to the newspapers. However, the events that make up the Wilsthorpe incident were different. These sightings left witnesses scratching their heads and squinting into the night sky. It was all definitely happening, but it defied explanation. Were all these things connected? I think so.

We had an alleged top-secret military exercise, police scientific investigations vans parked in remote areas, reports of black triangles entering the sea and multiple boomerang-shaped UFOs over the sea. Together with the archived UFO reports from my website, which were unchanged since 2009, no matter how far all of this stretches our beliefs, these events happened.

The Hunmanby Boomerangs

On the night of December 8th 2014 residents of Scarborough and the surrounding areas saw an object in the sky that defied all explanation – and it was seen by too many people to be considered misidentification.

They described a huge boomerang-shaped object moving slowly through the early evening sky. The first witness reports came from motorists and pedestrians in Valley Bridge, Scarborough. It was then seen two miles away over Scarborough Mere, as it headed out towards Staxton and Hunmanby. Whether this object is related to those seen over Wilsthorpe four years earlier is a question I cannot answer. I am only sharing the details here because of their similarity and high strangeness.

Jonathan Ellison was driving along Cayton Low Road. He was taking his wife and their young son back home to their farm in Hunmanby. It was early evening on December 8th 2014 and he remembers it was a bitterly cold and crisp night. The sky was clear and filled with stars and the surrounding roads and fields were white with snow and ice. During the journey Jonathan became aware of something very large and stationary in the sky ahead of them; he thinks the time was around 7pm.

At first, what he saw was just an odd combination of red and white lights that seemed to be in a fixed position or moving so slowly, that they appeared to be fixed. It just looked strange. He could not remember seeing anything like it before. They were very low in the sky and if all the lights were part of one object, he said the area it covered was huge. He said it seemed impossible that anything that large could be that low.

As the car got a little closer, Jonathan and his family could tell the object was slowly moving away from them. They also realised, from its direction of travel, that it appeared to be heading in the direction of their family's farm. Without a second thought he pulled the car over to call his mother and stepfather, who he knew would be at home. He wanted them to see it, but the thought of trying to explain it to them afterwards would not be easy; they had to see it with their own eyes.

When Jonathan arrived home, his mother and stepfather were waiting outside. The object was now just a distant set of lights slipping away into the night, but he hoped they had been able to get a good look at it. *"Did you see it? What was it? You must have seen it, it was so big."*

Boomerang-shaped object, sketched by Jonathan on the night of the sighting.

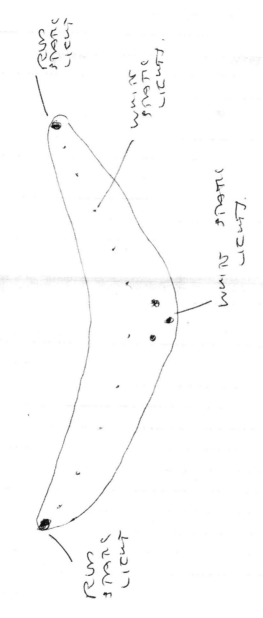

His stepfather explained what happened.

*"After you phoned it had already passed the farm and was heading towards Joe's farm. I don't know what it was, but it was big. All we could see was a massive, dark boomerang shape moving into the distance. If it was not for the lights we would have missed it. You were right, it was very low and we never heard a sound. What do you think it could have been Jonathan? You got a better look at it than us. Was it a UFO? I don't know what else it could it have been. Did you see the size of it?"*Jonathan told me he had no idea what they had seen. He just knew they had witnessed something highly unusual.

The family decided it was pointless standing outside any longer, the moment had passed and it was bitterly cold. They phoned their friend Joe who lived at a neighbouring farm, to let him know what they had seen and to urge him to be vigilant in case it passed over his farm. I was able to speak with Joe on two occasions myself and, although he was unable to meet me in person, he did confirm what the Ellisons had told me. He said he did see the object, but it was not as close as the sighting that Jonathan and his family had.

Joe said that something else unusual happened on the night the object was seen; something he could not explain. He told me he has two wind turbines on his farm, which have been trouble-free since they were first installed. Yet for some reason, on the night the object appeared in the sky, the two wind turbines stopped turning. It is impossible to say whether the object was responsible for stopping Joe's turbines. This was the first time they had ever failed and it has not happened since. Was it just coincidence or did the UFO have some kind of effect on the turbines? I think this is one of those occasions where I have to jump off the fence and say yes, I think something connected to the object caused these wind turbines to stop working.

Whatever energy or force it emitted must have been powerful to have such an effect. This makes me wonder whether being in close proximity to these objects could be a danger to health. I have no idea what technology could create a machine so huge that is able to travel silently through our skies. The wind turbines are at a higher elevation, therefore closer to the object, so perhaps this had some bearing on the process. I thought about Lesley Buttle's account from 1977 (described in TP1), where an unknown object was said to have stopped clocks, watches and machines at a nearby factory. So I knew that any combination of effects were possible if the unknowns ever came into contact with humans or machinery. I do not know whether Joe had to get his two turbines repaired after the UFO had passed or whether they simply started turning again.

Word of the huge UFO spread that night, and it was not long before more local farms were contacted and advised to look out for the strange silent craft. Just a few miles away from Hunmanby is another family-owned farm, where the object's presence may have been responsible for another equally strange occurrence that night. No one can say with any certainty that the UFO was directly responsible for what happened, but I think there is a strong possibility that it was. The third farmer told me he never saw the object, but he believes it may have been in close proximity because of what happened.

He told me they had a child's battery operated train - the rechargeable type that a child would sit on and ride – which had not worked for a long time and was in need of repair. In fact, they were advertising it for sale online at the time. I was told that, at some point during the evening, the toy suddenly came to life when its lights began to flash on and off. The family were shocked because it had not worked for as long as they could remember. Then after a minute or so, the lights on the toy went off and it returned to being broken again.

The UFO was the topic of conversation in the Ellison household the rest of the night. They were actually annoyed with themselves that they had not managed to get a good look at it. Sometime after 9pm Jonathan's stepfather went outside to smoke a cigarette. The temperature had been below freezing all day and the land seemed locked in an eerie silence as he stepped into the darkness. Thoughts of the boomerang-shaped UFO were still on his mind and at first he did not notice the unusual sound. Then he realised he could hear a faint humming, but so faint, that it almost seemed part of the silence.

As he smoked his cigarette, he looked up into the sky – which was now partly obscured by a huge dark mass above him. He called to his family and moments later they were all outside looking up at an unbelievable sight. The UFO was back. I think it must have been an incredible sight. They described it to me as being close in size to jumbo jet and the only sound it made was a gentle hum, as it hung motionless in the air - less than 500ft above them. Trying to guess why it was there was as pointless as trying to guess where it came from, who made it or where it went afterwards.

Just a few miles away from the Ellison farm is RAF Staxton Wold radar base. Is it possible that something the size of this UFO could have gone undetected? Are we to believe it literally slipped under their radar - even though it affected all things electrical it came into contact with that night in December 2014? The Ellisons estimated the object was about 500ft above them as they watched it. So surely the radar equipment at the nearby base would have detected it?

The Ellison family watched the unmoving UFO for over five minutes as it hung in the sky above their farm. Even though it was so huge, it would probably still have gone unnoticed, if not for the low-pitched humming sound it made. I asked Jonathan if he could tell me more about the object. I was interested to know if its lights flashed or were different in any way to other lights they were used to seeing in the night sky. The lightforms seen from Bempton and Speeton are very intense and vibrant, but Jonathan said the lights on this object were more dull than bright. He said it had a bank of three white lights in the centre and a single red light on either end, with smaller white lights between them.

He did not recall anything about it that resembled a conventional aircraft and none of its lights were flashing. In between there were a series of smaller white lights dotted around the main body of the UFO. He says overall it was a dark graphite-grey colour, with a very slight sheen. I asked if he could tell what he thought it might have been made of. I realise it was not really possible for him to give me an answer. He said he would need to have touched it to tell me that, but I still wanted his opinion. All he could say was that it appeared solid and very dense-looking; definitely a solid structured craft. His family did not notice any unusual smells from the UFO and it gave them no clues how it was able to hang motionless in the air.

Next page: impression of the object, as seen over the Ellison family farm.

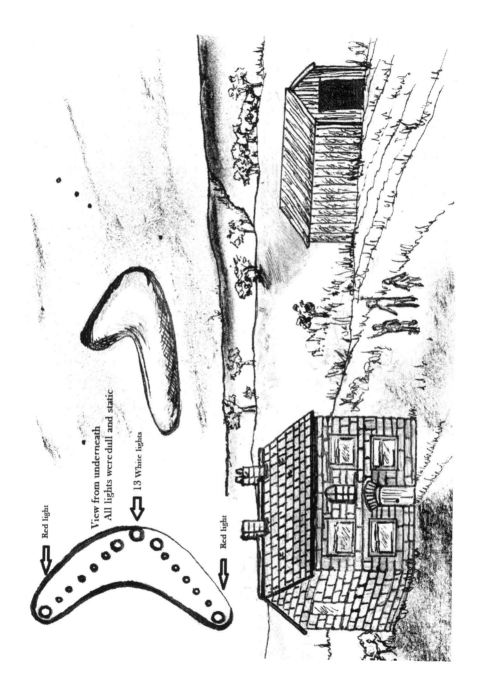

View from underneath
All lights were dull and static

Red light

13 White lights

Red light

213

I am convinced the Ellisons saw exactly what they described. If they were all of the opinion this object was man-made, then we have some incredible technology that should perhaps be made public. However, my own instincts tell me that this was something else. I don't want to jump onto the UFO bandwaggon and claim that every strange light in the sky is a spaceship from another planet - if the witnesses were all of the opinion this was a man-made craft, then that is exactly what I would report here, but this was not the case.

The Ellisons were convinced it was not man-made - but if this craft was one of our own, would its owners risk an accident by flying it so low over a populated area? I cannot imagine the sight of something that size coming down over a village like Hunmanby. Jonathan said that after his family had watched the object for a short time, it gradually moved away in the direction of the coast. It moved slowly and the humming sound never changed. It is possible there were more witnesses to this object that night. In time I hope they can find the courage to contact me so we can fit more pieces of this puzzle into the picture.

Body Found at Staxton Wold

December 8th 2014 proved to be a strange day in more ways than anyone could ever have imagined. Earlier that day, retired factory worker Alan Wilkinson left his home on Cayton Low Road to go for a walk. He was 65 years old and a few days earlier had been celebrating 44 years of marriage to his wife.

The weather conditions that morning were terrible, with snow and ice on the roads and fields, but Mr Wilkinson was a keen walker so there was no real cause for concern. But when he never arrived home later that day his family became worried. As night approached and he still had not returned, they became increasing concerned for his well being. The police, along with Scarborough and District Search and Rescue and members of RAF Leeming all began extensive searches in the area, but failed to find any trace of Mr Wilkinson. It was as though he had vanished off the face of the earth.

The last reported sighting of Mr Wilkinson was on December 8th at around 9.15am. He was described as wearing a blue checked shirt, jeans and a black jacket. He also wore a green body-warmer, black woollen hat and hiking boots. From this description, it would appear that Alan Wilkinson was dressed in suitable clothing for such a walk.

On January 16th 2015 police were informed that a body had been found in the woods at Staxton Wold. It was thought that it may have been the body of Mr Wilkinson. I understand that whoever found the body was out shooting game in a private area of woodland adjoining Staxton and Flixton Wold. The body was later identified as that of Alan Wilkinson, who was found away from the main path with his boots and some clothing removed. I am told that a possible reason for this removal of clothing may be due to the onset of hyperthermia. At the inquest, the coroner recorded a verdict of suicide.

There was evidence Mr Wilkinson had a disagreement with his wife the night before he went missing and there was evidence of alcohol and prescription pills near to where he was found. The report does not state if the alcohol and pills belonged to Mr Wilkinson but, due to the final verdict, we have to assume they did. This would therefore make the coroners verdict entirely accurate.

Mr. Wilkinson was known to have heart problems and tired very easily, so I cannot understand how he could have made that journey up onto Staxton Wold - especially in bad weather conditions. This does not mean to say he was unable to make it, but I challenge anyone who tires easily to attempt that walk in icy conditions.

The walking distance from Cayton Low Road to the area of Staxton Wold where Mr Wilkinson was found is over six miles. I have visited that remote area of woodland many times in the past and even though I consider myself to be quite fit, each and every time, the climb leaves me breathless. I cannot dispute the verdict, but I find it hard to imagine how a man who tired easily could reach that part of the woods in such terrible weather conditions. The incline from the foot of Staxton Wold to the top is a steep and uneven 500ft climb. With treacherous ice and snow already on the low lying land, it would have been far, far worse on Staxton Wold. The highest point of land in the area is where we find RAF Staxton Wold, which is also close to where the body was found.

Some may think my research is a leap too far into the darkness, but there is no escaping the fact that December 8th 2014 was a day of high strangeness. I have no evidence that links together any of the events of that day, except the location and the date, but just because something cannot be understood, does not mean it should be overlooked. We cannot see past the horizon, but we know there is more beyond it. All of these unknowns are just as real, it is only the understanding that is missing. What is it about these locations? Why Bempton? Why Staxton Wold? The questions have to be asked, re-asked and asked again, until a speck of light appears so that we are not just leaping into the darkness.

It is interesting to note that the area the Ellison family saw their UFO and the location Mr Wilkinson's body was found, is the same area where many accounts of the Flixton Werewolf originate and phantom big cats are seen. I am not proposing there is a connection between any of these things, but location often proves to be key. The land is littered with ancient burial mounds and earthworks - evidence of earlier man's association with the land. They are remnants of the past, which linger like ghosts to remind us they were once considered important places and they still are. We may not look upon them with the same awe as our ancestors, but these places are still producing jaw-dropping moments that continue to defy all explanations.

UFO Near RAF Base

Close to where these strange events took place, other unusual things were observed in the sky in December 2014. I received the following account from a couple who live close to RAF Staxton Wold. I consider it quite significant and was pleased the main witness took the time to write up this short report. They are a very private couple who rarely talk openly about such things. Although in September 2007 they did contact me to report a previous sighting which I published in TP1 under the title 'Encounter at Staxton Wold'.

Saturday, December 13th 2014 – 5.30am

"At 5.30am I opened the curtains to the bedroom that faces south-east. The sky was clear and stars were easily visible. It was still dark, but to the east the sky was slightly lighter. This was well before sunrise. We have a very good view of the sky and observe it on a daily basis, early each morning and at night, and have been doing so for the last eight years. We have no light pollution, other than traffic that passes on the A1249 road.

On this occasion, from that particular window, I noticed an unusual 'fuzzy' patch of light in the sky to the south-east. I expected it to be a cluster of stars, although I do not remember ever seeing it before. Through binoculars this fuzzy patch of light turned out to be something that looked like the bottom-left quarter of a round object, with a bright but still slightly fuzzy light shining from it. (See sketch on next page)

To the right, above and below it was dark, as if in shadow, but I could still see stars in the vicinity of it. As I watched, a white/silver light about the size of a star, came out of the shadow below and passed quite quickly across it, going from right to left. I wondered if I could see this without binoculars but I could not. As I continued to watch I realised the object was moving very slowly from left to right - but it was <u>behind</u> the stars, because I saw a normal star moving left to right in front of it! It continued to move very slowly from left to right and also upwards and backwards, just fading slightly as it did.

At 6am I went outside and without binoculars could still see the fuzzy patch. Unfortunately I could not spend any more time observing it, but

*each morning since then, if the sky has been clear, I look for this object
but have not seen anything unusual."*

I cannot explain what this lady witnessed that morning and I doubt
anyone will ever be able to explain it. Unless other witnesses come
forward or we learn more about what happened, her unusual account
just adds to the mystery surrounding the events of December 2014.

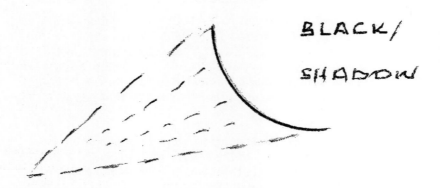

BLACK/

SHADOW

If You Go Down To The Cliffs Today...

There is often so much unusual activity around the Bempton Cliffs area I take every opportunity I can to go there, both day and night. I think good footage of the lightforms was my main goal for a time. Too many people see them for us to deny their existence is a reality. I just needed to catch them on film. I was sure that eventually my efforts would pay off and I would be rewarded by capturing something on film that was otherworldly. Even if that 'something' may lack an explanation, at least it would be undeniable.

On the evening of Saturday December 10th 2016 I went to the RSPB reserve with my friend Andi Ramsden. Earlier that week I received a phone call from Steve Cooper, a sea angler up at Speeton, who told me he had seen the lightforms. He even sent me some rough footage that he managed to capture using the camera on his mobile phone. Although the footage was poor, it did show the lights appearing out of the darkness and then vanishing just as quickly. With all my cameras charged and ready, I was happy that if something should appear, I would have the best chance of filming it.

The lightforms seem to appear at anytime during the hours of darkness or in the evening. If they constantly showed up at the same regular time, I would have to conclude that there would have to be a more Earthly explanation for them. However, this has never been the case and I am not so foolish that I would devote so much of my life in the pursuit of these anomalies, if I thought there was no real mystery to be discovered.

We arrived at the deserted car park of Bempton Nature Reserve at around 5.20pm and made our way to one of the cliff-edge viewing platforms. A short time later, with tripods set and camcorders in place, we settled our eyes on the North Sea and the surrounding area. It was a very dark night; quite overcast and bitterly cold. We could hear gunshots in the distance up towards Speeton, which was to the left of us. A twelve-bore I think, someone shooting rabbits no doubt. An hour had passed with nothing more than that distant gunshot to break the silence. I glanced down at my watch and its green dials glowed, revealing the time was 6.45pm.

A few more minutes passed and something caught my eye about fifty metres away to the right of us. It was a large shape that just seemed to appear from the edge of the cliffs. Something was running on all fours and fast. My immediate thought was a deer. I could not think of anything else big enough to fit the profile, but it was very dark, too dark to say for sure. Whatever this thing was, it was light coloured and that puzzled me. It covered a great distance in a short time, but I saw enough to definitely notice its colour.

For a moment my mind switched to Danes Dyke and the stories of the Danes Dyke Werewolf. I am not saying I saw a werewolf, because it was too dark and chances are, it was just a deer, but the stories played over in my mind. When it first caught my eye, the creature just sprung into life from the edge of the cliff; which has a sheer 200ft drop. Whatever this was also cleared the forty-two-inch-high wooden fence along the cliff's perimeter. Of course, this is something a deer would have no problem doing. I pointed it out in the darkness, urging Andi to look for himself. In truth, it was only because it caught my eye on the clifftop that I saw it at all, although I was still able to make out a vague shape as it ran into the distance.

This is where the story would have ended; a deer that suddenly appeared and ran off into the darkness. It was an unusual place to appear from, but apart from the light colour and it being quite heavy on its feet, there was nothing else that would make me think it might have been anything else. Andi and I stayed on the clifftops for over three hours that night, both of us hoping the lightforms would show up. At around 9pm the cloudy and overcast conditions took a turn for the worse and it began to drizzle with rain. That was my cue to pack away the cameras and tripods and within five minutes we were heading back up the path towards the car park.

Apart from the 'deer' sighting earlier in the evening, we had seen nothing of interest. Half way up the path I reached up and switched on my head torch. It has a very wide and powerful beam that lights up a large area. I stopped to let the light sweep the darkness and turned my head towards the old RAF base. Turning the other way I looked towards Flamborough and my torch beam reached out across the field known, on old maps, as the Leys. Then I stopped dead in my tracks.

"Can you see them?" I said to Andi in a slow quiet tone. Andi looked in the direction of my torch beam. *"Wow! What's that? What is it Paul?"*

What we saw were a pair of eyes glowing back at us; two large oval eyes that were only about 200ft away. I set my equipment box on the ground and we both fixed our own eyes on those that glared back at us. They were definitely not the eyes of a deer and whatever they belonged to blinked from time to time, in an almost slow and lazy way. We both agreed that the colour was a pinkish-white and looking at their size and the space between them, the creature's head must have been quite large. At one point it appeared to lower its head then lift it up again but it did not seem too fazed by our presence. In the past we have seen the eye-shine of badgers, foxes and deer, but this was different.

I opened the box of equipment and quickly took out my Canon 1200D camera. It was not suitable for the job but it was worth a try, even if the images turned out to be poor. Andi wanted to go back to the car and said so several times, but I had not just spent over three hours waiting in the cold to waste this opportunity.
"I'm going to see if I can get closer to it Andi. I want to know what it is. I have never seen eyes like that before. If it's that big black cat that's been reported, I think it will do a runner before I get too close."

Seconds later I set off across the field in the direction of the eyes, which still shone back at me in the darkness. I snapped a few images as I went in the general direction and hoped for the best. I think if I had used my camcorder at the time, instead of the SLR, I would have had better results. I saw it blinking, then it seemed to blink again and was gone. I turned to Andi and as quietly as possible I said, *"it's run away."*

When I turned back, the eyes had reappeared at about the same distance as when we first saw them. I was now about 100ft into the field and this thing was still there looking back at me. I'm not sure how close I might have got to it, because it appeared to be keeping me at the same distance the further I went. At this point I decided to turn back. I'm not sure what kind of animal it was, but it was clearly not scared of me. I actually felt like I was being lured into the field at one point. Anyone who has read TP1 would know this is the area many people reported seeing the big black cat in 2014.

Andi was relieved to find I was on the way back.
"What the hell was that Paul? I was worried you were going too far, because I could still see those eyes looking back. Was it walking backwards? It must have been, because you seemed to be getting

further away and that thing appeared to be keeping the same distance. Another thing I could not get my head around was why we could not see the outline of its head. I could not see anything except the eyes."

Andi had made a good point. We should have been able to see the shape of the animal's body or at least an outline, but we never did. When we first observed the eyes I estimated they were about three feet off the ground, but then they appeared to get lower, almost as though the animal was crouched. There is no other way to explain it. At one point Andi thought it was laying down, because we could see the grass and the eyes appeared to be a just few inches off the ground.

We both turned back and surveyed the field one more time. The eyes were back. The animal had moved closer this time and appeared to be in the same place we saw it ten minutes earlier. But now it was raining quite hard and I had no intention of setting off back across the field a second time. We watched it briefly, then carried on up the path to the car. On reflection I wish we had stayed around a little longer.

* * *

Two days after our sighting of the cliff animal, Andi was still fired up about our last visit to Bempton. He was hoping to see more of whatever had given him that rush of excitement last time. Then, quite out of the blue, he called to ask if I would go back there with him. This was really unusual for Andi as he lived thirty minutes away from Bridlington. He always had the routine of only joining me at the clifftops after he had dropped off his partner at her mother's place. Tonight was obviously different, which shows just how much of an impact this 'eye-shine' beast had on him.

He arrived at my place at 6.30pm and it was already dark. I was ready to go and a few minutes later we were heading out into the night towards Bempton. This time I took my infrared trail camera along, which records in dark conditions and its beam is invisible to most animals. The plan was to set it up on the path were I first saw the animal spring from the cliffs. It was a long shot and we had nothing to lose, but this was Bempton and anything could happen.

At 7pm we settled in to the same place we had been two nights before. This time the sky was bright with moonlight, so we could see much more of the surrounding land. I looked over to where the animal had appeared and said, *"You know Andi, for me to have seen that animal moving about in the pitch black the other night, it must have been quite light in colour. The deer around here are dark brown, but we better not read any more into it."*

In the bright moonlight we could see lots more, the land had opened up to us and I was optimistic that, if this thing appeared again, we would definitely see what it was. I set up my trail camera about 30ft from the cliff edge and walked back to where I had placed two tripods. Each had a camcorder attached and they were fixed and ready in case anything should appear. The lightforms had been our main objective before this, but now we had found something new to add to the mystery.

A few hours passed with nothing more interesting to break the silence than an occasional wave crashing against the rocks hundreds of feet below us. Even though we had wrapped up warmly, after a while of standing on the edge of the North Sea, the cold air finds its way into your bones. I looked out to sea and tried to imagine how the pilots of all those crashed aircraft must have felt, surrounded by nothing but cold and hostile water; it must have been a terrifying experience. Standing out on the clifftops in the cold is no comparison of course, but these thoughts still cross your mind. I glanced over towards Flamborough and two to three miles away something in the distance caught my eye.

"Andi, can you see that?" I pointed to some faint light which appeared to be moving in the distance. It was definitely on land. Andi looked in the direction I was pointing. *"Yeah, I see it. What do you think it is Paul?"*

I switched on my Sony camcorder and moments later I was scouring the land to get a better view. I noticed the lights appeared to be almost moving up and down. From this distance it was difficult to say for sure, but I thought it might be two people out walking. Andi agreed with me. *"But what would anyone be doing out on the clifftops at this time of night?"* I realised how daft my remark must have sounded to Andi. Then he pointed out the obvious to me, *"Why not? We're here aren't we?"*

I turned the camcorder off to conserve its battery, but we kept glancing over to the lights every now and again. They were getting larger and definitely moving towards us along the clifftop path. Another quick look through the viewfinder now confirmed what we suspected. I could see two people out walking and they were both wearing head torches.

I contemplated moving my trail camera. It was a good distance from the main path and it flashed red if anything came in range of its invisible beam. I knew that whoever was out there walking would see the flash if they triggered it. In the end we decided against it, after all, I had faced it towards the cliffs. We continued to watch the progress of the two walkers along the cliff path. We were on higher ground and I realised that, in the moonlight, they must have been able to see our silhouettes against the sky. As the lights moved closer I still questioned why anyone else would be out on the clifftops in the darkness. I just could not imagine anyone else having a reason to be there, but then, anyone seeing us must have been thinking the same thing.

The walkers stopped a few hundred metres away from us and appeared to be looking for something in the grass. It was impossible to say for sure that's what they were actually doing, but we watched them with interest. They must have known we were there. They would have seen us from miles away, because my camcorder emits a thin beam of red light that would have been visible in the dark. But they just stood in the darkness, like two people who had just bumped into each other on a street corner. Then something caught my eye. I turned to the right. *"Andi Andi, look at them. There. Just there!"* I touched Andi's shoulder as I whispered the words. Out of the darkness we saw another two people walk past us and continue up the cliff path towards Speeton.

I got one of those cold and chilling feelings that you only get when fear and surprise hit you. These two strangers had come out of nowhere, but they must have been there all the time. They were just a hundred metres or so ahead of the walkers with lights, who were still in the same place. Now this surprise pair, who were walking without torches in complete darkness, seemed more important. It might have been a bright night, but we both agreed it was complete madness to be walking the clifftops at night without a light. It is unlikely anyone would fall off the cliff, with its perimeter safety fence, but the land is uneven and full of hidden dips and changes. It would be easy to lose your footing and break an ankle.

Bempton never fails to surprise. We had originally come out here to look for unexplained lights, then days before, a strange animal was thrown into the mix. Now we had strange company of the human kind. The pair with the lights were now on the path and had begun to walk up towards the nature reserve car park. That in itself was odd. We had arrived hours before and my car was the only one parked there, so we knew they were not walking back to a car. The other pair, without lights, had now vanished into the night. Perhaps they were totally unconnected to the other two, but it was a strange set of circumstances and one I found quite unnerving.

We never encountered anyone on the clifftop path at night. In fact, apart from the rock anglers, who were sometimes on the cliff in their usual fixed positions, we were the only ones ever out there. The anglers were only there if the tide was favourable. We sometimes saw torchlights at night around the old RAF base, but no one ever came to the cliff edge. This whole scenario was over in less than five minutes and the two pairs of strangers went their separate ways into the night.

"Where the hell did they appear from Paul?" It was a shock to suddenly see two dark figures appear from nowhere. These surprise strangers made us both feel uneasy.
"I don't know Andi. Maybe we missed them because we were too busy looking at the men with lights. They can't have been more than a hundred metres in front of the other two all the time. I mean, we watched those lights for almost an hour as they approached from the Flamborough direction. And the camcorder has exceptional night vision, so I'm surprised we didn't see them sooner.
What confused me the most was, at first I could not actually work out what the two in darkness actually were. As they passed in the darkness I actually thought they resembled a pantomime horse. The one at the back had their hands on the shoulders of the one in front. So for a second or two I couldn't work out what I was seeing - and they were dressed in black from head to toe."

Both pairs of cliff walkers had now vanished into the night, but the experience had unnerved both of us. Bempton is one of those rare places that actually does scare me. This might be nothing more than my mind telling me to be wary, based on what I already know about the place. The two who passed us without lights were strange though. They were dressed all in black and it even looked as though their faces were blacked out. It was such peculiar behaviour, that it made me realise some places are just not good places to find yourself alone in.

The Beast Of Beast Cliff

The following first-hand account was shared with me one of two rock anglers I met up at Bempton in November 2016. They were seasoned anglers who had travelled almost a hundred miles from Durham, to fish from the Bempton clifftops. They could tell from my cameras that I was not up there to catch fish and, after explaining my reasons for being there, one of the men told me about a frightening animal he saw one night as he fished alone.

"It was further up the coast at a place called Sandsend, about thirty miles from here. I'm not the only one who has seen it; a few of the lads have said the same thing. Nobody wants to fish out there alone once they have seen that thing."

Sandsend is on the edge of the North Sea near Whitby and its rugged coastline is as remote and unchanged as Bempton's. The fisherman told me that this strange animal had been seen on more than one occasion on those lonely clifftops over the years. His own sighting of the beast scared him so much, he has never been back there. It was in November 2013 when he had the misfortune of encountering the creature.

"I remember the date because there was a fishing competition and I decided to try my luck at Sandsend. Some of the other lads were around, I could see their lights in the distance, but they were spaced out and miles away, so basically I was on my own. Only the glow of their headlights in the darkness gave them away. It would have been no good shouting for help. No one would have come.

I think I had been fishing for about two hours. I had only managed to catch a few small fish; nothing that I thought would win the competition. Up until that day I didn't mind fishing alone. I was always aware of the surroundings and nothing had really bothered me before. After all, this is the UK. There is nothing here to harm us except our own imagination on a dark night - or so I thought until this happened. I mean, look at me; I'm not exactly a little guy!

I think it was sometime after 11pm, I know it was quite late anyway, when I started to feel as though I was being watched. It's hard to explain, but I just felt like there were eyes on me. It spooked me right out it did. I can't explain it, the feeling just came over me all of a sudden. I double clicked my head torch to brighten it up; I'd had it on the dimmer setting until then to save the battery."

The angler leaned towards me to show me his head torch. He was quite proud that it was 5,000 lumens, which meant little to me at the time. What struck me when I looked at him, was that he had quite a hard face and, although appearances can be deceiving, this made him look quite formidable. His slightly bent nose and swollen ears told me all I needed to know. So hearing this man tell me how scared he was made his story even more interesting.

"As soon as I switched the headlight to its brightest setting I began to look around. I looked behind me and up and down the path. I just felt spooked and that's when I saw it standing there. I went cold. I just stared at first, trying to make out what it was. The light was only on it four or five seconds, but it was long enough for me to tell it was no rabbit or fox. Next thing, it seemed to lower its head, either that or it had run off, because I couldn't see it. Well my eyes were darting all over the place trying to work out where this thing could have disappeared to. Then I saw it again, only now it seemed a bit closer. I was thinking 'hold on, this can't be a deer. Not if it's got closer to me'.

I don't mind saying I felt more than a bit scared. I've seen just about everything over the years; deer, badgers, foxes and rabbits, but those eyes did not belong to any of those animals. For a start, they were too high off the ground. To be that high they would have belonged to a horse or a cow. And something else, the eyes were fixed in front just like mine and yours, and they were a bright yellow, almost orange colour. And here's the strangest thing; when I put the light on it the second time, it ducked its head down again, but it didn't just drop its head in reaction to the light, it was coming towards me down the path.

Once I realised this, I flipped the lid on my fishing box and began to throw my stuff inside. The thing is, I had to take my eyes off this bloody thing to pack up and every time I looked back it seemed a bit closer, but every time my light beam hit its face, it would drop its head. I don't mind saying I was terrified. Fear got the better of me and I cut my line, picked up the fishing box and got out of there as fast as I could. I s**t myself, well not literally, but I was really scared going down that cliff path. It might have been the fear that overtook everything, but I could still feel its eyes on me. I kept on looking back but saw nothing. I could *not shake off the overwhelming feeling that it was following me. It was as though its eyes were on me and really close. That was it for me, I have never fished in that place since and I don't fish alone anymore. My mate who's with us tonight, he's seen it as well. He won't go fishing at Sandsend ever again either. Not a chance."*

I told him about the strange animal that I saw with Andi a few nights before. I asked if he thought it might have been the same animal.
"I suppose it's possible, I don't know. What I saw sounds bigger than what you saw. From the shape of it I would say it was a massive dog. But I don't know of any dogs that stand that tall, and its eyes were like an amber colour. And it was smart enough to lower its head every time I put my beam of light onto it."

He was right. From the description he gave, the eye-shine from the animal we observed in the field did seem lower to the ground. It seemed smaller than the creature he was describing. Although at one point we actually thought it was on its belly.

Stories of an unusual dog-type creature seem to be ingrained in the land around East and North Yorkshire. The angler told me that quite a few of the men who go fishing around Sandsend claim to have seen the beast with the glowing eyes. If this is correct, then the stories from folklore have never really left these lonely places along our coastline.

In Kettleness, a few miles north of Whitby, stories of a huge black dog with glowing red eyes have survived to present day. Whitby has its own legend of a huge dog-like creature, named Black Shuck. Described as a monstrous animal with terrifying red eyes, its appearance is said to be a messenger of bad omens. Similar stories seem to form a pattern over the entire North and East Yorkshire coastline, including recent reports of large dog of gruesome appearance seen at Danes Dyke. Could accounts of the Flixton Werewolf be the same creature witnessed at Sandsend?

As recently as 2016 there have been reported sightings of a werewolf near the city of Hull. The Beverley and Barmston land drain was dug by hand in the 1800s and runs into the River Hull. It passes through open fields and remote areas of farmland where this fearsome creature has gained such notoriety, that it was named the Beast of Barmston Drain.

Could all of these sightings be the same creature? Could they even exist? I stand by what I said about this in TP1; that I do not think the UK has enough open country to support such a large and elusive animal. If it was indeed a flesh and blood beast, there would have to be a breeding population. But what if I am wrong? Could the remote inaccessible cliffs of East and North Yorkshire support this centuries-old beast? If you were to travel in a straight line from Sandsend to the Barmston Drain, your journey would take you through the Wolds near Flixton, Hunmanby and Staxton, where people have described seeing a werewolf.

I still do not subscribe to the theory that a large carnivore can be living in such close proximity to sheep, cattle and humans, but I wouldn't be doing my job as a researcher if I did not point out all of the possibilities. I have to admit, the locations the creature has been seen are very remote. Some of the sea caves on the coast are so inaccessible that human eyes have never even seen their inner depths. But could a huge and intelligent biped canine have evaded detection for centuries? I'm not so sure. In this world many things are possible. This is something I learned at an early age, due to the things I saw with my own eyes; things that should not have been possible, but clearly were.

The only way I can imagine such things existing alongside if us in the here and now, is if they survived in a parallel world, but had the ability to slip between their world and ours. Perhaps the creatures from folklore fit this category? I believe these creatures exist, but just not in the way modern man looks at existence.

A clue that suggests that something canine once existed can often be found in the place names they have been reported. Beast Cliff is the remote area of woodland on the edge of the North Sea near Sandsend, close to where the anglers saw their creature. Wolfland at Flixton, is so named due to an apparent infestation of savage beasts in ancient times. Old maps of Flixton give reference to Bandog House, in a time so distant that the maps are all that is left to prove it ever existed. 'Bandog' is a name given to fierce guard-dogs of old and there are stories from around the world that tell of such dogs being used to protect humans from werewolves. Then just three miles away from Flixton is the village of Hunmanby or Hund-manby which means 'hound-man'. All of this information ties in with the legends and perhaps the recent sightings of strange creatures around East and North Yorkshire.

Believing Is Seeing

If we stopped believing, would the sightings cease? I have said before that I think believing is seeing and not the other way around. I therefore wonder if it is something born out of the human mind. Perhaps a subconscious attachment brings on this 'interworld connection', which then allows such things to manifest in our reality?

Location has to hold the key to unlocking these mysteries, but for some reason there are huge gaps between the sightings of these creatures. Sometimes years pass, which allows the stories slip back into the realms of fantasy, until, out of the blue, someone reports seeing a werewolf.

I have recently been given a new account of the Flixton Werewolf that was claimed to have been seen in mid-2016 and stories of the Beast of Barmston Drain are still been reported today. In TP1 I described how the villages of Flixton and Folkton are so close they are inseparable, in all but name - and this latest sighting comes from a farmer who lives in Folkton. This was a daylight sighting of something described as a man covered in fur that was running across the fields of Star Carr.

The Carrs are an area of fertile wetland adjoining Flixton and Folkton. In ancient times hunter-gathers settled there, making their home on the edge of Star Carr. Eleven thousand years ago Star Carr was a great lake with islands and thick reed beds which extended for miles. This area is as rich in ancient history as anywhere else in the world. Evidence of sacrifice and shamanic practices have recently been discovered at Star Carr, along with the preserved remains of Britain's oldest dwelling house, which has been dated to 8,500BC. Starr Carr is truly a land of history and mystery, so I am not surprised that accounts of the Flixton Werewolf still surface in and around this most ancient of locations.

The farmer's sighting occurred in broad daylight in fields adjoining his own farm, which overlooks Star Carr. It was the erratic behaviour of some nearby horses that first caught his attention. He told me they were gathered at one end of a paddock and appeared skittish and nervous. Then he saw a creature running across open fields, just parallel to the paddock. He said it ran upright on two legs and was tall. He described it as being covered with dark fur and with a face like an Alsatian dog. He called it the wolfman.

For some reason the creature stopped half-way across the field and crouched down. He said the horses definitely sensed its presence because they were trying to distance themselves from it within the paddock.

Moments later this strange-looking beast was back up and running across the fields. The last the farmer saw of the creature was when it entered an area of woodland known as the Spell Howe plantation. Spell Howe is an interesting location and a fitting place to end this account. This small woodland is littered with burial mounds and is also very close to the burial mounds known as Sharp Howe - another ancient location where sightings of the Flixton Werewolf have been reported.

Next page: impression of the farmer's encounter with the 'wolfman'.

232

Green Object Off Hornsea

In 2016 I was told of a couple who claimed to have seen a rectangle of green lights under the sea. One evening in June they were walking along the clifftops between Wilsthorpe and Hornsea, near the village of Ulrome. In less than an hour they claim to have witnessed the same configuration of green lights twice, just beneath the surface of the sea. They say the object or formation was made up of at least six separate lights that were glowing in a florescent green colour. This was an odd story and there were no other similar reports from the time to back it up. So I had nothing more to go on besides the description. That was until August 15th 2016, when I visited the lifeboat station at Bridlington.

I arrived early in the morning as I did not want to take up too much of the officer's time. We exchanged the usual pleasantries and then he surprised me by saying that he was expecting my visit.

This off-the-cuff remark was amusing, because I only ever call in to the station when something of an unusual nature has been reported locally or there's something interesting I want to check via the lifeboat logs. I asked him why and he began to tell me about a strange callout they had received on August 7th, a week earlier. The lifeboat and its crew had been called out at 5pm to investigate a report of unusual green lights that had been seen off the coast of Hornsea. The witness who called described the lights as florescent green in colour and appearing in the shape of a rectangle.

So far, I have been unable to identify the witness and the lifeboat station officer had no more details to share with me. I am unsure if this is the same green object seen just weeks earlier by the couple out walking the clifftops, but it does sound similar.

The Cleo Porter Sighting

In August 2016 two girls, aged eleven and twelve, had a UFO sighting. They were staying with their parents at the time, near Wilsthorpe, at the campsite owned by the Royal Yorkshire Yacht Club.

It was after 10pm when they saw a stationary red light hovering over a field close to their tent. They say the light was stationary for some time before it moved away at speed. They remember seeing two horses in the field below the light, but they seemed unaffected by its presence. There was no sound heard from the object during the sighting.

I learned of this sighting directly from one of the witnesses, Cleo Porter, as she is my own granddaughter. When I asked her to tell me about it she said the object was red and it resembled half a ball in the sky. She described seeing a red light around the perimeter of the object, which moved anti-clockwise and at great speed. She thought it had multiple lights, but saw only one light up at a time, giving it the appearance of a continuous light moving around the edge.

Cleo and her friend were not the only ones to witness the UFO. The adults in the group also saw the object, but were unable to clearly identify it before it moved away.

Intelligent Lightforms And The Fire Fog

On Thursday January 19th 2017 I met up with a few of the trawlermen on Bridlington Harbour. I had received a call from a few days earlier asking if I could take a few photos of them as they worked on their boat in the harbour. I am always happy to help if I can and since they are a wealth of information to me, it was the least I could do.

Many of the things that happen out at sea never reach the ears of people on land. This is partly because the men just don't talk about work outside of their close-knit community – and, if it does not involve catching fish it simply does not interest them. The following story is one such example that was shared with me by trawlermen Danny Quinn and his father, on the morning I agreed to take the photos.

When I arrived they were busy repairing lobster pots ready for the next trip out to sea. The North Sea can be hard on the men and their equipment, but they are accustomed to the harsh conditions and are ready for whatever it throws at them. Over the years we have become great friends and they are always happy to see me and share interesting bits of information. Danny's father started the conversation;
"Have you told Paul about that weird fog that people reported when we were out at sea last Saturday." My ears pricked up as soon as I heard the word 'weird', although I'm not sure if that must mean I'm a bit weird? Anyway, there were two other men standing beside Danny and they glanced up, but said nothing. They just carried on weaving their green nylon cord in and out of the sea battered lobster pots.

"Well it was probably nothing really Paul," Danny said, *"but it came over the radio that all boats in the area were to be on the lookout for a bank of red or orange fog. It was reported to be about three and a half miles off Withernsea. This was a new one on us, no one seemed to have any idea what it could mean or what might have caused it."*

Danny explained that the sea was calm at the time and apart from the trawlermen exchanging various radio messages about the red fog, no problems were reported. They suspected someone had simply let off distress flares, but Danny said it was confirmed later that flares were not thought to be responsible. That was all they could tell me, but at the back of my mind I seemed to recall hearing about something similar before. I said nothing, but I wanted to be sure.

The next day I went to the lifeboat station. I wanted to know if any boats had been in distress and released flares on the day the red fog warning was given. Something told me there might be more to learn about this red fog and I still had the feeling I had heard something similar before.

I arrived at the station at about 10am; I had a donation cheque to drop off after a charity collection some months before, so it was a good opportunity for me visit. I asked the officer if there had been any interesting callouts lately. He told me about one, from 8am on January 16th, which was a bit of a strange one. I explained that I knew of the red fog callout from a few of the men on the harbour, which was why I was here at the station. He explained that it had been a request for boats to be on the lookout for orange lights. He did not say who made the call or where it originated, but orange lights had been seen out at sea.

This was even more interesting. The trawlermen had never mentioned anything about a warning of orange lights out at sea. I asked if he was aware of the red fog that had been seen.
"Yes, there were reports of a thick red mist or fog that was seen off Withernsea by a few fishing vessels, but orange lights had also been seen in the sky that morning. The fog was not thought to be connected with the lights and no boats radioed in to say they were in trouble."

That was all I could gather from the lifeboat station, so perhaps Danny and his father had just forgotten to tell me about the report of orange lights. I am sure there are many things that happen out at sea that are never spoken about, but I truly believe the small amount of information I manage to gather, is just the surface of a much deeper pool.

From the lifeboat station I walked to Bridlington Library. I wanted to check their archive because I still had a vague recollection of once seeing a newspaper article from the 1980s that talked of a red fog. As usual, I had my note book with me so when I arrived I spent a few minutes scanning through the pages of my notes. I was right, because I found a one-line entry entitled 'fire fog' alongside the words 'witness Mary Sexton'. I had obviously found an article on a previous visit to the archive, because I had also written 'Bridlington Free Press - March 12th 1987'. I found the appropriate microfilm in the archive and ten minutes later the reel was on the machine and I was looking at the article I wanted to read.

'Fiery fog' scare

A "fiery red fog" stopped Flamborough woman Mrs May Sexton in her tracks in Sewerby Road when she was driving home from Bridlington last Wednesday.

It was about 9 pm when Mrs Sexton came across the fog near Church Lane. "It was unnatural. I felt panicky," she said.

She thought the fog stretched for about 100 yards and she slowed right down because her lights could not penetrate it.

Mrs Sexton, of North End, Flamborough, said, "It got thicker and thicker, it was very frightening. I did not dare stop."

Launched

At about the same time, Bridlington lifeboat was launched after the keel boat Ubique reported a red distress flare off Dane's Dyke. Beaches on Dane's Dyke and Sewerby were searched but nothing was found.

Mrs Sexton said the red fog could have been caused by someone releasing a flare near to the road, adding that she saw three young men in the area.

'Flare' launch

Bridlington lifeboat launched last night after keel boat Ubique reported a red distress flare off Dane's Dyke. Coastguards also searched the beaches at Dane's Dyke, Sewerby and South Landing but nothing was found.

237

I only took an interest in the strange story of the red fog because I wondered if I might find similar stories in the library archive at a later date.. That single account could be the start of a sequence of events. As I first noted in TP1, one unusual event can sometimes act like a trip wire, that leads me to find whole series of equally strange but often related events. The story of the red fog could have been a piece of the puzzle that had previously gone unnoticed.

Now that I had confirmed the correct year was 1987, I began to read other news items from thirty years ago, in the hope it might offer clues to what was happening in the present time. However remote the chances of ever finding anything, I still had to check. To get a full picture of 1987 I read the newspaper headlines for the entire year. I needed to know if anything unexplained had happened that could tie in with the strange fire fog reported by Mary Sexton in March of that year. If I found anything, then it might help me to identify a similar pattern unfolding in 2017. I felt as if I was literally chasing smoke.

Later that week I spoke again with Danny and his father. I was able to ask them about the orange lights mentioned to me by the lifeboat station officer. They told me they knew nothing about a report of orange lights, but they had spoken with other fishermen about the red fog. They told me that those who had witnessed it all agreed it was a thick bank of red fog that blanketed a large area of the sea. They said it was not smoke from red flares or anything they could identify.

Smoke from flares produces a certain smell and acrid taste which carries in the air. But as far as they were aware, when I asked Danny and his father, no one had reported the smell or taste of flare smoke either. This was further confirmed by the lifeboat station officer who also thought the fog had nothing to do with flares. Danny's father also mentioned that a call came over the boat radio to say that someone had also seen a blue fog on the same day, but that was the only time he'd heard of that. Sightings of a blue fog were never mentioned to me by the officer at the lifeboat station.

The orange lightform activity off Bempton and Speeton had been particularly interesting over the past month or so. Many rock anglers reporting seeing the spheres on numerous occasions. I first used the term 'Intelligent Lightforms', or ILFs, many years ago when trying to find a way to describe the orange and red spheres of light that were being seen off the East and North Yorkshire coast and around the East Yorkshire Wolds. Even though the term is just a combination of words, it is the way the words are put together that makes them significant. I have noted that another writer claims to have coined the term, but this is not true. The phrase appears on my archived ILF-UFO website and mine is the first published use of the term.

The lightforms have been documented for many years, I have even been able to film them on more than one occasion. I can say with confidence that, what I have seen and filmed of the lightforms, they are definitely not flares.

I have been unable to find anything of significance to link Mary Sexton's 1987 red fog report to anything unusual, and if a thirty year gap is the norm between sightings, then I may not be here to investigate it the next time it occurs. For now, there are key points that stand in the way of this fog being some kind of meteorological phenomena. In 2017 the coastguard considered it to be of sufficient interest to warn all boats in the vicinity to look out for it. The lifeboat station officer told me there was talk of orange lights out at sea around the same time, but no one reported hearing the discharge of flares and no boats were reported in distress. This all seems a bit vague, since no one can say with any certainty what caused it.

My visit to the archive at Bridlington Library did reveal a few more interesting incidents of activity around the time of the 1987 report. It would seem that red lights had been witnessed out at sea on several occasions from the Danes Dyke area. Again, these lights were thought to be distress flares, however, no boats were reported to be in difficulty. Through word of mouth I learned this fog had been nicknamed 'fire fog', because those who had witnessed it described it as appearing to bristle and sparkle. In 1987 Mary Sexton was driving along Church Lane in Flamborough when she encountered her fire fog, just a few miles away from Danes Dyke and Sewerby. She later explained to reporters that it covered a large area and was far too dense to be smoke from any flare.

I noticed that Mary Sexton's sighting was published in the Bridlington Free Press on Thursday March 12th. It stated that she had encountered the fire fog on the previous Wednesday, which dates her sighting to March 4th. The 30-year-old news article also states that around the same time, Bridlington lifeboat was launched after a red distress flare was seen off the Sewerby coast. Yet a search of the beaches at Sewerby and Danes Dyke found nothing. I find it hard to believe that the fire fog Mary Sexton drove into was connected to the reported distress flare near Sewerby, because she was two and half miles away in Flamborough at the time.

With this in mind I was back at the lifeboat station a few days later. Armed with the right dates from 1987 I was hoping the old lifeboat logs might offer up some clues. As expected, I was shown a detailed log entry for March 4th 1987. There I found a discrepancy of one and a quarter hours between the time Mary Sexton encountered the fire fog and the time the lifeboat was launched. According to these details, the log suggests that the fire fog was present *before* the red distress flare was seen. The Bridlington lifeboat searched the sea that night for almost two hours, but returned after finding nothing at all.

There was log entry for another call out to a suspected distress flare around the same area on the night of March 25th 1987, but the boat was never put out to sea. These are just a few examples of unusual lights reported off the East and North Yorkshire coastline, but they are only a fraction of what has been witnessed over the years.

Seasoned lifeboatmen and trawlermen are now beginning to realise there could be more to these unusual lights - lights that have gone under the radar for such a long time. Until now, no one has ever bothered to gather all the relevant information and lay it bare. The sheer number of call outs and reports of these orange or red phantom lights off our coast, from the public and fishing boats, is staggering. I suspect East and North Yorkshire are not alone when it comes to phenomena of this kind.

Reports of the lightforms appearing over land and out to sea span decades of time. I think it is clear after studying the explanations offered up by professional bodies and the media, that in many instances, they have no idea what they are. It is not unusual to learn of three or even four different theories to explain just one sighting. Off-the-shelf explanations such as unusual atmospheric phenomena, flares, meteors, ball lightning and the now widely used excuse of Chinese lanterns, are all offered up. The reason they continue to get away with this is because their explanations fit with what the public know and understand.

Intelligent Lightforms are not just the occupants of our dreams, they are real and they have been recorded. We just do not have the capability to explain what they are. Not everything that surrounds the subject of UFOs has to revolve around the words *spaceship* or *flying saucer*. An event of high strangeness can hit at any level and leave little or no evidence that it ever existed.

Paul Sinclair lives with his wife and family in
the UK seaside town of Bridlington,
on the east coast of Yorkshire.

He began his research in 2002 after creating the
ILF-UFO sightings website.

Paul is also a talented artist who creates
huge surrealist artwork.
He enjoys countryside walks and
never leaves home without his camera !

Paul can be contacted via Facebook through the
Truth-Proof page. He also has a Truth-Proof
channel on Youtube and a website.
www.truthproof.webs.com